Bradman
vs Bodyline

Also by Roland Perry

Bradman
vs Bodyline

The inside story of the most notorious
Ashes series in history

ROLAND PERRY

ALLEN&UNWIN
SYDNEY・MELBOURNE・AUCKLAND・LONDON

Allen & Unwin
83 Alexander Street
Crows Nest NSW 2065
Australia
Phone: (61 2) 8425 0100
Email: info@allenandunwin.com
Web: www.allenandunwin.com

A catalogue record for this book is available from the National Library of Australia

ISBN 978 1 76087 915 0

Except where otherwise stated all photos are from the author's collection

Index by Garry Cousins
Set in 13/17.1 pt Adobe Caslon by Midland Typesetters, Australia
Printed and bound in Australia by Griffin Press, part of Ovato

10 9 8 7 6 5 4 3 2 1

*To Alan Young who loves a good cricket meal;
and Brenda Young, who just loves her Pies.*

CONTENTS

INTRODUCTION

Forget ball-tampering, illegal gambling, match-fixing and throwing. Nothing upset the world of cricket like Bodyline. This was the method of bowling designed by English cricketers to destroy the career of the greatest cricketer of all time, Don Bradman. It was a method to injure or intimidate the batsman by delivering bouncers at the body.

It had its zenith during the 1932–33 Ashes series in Australia—known forever as Bodyline—but had been in gestation in England's county cricket for years before that. Its ghost continued on for decades afterwards and is still scaring batsmen the world over. It will do so in the next Ashes series in 2021–22, which will mark 90 years since the most notorious Ashes competition ever.

Here, for the first time, is the real story of Bodyline and revelations about its inventors, imitators and victims that have been swept under the carpet as an inconvenient truth.

Until now, commentators in articles, books and films have described the events of the 1932–33 series without adequate focus on the drama before, after and even during the Ashes itself. Some writers have used the series as a vehicle to attempt to belittle Bradman. Others wished to besmirch the controversial England captain Douglas Jardine without regard to context or history. The Nottinghamshire and England captain Arthur Carr, with his cavalier approach to almost everything, mystifyingly, has been either ignored or given short shrift for his part in events. But not in this narrative.

Here, the roles of the key players in this grand sporting theatre—Arthur Carr, Harold Larwood, Douglas Jardine and Don Bradman—are brought to life. So are the essential minor characters, such as England paceman Bill Voce, Australian captain Bill Woodfull, and Marylebone Cricket Club luminary Plum Warner.

Bradman vs Bodyline covers cricket's greatest upheaval and threat to its survival as a 'sport', in all senses of the word.

PART ONE
1893–1919

I

THE INNOVATOR: ARTHUR CARR

Arthur Carr, born 21 May 1893, cared little for school-work. In 1907, at the age of thirteen, he was expelled from Eton, one of England's top schools, for being 'idle'. This was a quaint euphemism for a 'very lazy troublemaker', one who dared as a young teenager to more than flirt with female domestic staff. This latter predilection, along with penchants for smoking, gambling and drinking, were not barriers for a cricketing career at any level until well into the 21st century.

Arthur's father, Philip, a wealthy stockbroker, helped with money and influence to support his son in his passion-ate love of the game. His mother, Louise Smith, a beautiful Scot from Broughty Ferry, now a suburb of Dundee, would have preferred Arthur took up her passion for golf, which was *the* Scottish game of the second half of the nineteenth century. But from an early age she recognised his strong will and capacity for, and love of, all sports.

Carr's youthful distractions reflected a devil-may-care attitude. Often, when corralled into sports, this created an aggression and a fierce desire to win. Instinct ruled over intellect. It suited young Arthur. But they were impediments for the strictly disciplined 'muscular Christianity' of the British public (what we in Australia call private) school system.

When the sturdy sixteen year old fronted up for Nottinghamshire's Second XI in 1909, he knew he had to perform. This was his last chance at a dream career. He was good at rugby but never saw himself playing at the top level. He hated the idea of stockbroking, the profession in which his father and grandfather had thrived. Money was only useful for following hedonistic pursuits, never to be the font of life. Even Philip, who had been left a fortune by his father before him, never really loved the grey broking world. His passion was horses, so much so that he had moved the family from London to Newton Hall, a large estate near Great Dunmow, Essex. It was just 22 miles from Newmarket, the heart of the horse-racing business.

Arthur had little aspiration beyond cricket. He loved the game and watched the way his Essex heroes performed on the field and in the pavilion afterwards—drinking, bragging, betting, reminiscing and laughing until stupor or fatigue dictated when they should return to their families or single digs.

To a callow teenager, with his attitudes, this was heaven.

In 1908, the Carr family moved again, this time to another grand home, Rempstone Hall in Nottinghamshire. Once more there was a horse connection. Philip wanted to join the highly esteemed Quorn Hunt. He bought seventeen horses and hunted four times a week.

It was the move that made young Arthur's life.

His father encouraged him to try out with the county cricket team. Nottinghamshire was about the last of the counties to accept amateurs and did not encourage them to take up places of professionals but for a few matches each holiday period. The amateurs had a dressing room far bigger than their fellow *paid* performers and they entered the field by a separate gate, which reinforced the class difference.

The Nottinghamshire team was made up largely of miners; lads and men from the pits, who could earn extra shillings playing, and enjoy a break from the tough underground drudgery of their unenviable work in the coalfields.

Nothing was said to his face, but Arthur sensed a sullen indifference, even resentment, from the professional players. He knew he had to show he could really play the game, which he did for a few precious opportunities each summer. Arthur learnt respect for working-class men he would never otherwise meet. He managed a strong 102 in only his second appearance, against Cheshire, and in turn earnt some respect from his teammates.

The boy could bat.

The experience with the county side enhanced his batting record at Dorset's Sherborne School where he had been sent after being discharged from Eton. He topped the averages in 1910, hitting 638 at 45.41. He took most wickets with his exhausting medium-pacers, 32 at 15.06. He also excelled at rugby. His academic record did not improve much but he didn't care. He was gaining prestige from being the best summer/winter sportsperson at his school, in fact any school.

Carr knew Sherborne tolerated him because he was very good at sports.

'I was the biggest ass at [school] work,' he wrote. 'All of it was done for me by the clever boys.'

He was nearly thrown out of Sherborne for smoking once, and betting on another occasion. Yet this was inconsequential in terms of his advance beyond school. Carr was now on the cricket establishment's radar. The games of the leading public schools were recorded in the sport's annual bible, *Wisden*. The reports were read avidly in the never-ending search for future stars, and particularly leaders. England captains of sport, industry, academia, politics and the military almost always came from the public school system, or the upper and upper-middle classes. It had been the way for the most powerful nation on earth, and the system was exported throughout the British colonies. Its zenith was in the early part of the twentieth century.

This was the era of King Edward VII, who reigned from 1901 until 1910. 'Bertie' had revived the nation's image by being less constrained than his mother, Queen Victoria, in public at least. Staid discretion was replaced by ostentation; showiness in the way you dressed, gambled, drank, caroused and flouted your 'class'.

It was also part of the golden age of cricket where batting flamboyance in stroke play was encouraged and lauded. Carr fitted in with this setting almost too well. After Sherborne he was pushed to Oxford University for the 1911–12 year, again with his father's assistance, but again Arthur's indifference to developing his mind ultimately triumphed. He dropped out. As at Eton, he eschewed study and hated the 'stuffiness'. He padded up in 'friendlies' only and never officially represented the university.

Carr then did what many of the establishment figures did when they failed to enter Oxbridge: he applied for the Royal Military College, Sandhurst. Winston Churchill did; Douglas Haig (future Commander-in-Chief of Allied forces in the Great War) did without having to sit exams, thanks to his closeness to King George V; Edmund Allenby (future Commander in the Middle East War) did, though he sat exams. Arthur Carr did too, and failed the exams at three attempts. It may have been confirming to examiners that he was not too bright; more importantly, he was telling himself he really did not aspire to be in the officer class via his knowledge of the military and its history. Carr did the next thing possible by joining the Fifth Cavalry Brigade, officers reserve, in September 1913.

In essence this meant he would be into the action straight-away when England went to war. Conflict was looming and Carr, the adventurer, had long dreamt of joining a dashing cavalry outfit, as illustrated in colourful pictorial books of propaganda about British mounted swordsmen in wars in the last two centuries up until the Boer War. Carr enjoyed riding and racing like his father and his proficiency in the saddle, his pedigree and image of bravado and success on sporting fields, saw him promoted within weeks to second lieutenant.

He would have believed when he left school that he was born to lead. Yet he still had to master real leadership. He turned 21 at the beginning of the 1914 season, and by a series of selectorial omissions, absences and mishaps for the amateurs at the club, he found himself captain of Nottinghamshire.

It was premature. He did not have the respect of the rank-and-file professionals, who felt he'd been elevated because

7

his father had been president and donated funds to the club. They liked the youth and admired his courage and attacking play. But there had been a succession of amateur try-outs before him who had not shown the mettle required. Carr had a 'touch' with fellow players but it was not necessarily 'common'. His background and circumstances of breeding, education and wealth would not allow it. The only way to overcome unease in the ranks was to captain and bat with authority.

His first game as skipper—and eighteenth as a Firsts player—was a low-scoring, wet affair against Kent. It left him no room for daring moves or a batting performance of any note. Nottinghamshire lost. His second as skipper, again by default, was against Yorkshire, always a battle, no matter where the two were on the championship table. Carr was bold enough to send Yorkshire in on a good wicket. Perhaps the Yorkies were thrown by the move. They were dismissed for a desultory 75. Nottinghamshire fared better with a still modest 161. Yorkshire steadied in its second dig with 286. Then it rained. Nottinghamshire failed to reach the 201 target.

*

The knives were out before, during and after the game. The professionals had wanted one of their own, the proven Jim Iremonger, to lead. Some of them acted up. In the field, Jack Gunn remonstrated at an LBW decision. Jim Iremonger himself swore at a misfield by a teammate, loud enough for the Leeds members to hear; and when the game was slipping away, Tom Oates made derogatory remarks about Carr's decision to put Yorkshire in.

Young *Mr* Carr, the way amateurs had to be addressed, appeared before the Nottinghamshire Committee and reported on the trio's behaviour. It was less about him being a snitch, and mostly about his insecurity in leading the hard-boiled miners from the pits. The three miscreants were reprimanded. Gunn, a recidivist umpire-decision disputer, was to be given one more chance before dismissal from the club.

Carr's opportunities for future captaincy were rocky. He was replaced by a former leader, yet anything beyond 1914 regarding sport became academic, even insignificant.

War was about to intercede.

*

The traditional Bank Holiday weekend came amid the threat of conflict in Europe. Nottinghamshire played Surrey at The Oval in front of a packed crowd. Carr strode to the wicket at 3 for 110, flexing his considerable forearms, and tapping his bat hard as he faced up. He collected 2 fours with strong hits to leg and was in a forceful mood. At the end of an over, and with his score on 12, a telegram boy scurried onto the field and handed him a message. Carr, remaining expressionless, shoved the paper in his pocket.

Many spectators would have guessed what it meant. War was imminent. He would have to report *immediately* to his brigade headquarters. Carr knew that this would be his last hit for a while and began batting like it, swinging recklessly at deliveries he would otherwise have let through to the keeper, or ducked. He collected 30, including 5 fours before being caught in the deep.

That evening Carr packed and reported for duty at his brigade.

At the same time, the British government declared war on Germany.

The UK changed almost overnight into a military camp. Sports shut down for an indefinite period, and demonstrated how trivial and insignificant games were in the face of a world conflagration.

*

Carr was transferred to the Fifth Lancers to defend against the fast advancing Germans in Belgium. At Mons, the German First Army, its strongest, broke through British and French lines, forcing them to retreat. Carr found himself in a three-week rearguard action. He had no greatcoat for the cold autumn nights and contracted a fever. But he stayed in the line for the Battle of the Aisne River.

In a charge at a German machine-gun nest, his horse was shot in the head. It reared up and fell back on Carr, who was trapped underneath it. They were in no man's land between the two opposing forces and it took three hours, under the cover of darkness, before he could be freed and rescued. He was concussed and had a badly bruised body.

On the critical list, there was a fear he would die.

Carr was shipped back to England. After a fortnight in hospital he was taken back to Rempstone Hall, where he made a slow recovery over the next twelve months. He returned to the front in early 1916 and took part in the hideous Battle of the Somme in the summer.

Lancers were forced to play second fiddle to the newly introduced tanks that had been rushed into action. They were slow and broke down often, causing chaos in the British lines. The plan was for the tanks and infantry to breach the

German lines. The cavalry would then burst through the gap and slaughter the enemy. The tank failure retarded the British forces.

There was no breakthrough, only stalemate. Hundreds of thousands died.

The Lancers were reduced to patrolling no man's land. Late in September 1916, while on patrol with three other cavalrymen, Carr was caught in an ambush. The only man not wounded, he assisted his fellow Lancers and was mentioned in dispatches for this action.

On leave early in 1917, he had a quick relationship with Violet Borton, got her pregnant and married her, not an uncommon event for servicemen, who believed any such encounter might be their last before re-entering the fray. And it was deadly for the cavalry in this war where the horses were vulnerable to the heavy artillery that could target and kill them from up to 9 kilometres away. The Desert Mounted Column, 75 per cent Anzac Light Horse in the Middle East conflict against the Turks and Germans, was most effective in the vast deserts of Palestine, Jordan and Syria. But in the closer combat in Belgium and France, the cavalry was at an increasing disadvantage. Even commanders who had been brought up with the prestige of the mounted forces were facing the fact that they were becoming redundant.

So much so, that cavalrymen were being taken from their mounts and put on the front line as foot soldiers, a humiliating experience, not to mention having to face the horrors of trench warfare, which was anything but romantic.

Carr was back in England for the birth of his son, Angus, seven months after his marriage in September 1917. He returned to the battlefields of France but in November became a further casualty to horseflesh when his mount trod on his right foot and broke several bones.

This ended Carr's time on the front, and he could claim that horses saved his life. There was a fair chance that he would have experienced worse injury, even death, in the next year before the Armistice in November 1918. In that time several million men were killed. Carr spent much of his final twelve months safely carrying out special duties, with a limp for most of it, in the War Office at Whitehall.

*

The war experience left Arthur Carr with few detectable mental scars, except for a need for alcohol in excess that was the fate of many, if not a majority of all servicemen who had seen action. Alcoholism was so prevalent that it was a new post-war norm.

Strong of limb and constitution, he was a different man when he got home. He had an authority and sense of leadership after commanding the Lancers. He looked forward to seeing how this would literally play out on the more modest, yet still combative, contests on cricket fields of England and, perhaps, the world.

2

BEGINNINGS FOR THE IRON DUKE: DOUGLAS JARDINE

Douglas Jardine, born 23 October 1900 in Bombay, India, was a Scot whose heritage was from Annandale in Dumfriesshire, just north of the English border, known euphemistically for 300 years as 'The Debatable Land'. The only debate was over whether England or Scotland controlled the region. It was fought over in endless bloody battles, which bred violent, iron-willed men. Reflecting this, the Jardine family motto was *Cave Adsum*, meaning *Beware, I am here*.

Jardine's father, Malcolm, was a first-class cricketer who attended Fettes College in Edinburgh, and Oxford. His mother, Alison Moir, was a lover of the game, which meant the young Douglas was either going to be passionate about the sport, or rebel against it and hate it.

Malcolm's work as a barrister kept him in India but he wanted his son to have an education in the British public system. In 1910, at the age of nine, Douglas was sent to live with his aunt Kitty in St Andrews, Scotland and to board at Horris Hill School, near Newbury, Berkshire.

Jardine's dedication to the game began in grey, often bleak, St Andrews, where he came under the wing of a close friend of Aunt Kitty's, Andrew Lang, 66, a prolific Scots poet, novelist and anthropologist. But it wasn't his literature that inspired young Jardine the most. It was this substitute father figure's obsession with cricket. Lang added a philosophical dimension to the game beyond his father's passion.

'Cricket is a very humanising game,' he told Jardine. 'It appeals to patriotism and pride. It is eminently unselfish. It binds all the brethren together, whatever their politics and rank may be.'

Young Jardine was enthralled. 'We were in complete agreement that the two Cs—Cricket and Classics—were the two most important things in the world,' he said.

Lang later added fishing to Jardine's interests.

The boy now had an intellectual framework for cricket that meant more to him than any school subject. He was an average scholar but maintained for life a strong interest in Greek and Latin literature. Yet he couldn't wait for cricket practice after lectures, and matches on Saturday. The village green, with all its gentility, polite applause, ups and downs, character building and a desire to win, became a centring, stabilising force for him.

Lang, not much of a player himself, nevertheless gave the boy advice. 'Get your defensive play correct, and all else will flow from that.'

Jardine thought this was sound. It relieved him of trying to belt the cover off the ball with bats that were too big and arms that were not strong enough. He worked on his back-foot movement, feet in position, left elbow high. He found the cuts and pulls too challenging at nine but he could leg glance and flick through slips and gully. At age ten, no one could get him out in the nets, or in house matches. The cricket coaches noticed and chose him to bat at number six.

In 1913, aged twelve, he made the First XI, in the side for his solid batting and leg spinning. However, the team's coach was displeased with his lack of desire to attack or leave his crease for the classic one-two-one dance step against the spinners.

'Was he afraid of being dismissed?' he was asked.

'No,' came the pedantic reply, 'I was afraid of not being in. I love batting.'

The boy had in mind Andrew Lang's gratuitous advice, but he cited the writing of a greater authority, C. B. Fry, who published *Cricket: Batsmanship* in 1912. The book emphasised learning defensive play as the foundation for a batsman. Jardine's stubbornness or stoicism saw him cling to this approach; it did not colour the coach's decision to make him captain in his final year at Horris Hill.

The school team remained unbeaten. Jardine said little and gave little praise, which may have been due to shyness. He fielded with verve, bowled his leg spin with guile, and batted with style, as ever without pasting the bowling. He made good, instinctive decisions with field placements and bowling changes.

In 1914 as war loomed, Jardine entered Winchester College, an elite public school that was severe and at times gruelling. Cold showers in winter were endured and accepting pain was a principle, especially on the sporting field.

If struck on the body anywhere by a cricket ball you had to pretend you felt nothing.

'I couldn't actually hold the bat handle properly on one occasion,' Jardine wrote with pride. 'Two fingers were badly bruised. But no one on the field knew.'

'Never let the opposition see any weakness' was instilled into every boy on or off the field. Some flinched, others jumped around and rubbed the bruise. Young Jardine took it without a change of expression. He even enjoyed it, almost masochistically. On one occasion, a boy in the school rugby team suffered a broken leg, but he got up and played on. The spectators, including Jardine, applauded and lauded the lad as a hero.

Corporal punishment was rife there. Boys had to bear the cane on the derrière without complaint, no matter if they were nearly lacerated. All they were allowed to show was a red face; never tears. It was character building, allegedly.

Pupils were reminded that it could be important in preparing for war. England had been in battles with other nations for most of the past 400 years. The UK thrived on it, or at least the military class did, almost as if the occasional large-scale bloodletting was healthy for national unity, growth and regeneration. Global dominance of Britain and her vast dominions and colonies was also paramount.

Military leaders in 1914 could hark back to the Boer War when medals were awarded on an accelerated scale. But that conflict was fourteen years earlier. For most, easy advance in officer ranks only came when battles were on. There was a subtle pressure for something to happen and the Prussian Army was providing it. The German military-industrial machine was created and run on the premise that 'democracy'—the Germanic version of it—only worked if wars were never-ending.

In the UK, there was a gung-ho, 'let's get 'em' mentality developing even before war was declared in August 1914. Colonels, majors and generals were commenting and emitting warnings in the newspapers as the propaganda mounted.

When war was declared cricket shut down from the first-class level to the local village green. Many grounds were requisitioned by the military. Yet the turf on most public school grounds was unaffected. Games went on. The contests were publicised more widely. *Wisden* gave the matches more space than before. There was no county cricket on which to report.

Up-and-coming schoolboy stars such as Jardine were more than whispered about in the corridors of the game's governing body, the Marylebone Cricket Club (MCC). Sporting performances were now heightened in the recognition of a teenager's prestige. Perseverance, determination, dash in a cricket, football or rugby game was more respected than being good at arithmetic, or having the capacity to conjugate Latin verbs. Physical attributes in sporting competition on green fields all over the UK were far more redolent of what was happening on Flanders Fields of red poppies and blood, than any intellectual development.

In war, thinking skills were subservient to killing skills.

Jardine had changed from a shy, cautious lad to someone simply laconic and more confident. It came from good shows on the cricket pitch with bat and ball, in football as a goalkeeper, and at rackets. He made the First XI at sixteen in 1917 and stayed there through 1918 and 1919.

His coaches, all capable cricketers, worked on inducing him to attack spinners, not with the one-two-one dance, but with more intent and alacrity than he had demonstrated. A criticism was that he was a tad flat-footed. Stubborn young Douglas loosened up a fraction. He worked on his shots square of the wicket. He disdained lofting the ball.

Former Test all-rounder and coach, Schofield Haigh, with his slight shoulders and broad Huddersfield accent, pushed a sometimes reluctant Jardine more than the other two coaches to be more aggressive. The talented teenager had a near impenetrable defence. Haigh wanted him to take more risks.

Despite Haigh's weak frame and age (48 in 1919; he died two years later), the coach attempted to draw out any latent aggression in Jardine. Haigh could still bowl fast when he wanted to and in net encounters delivered head-high bumpers off a short run. Jardine used his height to dead bat them. Haigh urged him to use his feet to get into position for stronger responses. Jardine said nothing but refused to play shots.

Another of the ex-Test player coaches at Winchester, Rockley Wilson, an off spinner, reinforced Jardine's entrenchment at the crease, but advised him to take the one stride stretch forward more against the turning ball. Wilson, also a Yorkshireman, disagreed with Haigh about his emphasis on aggression. Wilson endorsed C. B. Fry's attitude of 'defence first, attack later' in a batsman's growth, and so supported Jardine's natural approach that had begun with Andrew Lang's advice.

The three coaches, including first-class cricketer Harry Altham, debated if Jardine should captain the school team in 1919. They agreed he was the best batsman, but his quiet manner, which bordered on aloofness, was of concern. Could he lead and inspire the team? And was that necessary at this level of the game?

In the end, they judged that his grit would be important. Cricket was often about not losing or not giving up.

Rather than being confused, in his final year at Winchester, Jardine subconsciously or otherwise fused the professional teaching with his own instincts and had a strong cricket season, topping the batting averages with 997 runs at an average of 66.46.

The crowning moment, that would be remembered by most boys and teachers at the school as long as they lived, was the annual 'grudge' match against Eton. Winchester had not won this game for twelve years. Unconcerned, Jardine led by example in the field with quick, thoughtful bowling changes, and determination with the bat, scoring slow but match-winning innings of 35 and 89. The latter performance was Jardine's most satisfying and favourite innings of all the games of cricket he ever played in his career.

Not far behind was his 135 not out against Harrow School. All old boys from Winchester, Eton and Harrow, who made up most of the cricket establishment at the MCC, took note.

They reflected on the match reports in *Wisden* and agreed that here was a possible Test captain of England.

3

FROM THE PITS:
HAROLD LARWOOD

Harold Larwood was born on 14 November 1904 into a Nottinghamshire family where the triumvirate of God, cricket and coal predominated. The Larwoods lived in Nuncargate close to the mining town of Kirkby-in-Ashfield, Nottinghamshire, that thirteen centuries earlier was settled by the Vikings, who gave the town the name 'Kirkby', Danish for 'Church Town'.

Harold was the fourth of five boys born to Robert, a miner, and Mary Sharman. Robert was a strict Methodist and treasurer of the local chapel. All boys traipsed along to church every Sunday morning without fail, and Robert himself more than once addressed the congregation about the evils of alcohol. He repeated the essence of his sermon to the village cricket team, which he captained and included at various times three of his sons.

The strict disciplines of the church underpinned the mentality of the team. You played it hard but fair; you never questioned an umpire's decision as a bowler or batsman; you never complained; you were always sporting to the opposition; and you never said anything 'intemperate'.

These principles were drilled further into young Harold at the age of five, when he attended Kirkby Woodhouse School. Football was popular but cricket was the key sport played. Even aged six and seven, the weedy little chap displayed something special. He could bowl fast with a tennis ball with pinpoint accuracy. His father noticed and when he turned eight, he handed him a cricket ball and led him into the nets at the club. He encouraged him to concentrate on his run-up and accuracy. Even at that tender age, young Harold had a smooth run to the wicket. There was never a loud heave of the ball. His follow-through was good. Robert gave him a few tips about bowling being a 'side on' action, where you looked over your left shoulder.

Harold was instructed not to fear the hard ball. He had a good eye and was adept in the field early. As a reward, the boy was allowed to bat to his father in the nets. The lesson here was to 'hurt' the ball; to hit it as hard as possible.

Robert, never one to overdo his praise for the boys, told Harold aged ten at the start of the 1915 cricket season, 'Keep on working at your game, and you could play for Nottingham.'

This was the highest praise he was capable of. None of Harold's four siblings received it.

*

The vision was extraordinary for Harold and allowed him to dream. He was an average student with no particular academic flare. He was happy to leave school at age thirteen and move on to the next phase of life, which began with him weighing flour at the local miners' cooperative store. At fourteen, early in 1919, a new, disenchanting future was shown to him at Annesley Colliery. His father organised a job at the mines looking after the pit ponies.

Young Harold knew the mining industry well enough. His father went down every day and would return covered in the grime of the underground work, which was exacting and unrelenting. Yet his father's faith in the boy's cricket was now a serious incentive for Harold one day to play the game for money. His reverie now was about aiming to avoid pit work. In the meantime, Harold did the dirty, hard work down the mines; the only virtue for him was that he gained strength in his upper body and legs.

In the summer of 1918, he made Nuncargate's Seconds. He was of less than average height and weight in the team of mainly adults. But his ability to hurl a cricket ball at speed with near perfect calibration gave him a bigger image. He avoided the pitfalls of drink, even though the side's elder players loved a pint or two. The teetotalling doctrine of his father, watching over him at the club, and the church, saw him eschew such temptations. Besides that, he wanted to be fit for his Saturday matches.

His self-discipline worked. In his first season he took 76 wickets at an exceptional 4.9 runs per wicket, all the more meritorious because he wore running shoes rather than boots, which were beyond his father's means.

Despite the foetid air in the pits, or perhaps because of it, he grew to 165 centimetres (5 foot 5 inches) by 1920. He was just fifteen and was selected to play for Nuncargate's Firsts, the same team as his father. It was an important step if Harold were to realise the possibility dangled by his father, that county team Nottinghamshire was not outside his reach.

*

Joe Hardstaff Sr, a Test and Nottinghamshire player, also hailed from Nuncargate and was a friend of Robert Larwood. He had watched Harold develop as a bowler and he asked for a net against him in March 1923.

It was a big moment for the eighteen year old.

He delivered accordingly, uprooting the experienced 40-year-old veteran's middle stump, and causing him to edge, miss and duck on other occasions.

After the net, Hardstaff took Robert aside and said he would arrange a trial for young Harold at the county's home, Trent Bridge, in the next month, April.

4

THE BOWRAL BOY: DON BRADMAN

A health issue in 1911 for Don Bradman's mother, Emily, caused the family to move from the remote country town of Cootamundra in the southwest slopes of New South Wales to Bowral in the Southern Highlands, some 120 kilometres south of Sydney. The air at more than 2200 feet above sea level was better in Bowral than just about anywhere in Australia. Don was the fifth and last Bradman child by four years, with one brother and three sisters.

Born 27 August 1908, he found life idyllic in the rural hamlet. He loved sports and excelled at them: cricket, tennis, athletics and rugby. If there had been any other popular games that needed a sphere or ball of some kind, he would have been competitive at them as well. Later he watched with interest as golfers played on a nearby course and decided it would be another challenge for him.

Don enjoyed his schoolwork and topped the class almost every year in mathematics, and sometimes English. Cricket, with its preoccupations with statistics, fascinated him the most. There was more substance in cricket history, especially involving the numbers.

There were no boys to play with close to home and this caused him to experiment. After playing cricket at school before class and during recess, he trotted home and played more, if Emily could take time from preparing the evening meal. She delivered her left armers and he played correctly with his first bat, fashioned by his carpenter father from a gum-tree branch.

If Emily was busy helping her daughters Islet, Lily and May or her other son, Victor, with their homework or piano, young Don would improvise by using a cricket stump to hit a golf ball against the brick base of a water tank. The ball would fly back fast. Bradman already had a superb eye and quick reflexes. This game, played for hours, sharpened his natural gifts even further. The boy improved his throwing arm and catching skills by aiming a tennis ball at the railing of a fence. If it went over, he would have the penalty of searching for the ball in thick, long grass.

There was no coach at school. His father, George, was not much interested in orthodoxy and this meant Bradman learnt to devise unorthodox shots. No one told him not to hit the ball from the off to leg with a cross-bat shot. He had the ability to be creative with shots off the front and back foot.

Don played his first real game of cricket for Bowral Primary at age eleven in 1919. He strode out in pads too big for his diminutive frame on the Glebe Park Oval (later to become Bradman Oval). He admitted to nerves as a tall, fast left armer from the neighbouring Mittagong School charged at him.

He was nearly bowled first ball.

Gathering some composure, he proceeded to score with enthusiasm all around the wicket until 55 not out, more than half his team's total. An astute observer would have judged that this first performance would set him apart in temperament and skill. It might just suggest young Bradman was someone who might even make club cricket in Sydney, a level just below First Class in Australia.

Nothing more could have been predicted for him in 1919.

PART TWO
1920–1928

5

POST-WAR COMIC
BOOK HERO

After World War I, Arthur Carr gained an image of a gung-ho mythical figure. He was seen as the dashing hero, who went on batting for Nottingham, when he was supposed to report to his cavalry barracks, *immediately*. He saw action on the Western Front, although there were gaps in the official War Office record with regard to his precise whereabouts at certain times. Carr was injured in and out of battle, which increased the 'glamour'. Added to this was his perseverance as a lothario, his marriage notwithstanding, and his capacity for prolonged and consistent drinking off and on the cricket field in an era when such behaviour was condoned and even lauded, especially by the ex-service community. His wealth, education and class allowed him to be a lovable rogue. It was the type of life as a sports star that many envied and aped, and to which some aspired.

Carr now knew how to relate to and lead men in the battle arena and on the sports field. There was a dash and dare about his batting bordering often on recklessness. When he got going in an innings, muscle overrode technique. There was terrific forearm punch in his driving and he cared little for wrist movement. He had weaknesses that opposition bowlers could exploit. He could not cut well. Either he didn't have the inclination or disdained the added flexibility required for this adventurous yet still refined shot.

Arthur Carr disdained refinement at anything.

He liked to remind everyone that the Nottinghamshire ground was founded behind the Trent Bridge Inn, as if it were a justification for inculcating a culture of drinking. He made playing for the county 'fun'. You could have a skinful the night before as long as you performed well on the field the next day. After play he created a licence to get legless. You could imbibe alcohol during the game too, as long as you kept the bottle or glass inside the dressing room and away from spectators and the eyes of the press.

Beer was issued to some instead of water in breaks. On special occasions, champagne was served.

Carr wrote in his autobiography, *Cricket with the Lid Off*, that every cricketer was aware 'amazing feats' could be achieved when 'under the influence'.

His philosophy was telling and a dangerous recipe for those under him, if they wished to avoid alcoholism. For some, such as his fast bowlers, it was a delicate balance of obeying the captain and not becoming addicted. 'All really fast bowlers need beer to help them keep going,' Carr said. 'You cannot be a great fast bowler on a bottle of ginger-pop or a nice glass of cold water ... he uses up immense amounts of physical strength in hard exercise, and he must have something to give him a kick.'

He went on to add, 'Beer is best. A pint too much may make him slightly tiddly for a little while, but only for a little while. He very quickly perspires it out of his system.'

His 1920 season with the bat was poor. He had been drinking moderately, for him, throughout the season but in desperation decided to get drunk the night before a game to test what it would do for his form. He awoke with a stinging hangover and thought the only way to get through the day in the field was by more boozing.

He went to the pavilion bar and swiftly knocked back three whisky and sodas.

'When it came to my turn to bat,' he said, 'I was in such form that I proceeded to make a double century.'

This was 204 against Essex, which was without its two best bowlers. Nevertheless, it was a thumping innings. Carr spoke of it every season thereafter, justifying his alcoholism. It added another dimension to the comic book hero he had become during his early career. The cricket community dined out on the anecdote as much as Carr himself. It sat sweetly next to the exaggerated tale about his ignoring the call to arms in favour of batting on for Nottinghamshire at The Oval.

Carr was selected for an MCC tour of New Zealand in 1921, and his average batting displays—apart from the occasional burst of brilliance—suggested he was chosen more for team harmony and conviviality than form. The year 1922 was better for him. He managed to be Nottinghamshire's best performer and was chosen by *Wisden* as one of the five cricketers of the year. It noted his 'straight-driving could almost have been described as the restoration of a lost art'. *The Cricketer* magazine listed him among the twelve cricketers of the year, calling him 'an excellent captain, keen and determined, who gets the best out of the men under him'.

This sort of praise led to him being chosen for two northern winter boat tours in the 1922–23 period, first to South Africa and then on to New Zealand again.

Carr was fast becoming a year-round cricketing amateur with a professional load.

He enjoyed the opportunity to play on and off the field, fuelled by wild nights and sun-filled days, away from restrictions of family and press coverage. Not much was ever written about these tours and this suited Carr particularly. He turned 29 on tour yet there was still the sense that he was an adolescent hedonist, which endeared him to many of his teammates, and opposition players, whom he embraced more than was normal for England teams.

The super comic hero image, more for male adults than schoolboys, was enhanced by his surviving several car crashes. He was an atrocious, careless driver. In 1923, when driving to play Worcestershire at Stourbridge, he hit a tree at Wychbold, writing off his old Bentley. Carr said the tree was perilously close to the road. A teammate in the car said it was five yards *off* the road.

Carr missed a day's play and turned up to bat as if nothing had happened. He did not care for unwanted publicity about his regular drink-driving 'events'. His short innings against Worcestershire was quick and devil-may-care, thus enhancing his 'crash and burn' image, at cricket, in fighting the enemy, and on the roads of England.

6

JARDINE'S EMERGENCE

Douglas Jardine's cricket seemed to mark time in 1920. He was nineteen, studying law at Oxford, and while he had shown the elusive 'potential' at his favourite sport, he also had a few drawbacks in the eyes of those who would have a say in his advance. His defence was always strong, but by 1921, when he made his first-class debut for the university, he seemed to struggle with the higher level of competition. Jardine relied on defence and wicket preservation rather than attack. His footwork deteriorated as a result.

Coach Tom Hayward, aged 40, tried to entice him to be more positive. Jardine was in awe of the former Test batsman, who had hit more than a hundred centuries in first-class cricket, only the second player to achieve this after W. G. Grace. Hayward first worked on Jardine's tendency to be flat-footed in his stroke play. He urged him to think he was playing real tennis, where his footwork and balance were good. He gave Jardine ballet exercises to sharpen his movements. Then he operated on his driving. Hayward was precise technically in his stroke play and this endeared him to Jardine, who prided himself similarly. Yet the coach had one of the most telling off drives in the history of the game. He was attacking for an opener, and had Jardine's confidence here too.

For a while it seemed Jardine was willing to learn from, and to please and copy the master. But that was in the nets. In competition, he fell back on holding on to his wicket. It was frustrating for the coach, the Oxford team, its opposition and spectators.

Hayward would glare down at his charge over an outsized moustache and urge him on in the nets. 'You can't score big if you don't go after the bowlers,' he said. Left unsaid was the fact that Hayward should know. Centuries at first-class level were his specialty. He had also scored a record (at that point) aggregate of 3518 runs in a season—1906. His utterances about making runs were adhered to. He was a professional who could berate anyone if he wished, even impressive young amateurs.

The following year, Jardine began the season as if he meant business, opening for Oxford with unusual intent and scoring three fifties in the first three matches. However, he was subdued after getting himself out to attacking shots when he wanted to go on to three figures, regardless of the team's situation.

Then came the game against Warwick Armstrong's powerful 1921 Australian touring team. It was mowing down all opposition. Showing disdain for the students, Armstrong demanded the university matches be two days instead of the three against the counties. The schedule was overcrowded and the colleges were forced to agree.

Jardine opened for Oxford. He was cautious but steady against speedster Jack Gregory, who delivered only four overs without even bothering to send the young man one bumper. Armstrong introduced leg spinner Arthur Mailey into the attack. Mailey loved batsmen who were loath to use their feet. He bowled four leg breaks in succession. Jardine watched and defended against two using his long legs to push forward, and two that caused the batsman to go back and keep out of his stumps, using his pads. Then Mailey delivered a perfectly flighted googly. For a split second it appeared enticing. Jardine went to drive but was caught in two minds as the ball dropped on him. He pushed at it and Mailey took a good caught and bowled.

Jardine trudged off unhappy that he had spoilt a chance to go beyond the still creditable 35.

Mailey proceeded to run through the students, taking 7 for 108 in 30.2 overs, almost half the overs bowled in Oxford's 180. Australia replied with 294 in quick time with Scottish right-arm fast medium Raymond Charles (R. C.) Robertson-Glasgow (Jardine's good friend and supporter, and later Bradman's favourite cricket writer) taking the best figures of 4 for 74.

Oxford batted again with a little over two sessions left on the final and second day. Unless the Australians could break through quickly the game would fizzle to a tame draw.

This time Gregory tore in as if he meant business, giving Jardine a minor working over, which was weathered well enough. Armstrong dismissed Jardine's opening partner for 19 with the score at 25. This was the possible opening for an Australian victory. Armstrong kept bowling himself, resting a tired Mailey except for eight overs, and thus sparing

Jardine from more stringent examination. Yet he batted well against all bowlers, including Mailey who sent down just 25 balls to him.

Jardine relied on defence again and that was understandable. He had to make sure his fellow students were not rolled for a low score. This was the approach Jardine himself had taken; the one you could depend on to bat stoically, if not stolidly, to save a game. It turned away spectators but was admired by teammates. They didn't wish to be humiliated by the tourists.

In the final session of the match he opened up a fraction more as Armstrong gave all but two fielders a bowl. As stumps loomed Jardine plodded his way towards a century. When the umpires called time, he was 96 not out and Oxford was 1 for 174. Jardine had batted for 157 minutes and hit 12 fours. Armstrong and his team were not interested in staying on for a couple more overs to let Jardine reach three figures.

The game had been over at tea, and the last session proved superfluous.

Armstrong was criticised for not letting Jardine become the first opposition player to reach a ton against the tourists. But the Australian captain was not in the habit of being overly generous to opposition teams; nor in doffing his lid to an Oxford player wearing a maroon and blue harlequin cap. Hundreds had to be earnt. Besides, when the pressure was off and the game was headed for a certain draw, Jardine had ample opportunity to increase his rate, even marginally, to take the coveted prize.

It was claimed that he took a dislike to Australians thereafter, which was unlikely. He would later have many more excuses to hate the plunderers from down under.

Had Jardine done a little more himself, and shown a second or third gear of aggression, even against the easier bowling Armstrong presented to him, a three-figure score may well have tipped him into England's Test team. As it was, he was being touted for the elevation by some influential voices, including that of former Test captain Pelham Francis (Plum) Warner.

*

Jardine continued on his dogged way in 1921 finishing the season with Surrey.

He missed most of 1922 due to a partial tear of his anterior cruciate ligament in the knee, that restricted his ability to lunge forward at the crease and turn quickly in the field. He was advised to wear a brace and stay off it until the following English summer, a frustrating situation for a talented youngster on the cusp of making the national side.

Jardine came back for Oxford and Surrey in 1923, his final Oxford year, but was not given the captaincy. His detractors said this was a character judgement. He was not the most popular candidate although such positions have rarely if ever been granted for being the most-loved chap. Leadership rarely equated to being the humorist, or most successful womaniser, or biggest party boy and drinker. The skipper would normally be picked on his capacity to win matches, even if he was not inspirational.

Jardine already had a tactical brain beyond the average 21 year old. As it was, the call was made for a more deserving and respected character: Australian Reg Bettington, an impressive leg spinner and hard-hitting, middle-order batsman.

The 194 centimetre (6 foot 3 inch) imposing son of an Australian grazier took 62 wickets at 16.55 for Oxford in 1923. In the big annual match against Cambridge he dominated with eleven wickets enabling an Oxford victory. It was the last game for the university for him, Robertson-Glasgow and Jardine. (Bettington went on to a life of exceptional achievement and service as a Harley Street surgeon and later as a doctor for the Australian Army on two war fronts over four years in World War II: in the Middle East against the Italians and Germans, and Papua against the Japanese.)

*

Jardine left Oxford with an unimpressive Fourth Class degree in modern history, which he could well justify because of other commitments, namely his cricket up and down the country. But it meant he would be just employable as a secondary school teacher. He was an amateur cricketer, so there was nothing there that would earn him a reasonable income.

On his father's advice, he began to qualify as a solicitor.

7

GENESIS OF A SPORTING GENIUS

Twelve-year-old Don Bradman was thrilled to join his father in February 1921 for a train ride to Sydney to see the first two days of the Fifth Ashes Test. On day one, a Friday, he was in awe at the sight of the Members Pavilion, other stands and the fabled 'Hill', all packed with more than 20,000 fans eager for the game to begin. On the English side were great names such as Hobbs, Rhodes, Hendren, Woolley and Parkin. The Australian team included the 'Big Ship' Warwick Armstrong, Bardsley, Macartney, Taylor, Gregory, Ryder and McDonald.

Bradman noted in his autobiography, *Farewell to Cricket*: 'Woolley's beautiful stroke-making, the smooth rhythm of Ted McDonald and the glorious catching of Parkin by Johnny Taylor [Bradman's favourite player]'. On day two he sat enchanted, watching a dazzling performance by Charlie Macartney as he displayed a range of shots from delicate leg glances and brutal pulls to slashing cuts and glorious cover drives on the way to 170.

The boy stood and applauded, as he did for a smashing 93 by paceman Gregory that also put Australia in a position to win by eight wickets. The game had been the most riveting 'show' young Don could imagine.

With the confidence that would become one of his trademarks, Bradman told his father, 'I shall never be satisfied until I play on this ground.' Modesty prevented him from adding 'and until I perform at the standard of Charlie Macartney'.

He acted as scorer for the Bowral town team, which played in the Berrima District Competition and other matches in the region. This needed sharp concentration, a head for figures and a good knowledge of the game.

At the end of 1921, when he was thirteen, the Bowral team was one short playing away against Moss Vale. Don asked his uncle, George Whatman, the team captain, if he could play. Whatman was concerned about him facing adult bowlers but he'd seen the diminutive lad in the nets. He could bat. Whatman gave him the nod and put him in second last in the batting order. Young Don marched in wearing pads that flapped against his stomach and holding a bat that was far too big.

Although restricted, he managed pushes, dabs and glances to reach 37 not out, much to the chagrin of Moss Vale's fast bowler, who threw everything at this 'child' with the extraordinary confidence, courage and defence. The next Saturday, when the game was all but over, Whatman let him open. This time Bradman scored 29 not out.

He filled in on another three occasions and scored 308 for Bowral in the 1921–22 season. He was never dismissed, meaning that his average in the adult competition stood at infinity.

There was no junior team in Bowral, and at the end of 1922, aged fourteen, he achieved a good intermediate certificate and high marks in mathematics and French. But school in country New South Wales did not go beyond Year 10, which meant the boy would have to look for a job when he dreamt of going on to finish secondary school and then university.

He had the intellect to do any degree he wished, but not the means.

The teenager became a clerk at local real estate agent, Percy Westbrook. There was no cricket path forward. This saw him turning to tennis for the better part of the next two summers and winning a local under-sixteen championship. His ability made him consider taking up this more opportunistic individual sport.

Yet cricket was still deep in his psyche and heart.

He turned out again, aged sixteen, for Bowral late in 1924, this time at number seven, scoring a duck and 66. The latter innings was enough to make him determined to continue in his first sport of choice.

*

The big cricket match for the next summer (1925–26) was against Wingello, which had an outstanding 21-year-old leg spinner, Bill O'Reilly, who was on the verge of state selection. O'Reilly was tall, and bowled a stock ball at medium pace. He had a good wrong 'un, and variety.

Bradman opened for Bowral and began well, forcing the Wingello skipper to bring on O'Reilly, who often was first change due to his speed of delivery. He had the over-adventurous lad pushing hard. Bradman edged one to slip and was dropped. O'Reilly remonstrated at his ill luck. The young batsman began to thrash the bowling, and noted that O'Reilly reacted 'like a disturbed hive of bees'. The angular, lanky spinner 'seemed to attack from all directions'.

But not well enough. Bradman became the beekeeper on that hot mid-summer afternoon. He obliterated O'Reilly with a rush of fours and sixes that left Bradman on 234 not out in 165 minutes, scoring more than a century in the last hour before stumps. Forty-eight of the last 50 came in boundaries.

'I could not assimilate that a pocket-sized schoolboy could have given me such a complete lacing,' O'Reilly remarked. (Bradman played against the spinner many times and there were further 'lacings' and reminders for O'Reilly of that humiliating afternoon in Bowral. No other batsman achieved or repeated such shellackings of the great leggie, whom Bradman judged the best bowler of all time, spinner or otherwise.)

It was beyond belief for O'Reilly that such a merciless talent could emerge from a neighbouring country town. It made the bowler rethink his budding career. Should he return to track and field competition, namely the hop, step and jump, at which he excelled? He stewed on the issue for a week.

The next Saturday, day two of the match, was at Wingello's home ground. O'Reilly opened with a very fast leg break and bowled Bradman. It restored some self-belief in the bowler's ability, although it took a few years to realise how good this batsman was, and to put that innings in perspective.

The regional press reported on Bradman when he made a dashing 300 in the final against Moss Vale, giving him a season's aggregate of 1318 runs at 94.16. His own leg spinners netted him 35 wickets at 8.5. These portents of brilliance were ignored by the Sydney press. They were seen as just country bumpkin figures. They did not even mention his triple hundred. Editors justified the spiking of the story by noting that the game was played on core matting and not turf.

His mother had a belief in the lad and sent him and his father to Sydney to buy a new bat as a reward for his efforts. Bradman, now seventeen, could not wait until the next summer season began.

In the meantime, he would read with interest about the Australian team's exploits in England, and dream one day that he would tour for his country.

8

CONVERGENCE OF LARWOOD AND CARR

Nottinghamshire coach and former champion, Jim Iremonger, along with Arthur Carr, were the modern equivalent of life coaches for Harold Larwood in the 1923 season. The captain thought him too small for a fast bowler in big cricket, and he was viewed more like a jockey than a cricketer. He lacked stamina.

Iremonger worked on Larwood's diet and exercise. The ruggedly handsome, lean youngster reached his peak height of 174 centimetres (5 foot 8 inches) and weighed in at 66 kilograms. The aim was to build his muscle everywhere and add about 4 kilograms. In parallel, Iremonger instructed him on the bowling arts, stressing accuracy more than speed, variations in his grip, and also a way to swing the ball in the air. Always he reminded young Harold that an increased pace would come naturally with his skills development.

Carr decided to treat him like a son. Carr was an experienced 30-year-old national hero, and he liked the lad's determination. He felt after two seasons, without saying it to Larwood, that he had the makings of a top county player. The protégé looked up to him as a cricketing god. Carr had one other task, not exactly connected to the game. 'I made it my business to see that he took to beer.'

When Carr proffered the demon drink, Larwood hesitated because of his strict Methodist upbringing. He didn't want to let his real father down. Iremonger endorsed the drinking by telling him it would do him no harm in moderation. The clinching argument was that it would add much-needed weight to his frame. Larwood succumbed, enjoyed stout and beer and added the aimed-for 4 kilograms over the next year.

The development showed on the field. Near the end of the 1923 season he took 8 for 44 for the county's Seconds against Lancashire. He was offered a player contract of 32 shillings a week, and was expected to carry out ground staff duties. The money was the same as his mining wage. He accepted without consulting his father and Robert was not pleased, telling his son that he would be working longer hours than down the mines. But Larwood didn't care. He considered anything was better than being in the pits, even if it were for only one summer. He would do everything in his power to make sure cricket kept him above ground for more than a year.

*

He succeeded but it took him nearly two more years before he was ready for a permanent place in the Nottinghamshire First XI. He sealed his position with an outstanding perfor-mance in mid-June 1925 against Yorkshire at Bramall Lane, Sheffield. He only took three wickets in a losing side but the twenty year old's pace had the knowledgeable crowd gasping. He troubled all batsmen, hitting and bruising a couple. When the crowd objected, Carr stepped in and told him not to be concerned. This was Yorkshire. The spectators were protective of their own.

His best drubbing was reserved for county star, Maurice Leyland, who was batting well on 52 when he popped a catch to Carr close in on the leg side when fending off a sharply lifting delivery.

The captain clapped and encouraged him. Larwood, always hard on himself, felt he was at last on the way to some sort of a career and security. Games were already earning a shilling or two more than he could make in the pits. He had the skills to climb away from the mines for good.

Larwood's confidence increased. He went on to take 73 wickets at 18.01 for the season. His best effort was a match-winning 11 for 41 against Worcestershire. He delivered with menace, forcing batsmen to take evasive action. The not so fleet of foot were hit on the shoulder and the arm. Larwood clean bowled eight of the opposition in a big win for Nottinghamshire at the end of the season.

Carr, a front runner to skipper England against the touring Australians, was already thinking ahead, if he were chosen, who might be his front-line bowlers?

He felt he had the right cattle prod for his star paceman. 'When I particularly wanted to get Larwood's tail up in order to get a quick wicket or two for Notts, I saw to it that he has not wanted for a drop or two [of beer].'

*

Around this time, Larwood began to feel more at home at Nottinghamshire. He thought his future might be fun and bright there. Nottinghamshire was supported by a rich Jewish merchant and philanthropist by the name of Sir Julien Cahn. He sold furniture in a chain of 300 stores throughout the UK in a business started and built up by his father, Albert, a German émigré. Julien Cahn also introduced hire purchase schemes to make it easier for customers to consider buying his products. He made no secret of his Orthodox upbringing and culture, despite running into an undercurrent of anti-Semitic sentiment, which he endured and dealt with by his financial largesse.

He loved cricket, and the game gave him a modicum of acceptance into the local establishment. It was a vehicle for his social mobility. He was ostentatious and well liked at the club. As soon as Larwood appeared, he showed him respect and supported him enthusiastically, recognising that like Cahn's father, the young miner had come up the hard way with his own special talents and an innate, though insecure, determination.

Cahn donated 30,000 pounds a year to Trent Bridge and its infrastructure. He organised games at his own private ground nearby, and always insisted on young Larwood being in his team. After a match he would slip the neophyte a quid, or on occasions even more, which would more than supplement the potential champion's weekly income.

Larwood was introduced to a world he could never have imagined while looking after the pit ponies at Kirkby-in-Ashfield. Cahn would throw lavish parties at his 35-room Stanford Hall home after games with other visiting clubs. Attractive young women entertained ten of the playing guests. The bowler who dared to dismiss Cahn, who batted in his own team, would miss out. It wasn't a scene Larwood would rush home to inform his hard-working father about. But he was amused enough to tell Robert about a pair of performing sea lions in one of the estate's swimming pools. Cahn's wife bought them for the man who had everything.

Cahn's fondness for young Larwood ran to paying for half of his house, which was built on two and a half acres of land. His backer had also lent him money, at no interest, to create his gardens of flowers and vegetables, which he sold at the local markets.

Carr was Larwood's cricket cultivator. Cahn was his early benefactor, the man who gave him a sense of financial stability, which depended on his staying on the track and performing at his best.

9

CAPTAIN CARR CRASH

When Arthur Carr received a letter from the national selection committee inviting him to captain England against the touring Australians in the 1926 Ashes, he celebrated with champagne and bought a new green Austin 7 car. On the way to Trent Bridge for the First Test he crashed into the back of a truck. The car was not a write-off but needed extensive repairs. Carr blamed the slippery road and bad weather.

He wanted Harold Larwood in the team and had support from selector and great player Jack Hobbs, especially after the speedster had removed him twice in a Nottinghamshire v Surrey game. Hobbs told the rest of the committee about Larwood's exceptional pace but was overruled by the other four selectors.

'You'd have a different attitude if you faced him,' Hobbs told them but to no avail.

The Tests were to be played over just three days, which seemed before and during the series to be a measure of austerity too far. Unless there were several substantial batting collapses the series was headed for tedious draws. Then the English weather had to be factored in and this, unless by divine intervention, seemed certain to curtail games further. What should have been a triumph for Carr in the Trent Bridge First Test ended up being a miserable time.

The game was washed out for all but 17.2 overs.

He lived to be skipper again in the Second Test at Lord's. This time he prevailed in having Larwood selected, using the argument that the young Nottinghamshire star had earnt a chance on his form in the trial match before the series when he took five wickets.

Carr had belief in the 21-year-old paceman who he said was improving with every match. Larwood's reaction to his selection was unique in the annals of Test cricket (at least in those recorded). 'I'm just not good enough, Mr Carr,' he said, 'I need more time.'

Carr cajoled him into a bit more confidence. He took him aside and went through the complete list of the Australian batsmen he would 'meet'. 'No doubt they are a good side, and they have a couple of champions,' he said, 'but they all have weaknesses. Macartney, for instance, likes to come at you from the get-go. This has left him vulnerable early, especially to a slips catch. You'll aim at his off stump with the ball moving away. He can't resist driving. I'll leave the off side a little vacant to tempt him.'

Carr went through the entire opposition on whom he'd taken notes, often from assessments made by others in the run-up games before the Tests. This calmed Larwood who nevertheless remained unsure about his ability to perform.

Carr kept boosting him and made sure he had a beer before he walked onto the field at Lord's. Larwood had performed well there before, but this was an Ashes Test in front of a packed crowd at the home of cricket. A far greater challenge.

Larwood was wayward. Carr believed it was simply nerves for the 21 year old. He made sure his paceman had another beer at the lunch break. Larwood came out and had Australia's number one batsman, Macartney, caught for 39. His confidence was up. Later in the day he bowled the dangerous Jack Gregory for just 7.

Australia went on to be all out for 383, with Warren Bardsley carrying his bat for 193 not out. Larwood sent down 32 overs, taking 2 for 99. England replied with 3 for 475. Carr declared, again with some controversy, and without him being allowed a hit. Plum Warner, still acting as if he were de facto England captain, ordered the innings' termination.

Carr did not protest. England had a lead of 92. The game would end in a dreary draw if he didn't keep it alive and give his team a chance to win.

Australia thought it would belt its way clear by opening with Jack Gregory but he made a golden duck. It avoided any dangers thanks to a dashing 133 not out from Macartney. Larwood removed Herbie Collins, a third very useful scalp, in a more than respectable first Test effort, taking 3 for 136 overall.

Australia played out a draw with 5 for 194.

Carr rued the lack of a fourth day.

Larwood was not so pessimistic after the game but was still down on himself, telling his captain, 'It [the performance] wasn't great. I wasted a lot of energy.' Regardless, or perhaps because of the beer, he remained on edge and was not as accurate as usual.

He still wasn't convinced he was right for Test matches, and this attitude seemed to be supported by the selectors who dropped him for the Third Test at Headingley.

Carr caused a stir by sending Australia in. The move looked an inspired one when Maurice Tate removed Bardsley for a duck first ball. He should have had Macartney with his fifth delivery, but Carr spilt a catch at second slip. Those who opposed his captaincy, or who simply didn't like his character and behaviour, were given an ounce more ammunition.

Instead of removing two top batsmen in an over, England and its fans had to endure a 235-run partnership between Bill Woodfull and Macartney, who went on to a dashing 151 in 172 minutes, including a century before lunch. Woodfull, aged 28, scored 141. The studious Melbourne mathematics teacher was the last man chosen for the tour and had emerged as the 'find' for Australia in 1926, scoring two Test centuries.

At the break, Carr was almost speechless. Plum Warner sat angrily close by and Carr was not sure if it was the decision to bowl first, or his dropping of a sitter in slips. 'Probably both,' the miserable England skipper felt.

Australia posted 494, putting the tourists in an unbeatable position in a three-day game. England made 294. Carr managed just 13. England was invited to follow on and ensured a draw with 3 for 254.

Knives were sheathed for the moment.

Carr remained himself. Two days before the Fourth Test at Old Trafford he was caught speeding at more than twice the legal limit, which was 10 miles per hour (16 kph). He was fined 40 shillings (2 pounds), and another 10 shillings for not renewing his licence. The reporting in the papers was straight but the fact that he made the news for minor traffic offences, with the inference of irresponsibility, both garnished his image with supporters, and tarnished it with detractors.

Carr's mood was not helped by Australia winning the toss at Old Trafford and batting in inclement weather even worse than at Nottingham in the First Test. Yet 20,000 rugged-up spectators still filled the stands in hope, which was all they were left with after only a couple of overs were bowled. The game was one of just two days, which compounded the problem of these shorter version Tests.

Carr went to dinner with his wife and friends at the Midland Hotel on the rest day, Sunday. They all drank champagne, Carr having just one glass. During the dinner he complained of feeling unwell. He awoke the next morning with a temperature and a burning sore throat. He could not play and was replaced as skipper by Jack Hobbs, who Carr said in private at the time was a poor choice. He would have opted for an amateur. Surprisingly, Hobbs later agreed, writing in his autobiography, *My Life Story*, that he preferred 'to see an amateur as captain and most professions prefer it, especially in international cricket, chiefly because of the social side and because of the natural dislike of the professionals to boss their own fellows'.

Hobbs disliked the tedious parts of captaincy, such as glad-handing, speech-making, being the team spokesman and doing press interviews. Class divide attitudes were alive and well in English cricket in the 1920s.

It turned out Carr had tonsillitis. He was too mature to be operated on. Doctors told him to rest, keep warm, and take aspirin to keep his temperature down.

But his reputation got the rumour mill whirring. The thinly veiled, false innuendo in the press, and the freer gossip in the cricket world, was that the England captain had been drinking hard, as he was known to do, and that he could not appear on the Monday morning, day two, for play.

Australia was dismissed for 335, and England replied with 5 for 305, the game ending with the fourth draw in succession.

*

Despite his condition, Carr fulfilled a promise to play in a benefit match for Hobbs in the August Bank Holiday game, Nottinghamshire v Surrey. Carr, suffering from his illness, turned up with a neck bandage and still showing signs of fever. He did the right thing by Hobbs but didn't help gate takings by making a duck in the first innings. He made up for this in his second innings, scoring a bright 33. Hobbs notched 24 and 60, which didn't hurt his big pay day.

Carr insisted on playing for Nottinghamshire again, the next game being against Sussex in Hastings. He and three fellow Nottinghamshire players had a convivial dinner in London and then Carr drove them off in his repaired Austin 7. This time he managed to crash into a telegraph pole. Luckily, he and his three passengers lived, but one, Fred Barratt, emerged 'very badly cut by broken glass'. The car was damaged but they managed to get it running. There were benefits in cars that had top speeds of 50 kph. The passengers would have something to dine out on for years and add to the legend of Carr's exploits on and off the field.

In Hastings, Larwood was in fierce touch, taking 6 for 60 and 6 for 67. His pace was too much for several batsmen, who took blows on the torso.

Carr nurtured him in short, blistering spells, which led to a Nottinghamshire win by 77 runs. Carr, however, still suffered and looked out of sorts in his two innings of 16 and 15. There was also the possibility that he incurred delayed shock from the car accident, something not even considered at the time for such a hardy hero.

He then drove back to Trent Bridge, this time with three other intrepid cricketers, for the game against Derbyshire on a Saturday. He won the toss and batted, knowing it would be useful to get a decent score in order to shore up selectorial confidence for the upcoming Fifth Test at The Oval, beginning in a week.

He scored just 20.

His string of low scores were not helping his case. Nor were the rumours about the reasons for his ill-health, along with the badly timed car incident, which had trickled into the newspapers.

Nottinghamshire was all out for 360. Still in tip-top form on the Saturday evening, Larwood knocked over two Derbyshire batsmen, leaving the county 3 for 36 at stumps.

Carr had another moment of *cricket interruptus*, this time for a dash down to London for a selectors' meeting. Chairman Plum Warner greeted him in the MCC board room in his decidedly polite manner with the invitation to *stand down* as the Test captain. The selection committee had split three to two against him.

Carr was stunned. He argued that it was not the right time.

'We want you to do this for England's sake,' Warner said. 'You know you are not fully fit, Arthur.'

'I'm over the tonsillitis,' Carr protested. 'I've played the last three county matches.'

'But your form, Arthur . . .'

'I've had one hit in the Tests!'

'Your county form has not been strong. This is a timeless match. We need a very fit eleven.'

'So you're dumping me as captain right at the time the team needs stability for a win at The Oval.'

'I'm afraid so, Arthur. You are not in the eleven, either.'

Carr was flabbergasted. He left the meeting in high dudgeon.

The standard official press statement with the usual face-saving hypocrisy stated: 'Mr. A. W. Carr, the England captain, who has not been in good health recently, generously offered to resign his place in the eleven. On consideration, this unselfish action on the part of Mr. Carr was accepted by the selection committee with the greatest possible regret.'

The press was further shocked to learn that ex-Cambridge and Kent amateur Percy Chapman, with the experience of two Tests against South Africa in 1924, including one innings of 8 runs, and a scant county career, was chosen to lead the side.

Chapman was a kind of *Boy's Own Annual* ideal of a dashing England captain. At times he batted with Gay Abandon, when Gay was not always the perfect partner for the occasion. Neville Cardus described him as 'tall, slim, youthful and pink and chubby of face. His left-handed batting mingled brilliance and grace . . . His cricket was romantic in its vaunting energy while classic in shape.'

Carr, rougher hewn as a batsman, also suffered by compari-son in physical appearance. A UK *Daily Express* reporter, sizing up the England team, saw Chapman as 'the Apollo of the XI'. Carr's face, the reporter said was 'interesting. You receive from it an impression of brain and brawn and something else—I cannot discover what. His nose is crooked, his underlip juts out, he scowls ferociously, but what a head! The enormity of it is almost frightening—shall I say sinister? I hope it frightens the Australians.'

The selectors didn't think it had scared them enough. He was denied the opportunity to take his side on to the first Ashes win since 1912.

A consolation for him and Nottinghamshire was the re-selection of the in-form and more confident Larwood.

As it turned out in the deciding Test, left-hander Chapman acquitted himself well with a 49, second top score in England's first innings, and the home side went on to win by 289 runs, thanks largely to hundreds by Hobbs and Herbert Sutcliffe.

Larwood played a strong part, taking 3 for 84 and 3 for 34. England's win wiped away the criticisms of the selectors, who were now lauded as wise, if not geniuses, as the team and the nation basked in the glory of defeating Australia for the first time in fourteen years.

Carr was left with his wounds and humiliation, and his chances for a return to the top level hovered uncertainly. As if to mark 1926 his *annus horribilis*, Carr managed to roll his not so lovely green Austin 7 late in the year. It too had taken a battering.

*

By contrast, his protégé Larwood's star was very much in the ascendant as the most potent England fast bowler seen for some time.

He played for an England XI v Australia at Folkstone early in September and gave the tourists a hefty send-off, taking 7 for 95 in the one innings he bowled. He struck three of the batsmen, when few were quick enough to get out of the way.

Larwood took 137 wickets at 18.31 for the 1926 season. He was stamping himself on the game—and more than a few bodies. Carr never discouraged him roughing and softening up batting opponents.

Despite later protestations, Larwood from 1926 had been moulded by Carr into the most dangerous bowler in England.

*

Douglas Jardine's 1926 season was his best to date, scoring 1473 for Surrey at the more than creditable average of 46.03. But he was overlooked for the Tests and remained in a second group of batsmen in line for Test selection. In order to gain recognition, he stepped up his scoring rate towards the end of the season, which several coaches over the last decade had urged him to do.

It was too late to face Australia in this Ashes, but at age 25, Jardine still had time to make his mark.

BRADMAN'S BREAKTHROUGH

Bradman's batting record until the age of eighteen in country New South Wales was literally *incredible* to Sydney sports editors. However, his leg-spinning figures were more comprehensible. This led to him being among twenty young bowling and batting hopefuls invited by the NSW Cricket Association to try out at the Sydney Cricket Ground (SCG) nets in front of a small group of state selectors and former Test players.

The least influential was freshman selector, Harold 'Mudgee' Cranney. He noticed the smallest lad, who was batting to the hopefuls. Cranney was drawn to his quick foot movements, his rapid bat speed, and shots in every direction. He moved around behind the nets for a better view.

The batsman was wearing spikes for the first time and he occasionally had trouble in pushing forward. Cranney was taken by his back-foot defence, his steady head, his readiness to dance down the wicket to the slow bowlers, and the aggression towards anything fast and short, which he dispatched with rolling wrists and no fear.

Cranney moved in front of the nets again and asked a big young bowler to deliver as hard as he could to the nimble little player.

The big speedster was handled with ease.

Cranney asked an official who the batsman was.

The official looked at a list. 'Bradman,' he said, 'J. Bradman from Bowral.'

'J for what?'

The official didn't know.

Cranney asked the more senior selectors to have a look at the fellow who had so intrigued him. They liked what they saw, but not enough to invite him to their club. Cranney, a state opening batsman, backed his judgement and invited Bradman to join Cumberland Club, subject to a board meeting. They had to consider if this new lad, *Don* Bradman, was worth the 8 shillings and 6 pence for the round train trip from Bowral. Not having seen him in action, the cost was seen as prohibitive.

It was a blow, but the confident teenager responded the best way he could by returning to Bowral and belting a chanceless 170 not out in two hours for Bowral against Exeter. The state selectors took more notice. They could now marry the figures to a character, instead of a regional country match report buried deep in the daily newspaper sports pages.

Bradman was selected to play for the 'Possibles' against the 'Probables' before the first Shield game of the 1926–27 season. He made an impressive 37 not out, batting at number seven. That convinced St George to take a punt on the country lad with the astronomically high bush-batting record.

In late November 1926, Bradman played in Country Week and at the end of five one-day matches, in which he scored consistently, he was chosen for his initial St George match playing Petersham on a Saturday. Bradman made the most of this moment, scoring 110 (run out) at a run a ball, one of the most audacious and impressive debut performances ever in club cricket.

Two days later, he followed this with a superb 98 playing for the Combined Country team against the City XI, which was captained by Charlie Macartney (now aged 40), Bradman's boyhood hero, who a short six years earlier had enthralled him with his 170 at the SCG.

Bradman had now had seven innings in eight matches in which he consistently performed better. At the end of this burst, he had full confidence in a cricketing career, yet emulating Macartney in a Sydney Test was still just a dream.

He still had to prove himself beyond one- or two-day, short-form cricket. He was selected in the NSW Second XI, and top scored with 43 on New Year's Day 1927. Bradman continued performing with distinction but not big scores for St George, putting together an aggregate of 289 at 48.1 for the 1926–27 season.

He went back to Bowral at the end of the St George season and hammered 320, including 6 sixes, 1 five and 43 fours.

This performance demonstrated how far he had come in a year since his previous triple hundred.

A MAN'S GAME

Arthur Carr was profoundly affected well into 1927 after being discarded for what would have been the most glorious moment of his career—captaining England to an Ashes victory. Most observers sympathised, but it could not salve his deep hurt. His mental doldrums were exacerbated by shingles, a viral infection that caused a painful rash on his lower stomach and groin area. Doctors told him that his cavalier reaction to his tonsillitis the year before may have compromised his immune system, thus allowing the virus to enter his nervous system. It affected his cricket. He missed games because of it and dropped himself down the order to number 8. His average for the 1927 season dipped to an alarming 19.02, when it had always been about twice that, with an exceptional 56.12 when he opened the batting in 1925.

Carr prided himself in being almost impervious to pain, when he went down on the battlefield under his mount, or if he tumbled on the hunting field. His now many car crashes had left him cut and bruised but with no lasting physical hurt. He had endured a broken nose and thumb through cricket, which he bore easily and claimed they led to little discomfort. But shingles, largely unseen, caused him to suffer burning sensations and agonising, hideous blisters.

*

Carr drank more, turning to spirits with enthusiasm, at times to anaesthetise himself from the permanent itching that accompanied the virus. Yet he was still in charge at Nottingham where everyone looked up to his leadership, none less than Larwood, and his new partner to be, left-armer Bill Voce. The novice was aged seventeen and 191 centimetres (6 foot 3 inches) tall and, like Larwood, had come from a mining town, Annesley Woodhouse, which bordered on Nuncargate.

Voce's father had died young, putting more pressure on the boy from a poorer part of the mining region. He too had come from the pits, where he had been working for four years. Young Voce wanted a job at Trent Bridge to support his widowed mother and younger siblings. The teenager admired the straight-talking, hard-hitting, hard-drinking skipper, who in turn coached the new teenager in life and cricket.

Carr urged Voce, even more than Larwood, to be tough on batsmen. If the opposition incurred bruises and broken bones, it was said to be 'bad luck'. If the batsmen didn't like it, then they didn't have to play. It was a 'man's game'. Times were harder after the horrors of the 1914–18 World War, where tens of millions died or were injured. The male of the species was expected never to complain. He was alive when countless others had paid the ultimate price. Post-war, a man was expected to be strong and front up to adversity, or fade away. This applied more to top competitive physical sports such as cricket and rugby, than any other field.

Carr, as much as any county captain, led the way in the macho stakes, and despite his setbacks, his legend, swollen by myth, had not diminished.

Voce began at Nottinghamshire delivering spin and medium-pace inswingers. Carr instructed him to bowl quicker and asked Larwood and the team coaches to work on all aspects of his delivery. But there was not much to do. Voce was a natural with a loping run-up. He didn't quite have Larwood's smooth fluidity, but very few in the game did.

Larwood led the way taking 100 wickets at 16.95, and was chosen as one of *Wisden*'s five cricketers of the year for 1927; not quite enough to give Nottinghamshire the championship, although it came second, only losing its final match to Glamorgan. Larwood now felt a sense of security about a career at the top of the game. In September 1927, he married his girlfriend, Lois Bird, aged twenty, an attractive miner's daughter he first met two years earlier.

*

Disappointed as he was with being relegated from Test to county level, Carr now had a powerful, left, right opening bowling combination equal to, or better than any other county. He set out to manage them together through the next season and predicted that they would soon be England's most lethal opening pair.

*

Douglas Jardine qualified as a solicitor and found low-key, undemanding employment at Barings, banker to King George V and the Royal Family.

He was at the cusp of whether as a cricketer he would go on to play Tests, or stay in the ranks of county cricket to become an 'interesting' *Wisden* footnote. His new employment allowed him just eleven matches, which demonstrated Jardine was teetering over taking his game or his banking career further.

The latter had to hold sway. But the security he felt allowed him to free his mind at the crease. He moved his feet more than ever before and loosened up his shot range to include the cut and pull. He even on occasion used his feet to the spinners, a daring move against orthodoxy. He admitted that watching Macartney play spin in the 1926 Ashes had influenced him, but it was yet to be seen whether he went on with such an approach.

Jardine the dogged had become Douglas the daring. He opened the 1927 season with three centuries in the first three matches, and notched 1002 runs at the sweet top average at Surrey of 91.09, all during an unusually wet summer, even for the UK.

Along with Larwood, he was named one of *Wisden*'s five cricketers of the year.

At age 26, Jardine could not avoid his image as standoffish that friends passed off as shyness, yet he had eased into national prominence without a big profile. The MCC jotted him down as a future Test player. Its committee cared little if he had an austere manner. Steel in the soul was good, especially in playing Australia. He, Carr and many other English players of the era regarded contests with all other nations as pleasant, sometimes leisurely affairs. But Australia was seen as the sporting 'Hun'. You had to be rugged matching them. It wasn't quite war on the pitch, but the nearest thing to it.

Jardine's timing to impress selectors had improved. He notched a century in the Gentlemen v Players matches. The entire MCC Committee, and anybody who was anybody in the cricket establishment, watched. His correct style, predicated on perfect defence, was balanced by enough attacking strokes to stop the members from not nodding off over their gin and tonics. He was clapped for his effort, *thoughtfully*. This narrow-eyed, lean figure with the aquiline features had the qualities needed for a step up.

He was chosen for an England XI against The Rest. Percy Chapman, slated as captain, pulled out at the last moment for health reasons. Jardine was made skipper. Onlookers and the press were impressed.

He was more a field commander than a cajoling skipper, and he hated losing.

12

PRELUDE
TO GREATNESS

Don Bradman strode onto the lush green Adelaide ground under the spire of St Peter's Cathedral for his initial first-class innings for New South Wales. The sun was hot; the score was 4 for 250; the pressure was off the batsman to a point. Yet the nineteen year old still had to face Clarrie Grimmett, the world's finest, pure leg spinner. He had just dismissed keeper Bert Oldfield for 12. The South Australian side was back in the game. With this neophyte at the crease, after New South Wales's captain Alan Kippax wilted in the heat and retired hurt, Grimmett was keen to eat into the middle order and finish off the visitors.

He stood at the top of his bowling mark. Bradman stepped away from the crease and noted every field placement. He blocked the first ball. He moved back to the second delivery, which spun across him sharply. Bradman did the unthinkable for a batsman facing this spinning star. He played a cross-back pull through mid-wicket for a thumping four. A few balls later, the confident new youth drove Grimmett for a *second* four in his first-ever over at this level of the game. No one in the history of first-class cricket in Australia had made such a cool, unhurried and auspicious start against such an accomplished bowler.

He went on to a chanceless 118 in three hours' batting, with Grimmett being given the most punishment. Like O'Reilly before him, the spinner wondered if he were slipping after such a belting from this young man from the bush. The South Australians had heard about the brilliance of Archie Jackson, who missed the game through injury, but this new lad was unknown.

Hardly anyone noticed the grandeur of the performance, except the local press, who did not rave about Bradman's first effort. All eyes were on reports from Melbourne where Test player Bill Ponsford was climbing cricket's Mt Everest with a massive score that reached 437, a new world record. It was the second time he had topped a quadruple.

Bradman's first ton was followed by a mediocre run of scores—33, 31, 5, 0 and 13. He moved out of the slump with 73 against South Australia and Grimmett, this time in Sydney. Another century in his last innings of the 1927–28 season gave him an average of 46.22.

He had not set the cricketing world on fire, but he had sparked a promising beginning. Bradman had taken a step up every season since his prodigious scoring for Bowral in 1925–26. He was being overshadowed by the big guns such as Ponsford and Bill Woodfull, and the stylist Kippax who hit a fine triple hundred late in the season. The taller new NSW batsman, Archie Jackson, was taking more of the accolades. He looked more orthodox and elegant than Bradman. The latter was left out of the end-of-season Victor Richardson–led tour of New Zealand.

Yet this omission worked in Bradman's favour. He had been named as one of three standbys. The expectations were lower. His rise had been rapid from country to state side, then to the verge of national selection.

Bradman could edge higher at his own pace without too many expectations.

13

CARR STALLS, LARWOOD SPEEDS UP, JARDINE STEPS UP

Arthur Carr's shingles made travel awkward, so in the northern winter of 1927–28 he and his wife moved closer to the Nottingham ground at Bulcote Manor. The property featured a big garden and paddock which allowed him to indulge his second sporting love of riding. His days of drinking and carousing in Nottingham hotels for six months a year were over. When not chosen for the MCC tour of South Africa, he joined the South Nottingham Hunt, a pleasant break from cricket travels, although he missed the chance for more carousing and drinking in warmer climes. Carr was now 34. Yet despite this lapse no one close to him expected him to slow down once he overcame his illness.

The Nottingham Committee was split about reappointing him as captain for the 1928 season, and it was left until April to make the announcement. The delay reflected a hesitation about his age, his form, his illnesses, his reputation and the way he captained the team. In Carr's advantage was his career record so far, his huge popularity at the county, and the fact that Nottinghamshire had nearly won the championship in 1927.

Carr noted in his autobiography, 'They [some of the Committee] wanted to chuck me out of Notts cricket. They said I was not exactly teetotal and rather too fond of sitting up late at night [a reference to his hotel life].'

Letters had come in 1928 from other counties about the way Larwood bowled. Too many batsmen were being injured. Carr began experimenting with 'fast leg theory' as opposed to simply 'leg theory'. The latter had been around since the middle of the nineteenth century. It was a mostly negative ploy. A bowler would send his deliveries down the leg side, with a field stacked there, the main object being the slowing of the scoring rate. *Fast* leg theory was a very different tactic, with the 'theory' being euphemistic, giving it a dignified, academic image. The only similarity to 'leg theory' was the stacking of the leg-side field. The object was to deliver fast at the leg stump with the ball lifting into the ribcage, a very awkward proposition for most batsmen, even the agile.

'It was invented because we found that when the shine was off the new ball, Larwood could not swing it,' Carr wrote, 'so, the natural thing to do was to break it [the ball] back [into the right-hander] and switch his field over for catches on the leg side.'

Larwood had unusually large hands and strong fingers, which allowed him to move the ball off the pitch.

The important corollary to this was that Larwood's speed was intimidating to most batsmen. Sudden field switches concerned them. Carr and Larwood, and later Voce, exploited this, but not yet systematically. Larwood was not yet accurate enough, and relied on sheer pace and lifting the ball up around the ribcage. It was still a worry for opposition teams, but just the beginning of its effectiveness.

Carr would push Larwood any way he could to squeeze more determination and speed out of him. If beer, even the odd glass of champagne, didn't do it, he'd goad him by saying a certain batsman had said he (Larwood) wasn't that fast.

The bowler reacted appropriately for the captain's purposes.

There were early drawbacks to Larwood letting loose like a snorting bull and fielders switching to the fast leg theory mid-over. He would spray the ball about and make it difficult for keeper and slips either side of the wicket, who had to watch out for flying mishits.

One consolation for Carr that season was Nottinghamshire's performance. It ended up third in the 1928 championship and lost just three out of 32 matches. This helped his demeanour around the pavilion and in dealing with the committee. Those who had called for his sacking were muted, for the moment.

*

Jardine had his sensibilities hurt during the 1928 Gentlemen v Players match when he was slow hand-clapped early in an innings, then booed for scoring 2 runs in half an hour. He set his jaw intractably against this behaviour and crawled on, weaving his innings at his pace, until he reached 140. Then, still with grace in his straight-backed shots, he pulverised the bowling for 53 runs in 28 minutes, lifting his score to 193, and earning cheers from the patient spectators, who had endured his tardy start.

No one was going to divert Jardine, the rigid Scot, who was seemingly impervious to crowd reaction, at least in England. He knew what he was doing. He was appointed captain of The Rest against England in a Test trial with the 1928–29 Ashes tour of Australia in mind. Jardine had to face Larwood in a belligerent mood, and the wile of Maurice Tate, the Sussex and England all-rounder, who had developed into the finest seam bowler of the era.

Jardine was at his rearguard best, scoring 74 not out—the highest of the match—on a rain-affected pitch. It saved his team from defeat and gained him his first-ever Test, versus the touring West Indies at Lord's. The visitors were not strong, although they had three good pacemen: Learie Constantine; George Francis; and Herman Griffith, who trapped Jardine LBW for 22 in his only innings of the match, won by England by an innings.

Jardine's determination to stay at the wicket, especially if a tour of Australia was at stake, took on another dimension during the July Second Test at Old Trafford. Batting at number five in a partnership with Wally Hammond, he reached 26. He played a shot and began a run, hitting his wicket in the process. The West Indies appealed.

The umpire gave him not out. The West Indies were not happy. They believed he was out, hit wicket. Bowler Constantine said after the day's play, 'He [Jardine] was only given not out because he told the umpire he had completed his shot.'

Only a slow-motion action replay *may* have been able to tell, but it did remind observers of the time W. G. Grace, 40 years earlier, had been struck on the pads while batting in a county game. He ran down the wicket towards the umpire, shouting in high-pitched anxiety, 'Out if I hadn't hit! Out if I hadn't hit it!'

An intimidated umpire also gave England's most notable nineteenth century cricketer not out.

Jardine carried on to a polished, methodical 83 in 160 balls, before being run out by Maurice Tate, who refused to answer a call for a single. Jardine's score was enough, good judges said, for him to be chosen for the squad for the 1928–29 Ashes.

Business commitments at Barings kept him out of the Third Test, which ended in a clean sweep of innings wins for the home side.

*

Larwood played in the First Test, took 1 for 27 in the West Indies first innings, but injured a foot, which stopped him bowling in the second innings and the entire Second Test. He came back in the Third Test and took 5 for 87 over the two opposition innings.

His bumper 1928 season for Nottinghamshire sealed his Australian tour. He took 138 wickets at 14.51, which saw him top the national bowling averages again. Larwood's form, and the strength of the MCC squad overall, especially in batting, meant England was confident of retaining the Ashes in Australia.

*

King George V and Queen Mary arrived at Trent Bridge in early July to watch a little of the Nottinghamshire v West Indies match, and be introduced to the teams. Carr marked the occasion with a dashing 100 in 125 minutes before being bowled by Constantine when going for another big hit. George V spent more than the usual amount of time chatting informally with Carr. The King kept personal files on 'famous subjects' of whom the cricketer was one.

George V's private diary entry about the visit was brief, 'Met West Indies and Notts team led by Mr. Carr. Captain for the Ashes, I wondered?'

This was in reference to the coming announcement of the squad for the 1928–29 Australian tour. The team was announced on 30 July, with Percy Chapman retained as captain. Carr had been left out of an earlier trial match that went a long way to deciding the touring seventeen players.

He expected to be left out. Yet it was still a blow after his stated aim of leading England in an Ashes series down under.

PART THREE

1928–1929

14

ASHES 1928–29

Bradman opened the 1928–29 season in September with an electric innings of 107 in just over two hours for St George against Gordon at Chatswood Oval. He was selected for a trial game, Australia v The Rest, but failed in both innings with 14 and 5. He redeemed himself soon after with 131 in the opening Shield game against Queensland in Brisbane, and then followed it up with 133 not out in the second innings, becoming only the tenth player to gain the double in a Shield match.

If ever someone had announced himself for Test selection it was the twenty year old. Still critics were ranking the elegant Archie Jackson higher and suggesting he was the heir apparent to the late Victor Trumper.

*

The England squad arrived by boat into Fremantle in October and Jardine sailed on with three successive centuries against the states. In the game against New South Wales, he hit 140. When Bradman was asked about his impression of Jardine, he replied, 'I had no way of assessing his character. I could only assess his batting. Jardine was a very good bat indeed.'

The more than 43,000 spectators at the SCG were less circumspect in their feelings. They did not like Jardine's patrician bearing and dress—notably the silk neck choker and Harlequin cap from his Oxford days—that brought ridicule from the SCG Hill. Nothing offended the locals as much as 'pommies' presenting an image of superiority in egalitarian Australia, still sensitive to its mainly convict origins. Jardine's sharp features aided his nose-in-the-air demeanour.

He endured abuse when he chased the ball near the boundary. While fielding, he flicked at the flies. One wag called, 'You leave our flies alone!' When batting, another yelled, 'Hey, Jardine, want a batman to hold your bat for you?'

Instead of rolling with the comments by bowing, or waving his cap, or even just smiling, Jardine looked grim.

A fellow English player said to him, 'The crowd don't seem to like you, Douglas.'

'The feeling is fucking mutual!' he snarled.

Jardine was not humourless, according to those who knew him well, but the Australian wit was too rough for his liking. He judged the crowds as unruly and 'uneducated'. It was a reaction to them making fun of his Oxford headgear, which may have been calculated. England amateurs often wore their university or even old school caps when batting, but it was 'not done' in the field when players were supposed to look unified under the team's approved cap. Percy Chapman only wore his less dazzling Cambridge University headgear when batting, and there was not a murmur of disapproval from the judgemental Hill. Barrackers saw him as jolly and more acceptable.

*

England piled on 734 in its innings. In the few minutes before close of play on day two, New South Wales lost two quick wickets. Bradman came to the wicket to join Kippax. Chapman was well aware that Jackson, who'd just been dismissed, and Bradman were Australia's two new 'hopefuls'. He brought on Larwood. The idea was to rattle Bradman early. Bradman had been following events in England and was cognisant of the Nottinghamshire star's record as the fastest man in England, if not the world.

He took block nonchalantly and his usual half-grin, which meant confidence and calm, was read as 'arrogance' by some bowlers, including Larwood.

He was 6 not out at stumps, with Kippax on 22.

Hostilities resumed the next day with Bradman quickly into stride. He took to Larwood as if it were a challenge to control him rather than the other way around. He reached 50 in 85 minutes and saw a dejected Larwood off with a burst of fours that had the outstanding paceman second-guessing himself. Bradman went on to 87 before being bowled by an unplayable ball from the spinner 'Tich' Freeman.

New South Wales struggled to 349 and was forced to follow on.

This time Jackson made a scintillating 40 before being run out. Selectors saw enough to consider him almost right for Test selection.

In came the still underrated Bradman to join Kippax again. Larwood was on. Fuelled by beers in the dressing room, he was fast and more accurate than in the first innings. Kippax went on the defence against him. Bradman was more adventurous in an attempt to stay on top in the second encounter. He took most of the strike against Larwood and targeted him with attacking shots all around the wicket. He reached 50 in 65 minutes. Once Larwood was relegated to the field and licking his wounds at mid-off, Bradman was a fraction more circumspect, especially against Freeman, yet still reached his century in 128 minutes.

Until this innings of 142 not out (14 fours) in 156 minutes, many England players, particularly the batsmen, expressed cynicism about the adulation around the country for Bradman before he had been tested at a higher level. Now people understood what all the fuss was about. His defiant 87 and a dashing unbeaten century had all the shots against all comers, including now the spinners, whom he had worked out like a raptor stalking a prey, after they had troubled him earlier.

His concentration allied to his courage against Larwood's deadly head-high bullets, and his power in attacking and removing him from the bowling crease, had the touring squad concerned. It all indicated a special temperament. Larwood grumbled more than once in the dressing room about Bradman's manner, which he branded as smug.

On the Australian supporters' side, critics were now placing Bradman on a par with the amiable and brilliant Jackson. The England players felt more comfortable with him. No one anywhere had a bad word about Archie. He seemed less sure of himself and more respectful, whereas

Bradman, who let his bat do the talking, appeared less approachable, even remote.

These spoken and secret revelations were at the margins. England was searching for psychological advantages. They were not yet demonising Bradman, but looking for derogatory labels that would build to a grudge, a dislike, even 'hate'. In war, it helped to make killing the enemy easier. In sport, it wasn't much different. The long contest—timeless Tests to come in this case—created a lot of downtime in the trenches and not on the battlefield. If an opposition star could be tagged with a perceived character flaw, then it would be a factor in the contest.

It worked both ways. Jardine was receiving unfair abuse for being apparently aloof and forbidding. He was branded as a 'toff', which he was not. He was educated with an establishment background, yet his Scottish and Indian experiences added a dimension that was 'different' even in the England squad's ranks. The crowds had exhibited a mob-like 'judgement' on him and were letting him know it. How Jardine reacted on and off the field would be another factor in the series.

Jardine chose not to breakfast with the professionals in the squad and preferred to be alone, whereas the other two amateurs on tour, Chapman and Jack 'Farmer' White, did mix easily with them.

*

Jardine's excellent run of scores ended in the MCC v Australian XI game in Sydney beginning 16 November when his old contemporary from Oxford, Reg Bettington, dismissed him twice, first bowling him around his legs for 6, and then trapping him LBW for 13.

Each morning, Jardine made a point of breakfasting with Bettington, happy to put his former Oxford teammate above fraternising with the rest of the team. Each evening in Sydney and all other cities, he disappeared for social engagements with former Oxbridge companions.

England beat the Australian trial XI easily by eight wickets. Bradman was the mainstay of a weak first innings of 231, scoring 58 not out, but only 18 (bowled Tate) in the second.

In good form, Larwood was delivering at top pace. He troubled all batsmen except Bradman, who once more scored too freely off him for stand-in MCC captain White's liking. Twice Bradman drove and hooked him out of the attack. This set up future entertaining encounters between the pair.

*

They didn't have long to wait. Bradman was selected for the First Test in Brisbane, beginning 30 November. England won the toss and piled on 521, making their position almost unassailable in a game without time limitations. Australia batted late on Saturday, day two, and Larwood, at his magnificent best, ripped through the early order, clean-bowling three and leaving Australia in trouble at 4 for 44. On the Monday, day three, Bradman came in at 5 for 71, in his first-ever Test appearance.

Chapman had witnessed the newcomer's toll on Larwood at every encounter. Despite the quick's devastating form, the captain spelled him to avoid damage to Larwood's sometimes fragile ego that often needed the Arthur Carr endorsed 'beer boost'.

Chapman loved a drink as much, if not more than Carr, yet he was not prepared to allow beer on the field mid-session.

There was a double standard here, for Chapman himself was tippling during play. But he felt he had to engender a certain amount of discipline among his professional charges.

Chapman replaced his major asset with Tate and his swing in order to tie Bradman up at one end. This worked better than expected and Tate snared him LBW for just 18.

Australia was rolled for just 122, and the dependable Woodfull, the Australian vice-captain, carried his bat for a stubborn 30 not out. He was one measure of resistance and on the rise in the national game, having been named one of *Wisden*'s five cricketers of the year during the Ashes tour of 1926.

The destroyer, however, was Larwood. He took 6 for 32, to go with a power-laden 70 with the bat.

Chapman decided to bat again and took their lead to 741 before declaring. It rained and created a serious 'sticky' wicket, a veritable 'glue-pot'. Jack White crowded Bradman with close fielders and induced a catch to silly mid-off, for just 1, ensuring a most inauspicious debut Test in a massive 675-run loss.

As Bradman left the field, Tate moved to White and joked, 'I wanted him. He was my rabbit.'

15

LARWOOD
UNOBSTRUCTED

Bradman was the sacrificial bunny for the mid-December Second Test in Sydney. The selectors dropped him to twelfth man, when any one of nine others deserved to be omitted. He had to look on as captain Jack Ryder won the toss, batted and Australia ran into Hurricane Harold again, who was relieved he did not have to deliver to the grinning 'boy'.

Larwood dismissed two batsmen early and broke Ponsford's wrist, putting him out of the game and the series. The solid Victorian run plunderer was not nimble enough of foot to avoid Larwood's thunderbolts. His method had been to turn his back and considerable rump to the ball. This time he hadn't had time to do even that and paid the price of a season lost.

Australia struggled to 253. Wally Hammond, in fine form, nearly wiped Australia's score off his own bat with 251 as England amassed 636. Australia did better in its second dig with Hunter 'Stork' Hendry and Woodfull showing strong resistance. Chapman reacted with 'leg theory' from Tate and George Geary, pitching outside leg stump with two short legs, a long leg, a mid-wicket, mid-on and one slip. It was utterly negative and meant to slow the scoring rate.

Larwood joined in with 'fast leg theory', with the off-side slip edging over to leg slip, along with the others placed on the leg side. Larwood bowled on leg stump, and did his best to lift the ball into the body of the batsmen. His aim was not to bog them down, but to blast them out.

Warwick Armstrong, not given to hyperbole, or taking a backward step, reacted in a London paper, 'Larwood appeared to be bowling deliberately at the batsmen. He had great pace and could afford not to bowl at the man. If he continued these tactics the spectators here might think there are more sporting ways of getting results. It would be a pity if a player like Larwood ran the risk of unpopularity when he has the talent to send the ball up differently.'

Another former Australian captain, Monty Noble, was even more to the point, 'Despite his direct method of attack on the wicket, at times he is not over-particular about where the ball goes, delivering it well outside the off stump, outside the leg stump, or direct to the body or head.'

Noble had stumbled on Larwood's capacity to fire up in a sometimes haphazard way, which had been a rule rather than the exception under Carr at Nottinghamshire.

Noble went on, 'The working of this trap is easily discernible from the pavilion, for a man is always placed in position to bring about the batsman's downfall in the case of a mistake. It may be that this method is adopted to impress the faint-hearted with the possibility of injury. This would cause them to draw away or nibble at the ball instead of boldly facing it with the bat well in front of the body, or allowing the bumpy ones to pass harmlessly over the wicket.'

This was fair 'pavilion' analysis by Noble, except for one further observation. Only one batsman, Bradman, so far in the summer had proven nimble, skilled and confident enough to counter-attack Larwood's blistering pace. This left the home team vulnerable to a possible whitewash 5:0 Ashes loss, especially if the one successful combatant remained on the sidelines.

*

During the innings Jardine had to field on the boundary in front of the SCG Hill again, as Hammond and Chapman were close-to-the-wicket specialists. Once more, he made the mistake (or was it by design?) of wearing his harlequin cap. Once more, barrackers piled on the verbal barrage, which they had first let loose in the earlier game against New South Wales. Every time Jardine moved to field the ball he was catcalled. His throwing was mixed, for he had not worked on his outfield skills. He was jeered if he was off direction.

Chapman could not tell from Jardine's stony façade if he was tormented, but motioned for him to move to the outfield in front of the less hostile members. Jardine turned and spat in the direction of the Hill hounds before trotting off.

This indicated to all that they had got under his skin.

His reaction was noted by the press and reported on, thus giving an invitation to crowds all around Australia to take up the vocal cudgel against him for the rest of the tour.

*

Australia battled along to 397 in the second innings with Woodfull completing a gritty double of 68 and 111. He had a strong defence but not the capacity to attack and take the initiative.

England needed just 15 to win. Chapman completed the humiliation by sending in tailenders to mop up the runs for an easy 8-wicket victory.

16

RESTORATION

Bradman scored a timely 71 not out for New South Wales in the big state game against Victoria late in December, which propelled him back into calculations for the Third Test, beginning 29 December 1928. The Melbourne wicket was known to be hard and bouncy, and therefore conducive to real pace. His mastering of England's firebrand Larwood swung the selectors' divided opinion and he was chosen. Besides that, Ponsford was out and a new batsman was needed, along with an injection of youth.

The Ashes were in the balance.

Woodfull won the toss and batted, but was soon back in the pavilion for just 7 and Vic Richardson for 3. Two were down for 15. At lunch, in front of the large Melbourne crowd, Australia was slipping at 3 for 63. Kippax (100) and Ryder staged a recovery to be 4 for 218.

Bradman walked out to a huge reception usually reserved for champion Aussie Rules teams that surprised even the

Australians, and definitely the England players. What had he done to deserve this? they wondered. He failed at Brisbane, and yes, his season was full of scoring highs, but not yet in the Tests. It was as if the supporters had a special prescience. More likely it was a combination of hope that he would pull off a stellar exhibition, and also support for the underdog.

Bradman was cautious facing Larwood for two overs, and then decided to attack him, taking 10 runs off his third over. Larwood's head went down; his shoulders slumped. Chapman had a solicitous word in his ear, but once more removed him from the attack. Bradman made eye contact ever so briefly, still with that maddening half-grin. Larwood took it personally. It was no compensation to know that Bradman had made him his special quarry for the series. Then again, once Larwood was out of the firing line, Bradman set his eyes on others for further conquest. He was wary of Tate's swing and White's spin.

Bradman was 26 not out with Ryder relaxed after a defiant century. The next morning Tate removed Ryder for 112, then Oldfield quickly. New Victorian Ted a'Beckett, aged 21, joined Bradman. Chapman brought on Larwood again. Bradman took most of the strike from him, nullifying his influence until the bowler tired.

The two youngsters batted carefully through to lunch, with Bradman reaching his first Test 50.

After the break, Chapman ignored Larwood, even though he'd had a couple of beers and was ready to go again, and brought on Hammond for his delivery of jagging medium-pace cutters. Bradman had dealt with him before and now launched into him with 12 off ten balls. His enthusiasm got hold of him and he played the wrong shot to a good yorker and was bowled for 79. Larwood was effusive in his congratulations for the champion all-rounder. Hammond had saved him a lot of drudgery at the crease, had Chapman brought him on again.

Once more, Australia was all out for 397. Larwood, who had started well against the early batsmen, taking three of the first four wickets, had been attacked and then blunted by Bradman and Ryder, and finished with the unflattering figures of 3 for 127.

Hammond again dominated in England's attempt to get in front. Jardine incurred the further wrath of the Melbourne 'uneducated'. He was booed, catcalled and slow-clapped.

'Jardine, we've all got New Year's hangovers!' one character yelled. 'Brighten it up, will you?'

'Will the bloody bagpipes help, Jardine?' another called.

'You're the definition of a mean Scot!' was a further cry, and on it went with each wag trying to outdo the others. Most were tedious outbursts, with one or two gems, that Jardine admitted much later he had heard, and even appreciated.

He kept his Mt Rushmore visage throughout the onslaught of insults.

A chant of 'Jardine, sardine' went up and soon fizzled out. Spectators began to walk to the exits as stumps approached.

Unperturbed, Jardine went on with his job of putting his country in front.

*

During England's first innings, Herbert Sutcliffe was in partnership with Hammond when Bradman prowled the covers and nearly exacted a run-out. He had already dismissed

Hobbs and Hammond on the tour, and had made himself a reputation for being a fast, pinpoint accurate throw.

One return came close to Sutcliffe's head as it speared into the keeper's gloves.

'Hey!' the batsman cried, 'that was aimed at me!'

'If I had aimed at you,' Bradman said calmly but clearly, 'it would have hit you.'

Sutcliffe and Hammond took this as cheek or arrogance. But it was neither. Rather, it was the young man being his pragmatic, confident self.

Athletic Aussie Rules football star a'Beckett took a superb catch off 46-year-old off spinner Don Blackie the next morning to dismiss Hammond for an even 200. Jardine came out of his shell and startled everyone with 4 fours off Blackie, before the bowler took a return catch.

Despite the criticism, Jardine had done the job, albeit an overly patient one, for 62, and England edged ahead by 20.

Larwood broke through Vic Richardson (5) again, but Woodfull led the way forward with his own snail impression and had Australia 2 for 118 at stumps, the lead 98.

The following morning, Bradman came to the wicket at 4 for 148, once more with a reception several decibels higher than for any other player. For some reason never explained, this Sydneyite was already the national favourite for a *Victorian* audience, something rarely seen in the parochial states. Only the legendary Victor Trumper had reached such an accolade in recent times.

Ryder had instructed Bradman to defend and stay with Woodfull. He wanted a lead of at least 300.

The two defended on at not much more than the rate of the Jardine/Hammond plod, but there was no abuse, not even a 'Have a go, ya mug!'.

Chapman brought Larwood on. Bradman could not help himself and stepped up the scoring. Larwood limped out of the attack with a pulled tendon, giving Bradman honours again in their continued contest within a contest, although the injury made this an uneven battle in their seventh encounter, which had all gone to the Australian.

Woodfull made it to 105 before Tate removed him as Australia reached 5 for 201. Bradman was 24 not out, and the game finely balanced. Bradman reached his 50 in 143 minutes, now accumulating at a slower rate than Jardine, and was cheered as if it were his hundred.

Australia was 7 for 250 at tea. The afternoon crowd had swollen to nearly 50,000 as the word filtered around the city that Bradman was in and approaching his first century in Test cricket. He was also freer now as his skipper Ryder told him to hog the strike and build the score.

Bradman was 96 at 5.30 p.m. He drove a well-flighted dipper from White past Chapman at mid-off. The crowd, estimated at 57,000 by this stage, got to its feet to cheer Bradman and the ball as Jardine gave chase. Partner Ron Oxenham ran as hard as Bradman to take three as Jardine reached the ball just inside the boundary. Oxenham, running to the danger end, called Bradman through, and just beat Jardine's accurate hurl, with a long stretch of arm and bat.

Bradman had his breakthrough 100. His second 50 had taken 80 minutes. At twenty years and four months, he was the youngest ever batsman to make a century. The crowd appreciated his dream rise from a teenager making telephone number scores in the bush three years earlier to the ultimate in elite cricket. They reacted at the MCG like never before for any sporting spectacle. It went on for several minutes. The England players sat down on the field. Oxenham wandered down to shake Bradman's hand. This precipitated more cheering and clapping.

After five minutes or so, the noise subsided. White walked back to his mark. He was about to bowl when the umpire's arm went up. Bradman was taking block again. Another roar went up. The spectators got the message. The batsman was setting himself for a lot more. This ploy was becoming a Bradman trademark.

In this case, he only added 12 more, but it seemed enough. He had done most to turn his team's innings around and make it competitive.

It rained overnight and Australia was all out the next morning for 351. England were set 332 for victory on a 'sticky dog' of a wicket, a difficult task even for England's batsmen who knew how to play on rain-affected tracks.

The first six bats dug in for the battle, with Hobbs (45) and Herbert Sutcliffe setting up a win with an opening stand of 105. The standout was Yorkshire's Sutcliffe in his element staying at the wicket for 6 hours 24 minutes, facing 462 balls and making 135.

His grand effort did the most to give England a three-wicket victory and the Ashes.

17

OPERATION
SALVAGE

There was a four-week break before the Fourth Test in Adelaide. Jardine joined the tourists on a trip down to Tasmania for games against that state. It was the most pleasant part of the gruelling tour for him. He scored his best innings of 214 against a surprisingly good attack at Launceston. His grand form as a stylist returned to that of the early part of the tour.

He avoided the second game at Hobart by indulging his love of fishing, first shown to him by Andrew Lang when he was a young boy. A friend from his school days at Winchester whisked him into the state's interior and the Penstock River where he scored nearly as many fish as runs in waters abundant with brown trout. Refreshed, he fashioned another century back on the mainland in Adelaide against a Vic Richardson–led South Australia.

*

Bradman made the most of the break between Tests, not relaxing but performing in the return match between New South Wales and Victoria at the SCG beginning 24 January 1929. He broke several records in compiling 340 not out before captain Kippax declared the innings at 6 for 713.

Bradman had transported his prowess for making high scores from the country—where he had notched two triple hundreds—into the first-class arena. He'd also managed to do it on the ground on which he most wanted to succeed ever since first seeing Macartney.

Bradman's score was the highest at the SCG to that point, the highest by a NSW player and the most ever made in one innings by a player in matches between the two strongest states. He had been 488 minutes at the wicket, and scoring right through the innings at an entertaining rate.

This kind of show was making turnstiles click all around Australia wherever he played. Even Sydney club games on Saturday afternoons had to shut the gate on spectators wandering down to St George's Hurstville Oval to see this new lad who'd captured so much of the collective national imagination.

In short, Bradman 'got on with it' with unmatched powers of concentration. His competitive nature was forever calculating—fast and on the spot—how to overcome a bowler. He had taken on and obliterated England's great striker Larwood. He was learning how to combat the guile of Tate, the wile of White, the cunning of medium-pacer George Geary, and the others. Bradman enjoyed the challenges, hence that half-grin that was now unsettling opposition players both in Test and state games. It had bothered O'Reilly and irritated Grimmett. This new pocket rocket of a batsman was creating a legion of adversaries who wanted to defeat him.

Already, it was becoming a considerable boast to say, 'I got Bradman at . . .'

*

England won the toss and batted in the Fourth Test in Adelaide and was 5 for 246 at the end of day one. Honours were even, and in the series as a whole, they were evening up. The difference between the teams, as it had been all series, was Wally Hammond. He too had annoyed crowds with his majestically slow batting. He came in at 1 for 140 and was 119 not out on day two in a total of 334.

Hammond (or 'en-eggs' as in 'Ham 'n' eggs' as a spectator called him) had batted for more than six hours—effectively a day—for his runs at a strike rate of 31.81. So far, he had scored 44, 28, 251, 200, 32 and 119 not out.

*

All eyes in Adelaide turned to the pavilion for the first glimpse in a Test of nineteen-year-old Archie Jackson, opening with Woodfull. He hit an elegant, refined 164 from Australia's response of 369 and along the way had an 83-run partnership with Bradman (40). In one Test the teenager had taken a record off Bradman as the youngest Test century scorer ever. Jackson took Bradman's lead on attacking and subduing Larwood, who took 1 for 97.

In England's second innings, Hammond (177, strike rate 29.35) and Jardine (98, strike rate 27.35) had a 262-run link that had fans objecting as they crawled England into a strong position. Jardine received intermittent abuse as he stayed in his immovable zone, his face a granite mosaic. He had continued on his return to top form in Tasmania and left the Adelaide field to jeers and polite applause, disappointed he had just failed to notch a century, as he had for Oxford against Armstrong's team in 1921.

By contrast, at 4 for 296 Chapman marched out in a garish, multi-coloured cap and drew laughs and applause from the fans in a brief moment of levity after the dreary England batting to that point. This headgear was given to Cambridge players who made a 'pair'—naught in both innings of a match. It featured two big zeroes on the front while the word 'chaps' in capitals was on the back. Perhaps the happy captain, having retained the Ashes so easily in the previous game, had tippled before coming into bat with such a self-deprecatory cap in this setting. The crowd jeered and cheered him, and he grinned a lot.

Whatever the reason, he was out after eight balls, appropriately, for a duck, caught Woodfull bowled Blackie.

England reached 383, a lead of 348. The tardy batting by both sides dragged the game into day six. Jackson was removed by Geary's movement off the pitch, caught behind for 36, which gave him 200 even for the game. Bradman came to the wicket at 4 for 211, with many good judges saying he should have been in earlier. He was still there at stumps on 16, with Oxenham on 2, and Australia at 6 for 260, with a key series batsman, Ryder, out for 87.

The home team was 89 runs short of victory.

The odds were even for one reason: Bradman was still in.

Day seven was blustery and hot. Larwood, with a couple of beers in him, began with terrific pace and fast leg theory. He had three men close on the leg, and three in the deep.

Half the deliveries in his two overs were aimed at the batsman's body with the intention of bouncing and bruising him out. Once more Bradman met the challenge with some fine shots. He took 22 runs from Larwood, ending with a courageous hook off his eyebrows, which sped to the square-leg boundary.

Chapman took the sweating Larwood off. He had given it everything. It was another 'win' to his twenty-year-old nemesis, who the bowler admitted was giving him nightmares.

Former England Test player and contemporary Surrey captain, Percy Fender, an early and assiduous Bradman critic, observed from the press box, 'Bradman found Larwood so much to his liking that he was too expensive to be kept on in that crucial stage of proceedings.'

Australia was closing on 300.

Bradman moved to 50, his 36 in the morning taking just 43 minutes. Oxenham drove at White and was out for 12 with the total at 308. Those extra 41 runs suddenly seemed a lot with just three wickets left.

A nervous Oldfield came in and attacked instead of defending. He left everything to Bradman, whose calibrated nerve, despite, or because of his youth, was built for the occasion. The new man at the wicket was too eager. He drove into the covers and called for a run. Bradman ran through and was relieved to see George Duckworth crash his glove into the stumps after the ball had spilt free. But the umpire, who had not seen the ball leave the keeper's grasp, raised his finger to vociferous appealing. Bradman did not glare at the umpire. He tucked his bat under his armpit and strode off, for 58; the score on 8 for 320, still 29 short of a win.

The remaining batsmen, Oldfield, Grimmett and Blackie, battled on but succumbed to nerves in trying to belt their way to victory rather than take it gently.

Australia fell short but by just 11 runs.

The home team had let two games in a row slip from their grasp. Yet hope emerged from the two losses after the disastrous two early defeats when England made the opposition look third-rate.

There was nothing now between the two teams. Australia had not won a Test in nine matches. It was due, and there was no less interest in an outcome in the Fifth and final Test in Melbourne.

*

There were still games for the tourists to play, including against Ballarat, and Victoria at the MCG. The affable Chapman was disappointed at being abused in the Ballarat game for letting his non-bowlers bowl, which the locals saw as patronising and insulting.

The reverse occurred at the MCG in the match against Victoria at the beginning of March. The state, led by Ryder, piled on 9 for 572 into the third session of day two. Woodfull was on 275 not out and Bert Ironmonger, aged 46, on 4 not out. Chapman, frustrated by the state side batting on for so long, brought on Larwood to let rip at the hapless Ironmonger, a number 11 batsman.

It was also to end Woodfull's chances of reaching 300. The Victorian crowd booed and abused Chapman. He told his team to sit on the ground until the fans settled down. They refused. Chapman walked to a section of the crowd that seemed most offended by his captaincy. He made a few hand gestures but it did not placate the mob, who howled more. Fearing an incident, Ryder declared the innings closed. As the team filed off the ground through the members' stand, Chapman was jostled by angry fans.

When the MCC batted, Jardine was dismissed for just 4 and had to endure further unfavourable epithets as he walked from the field. The next day, late in the MCC innings, Ironmonger, with his left-arm orthodox (off-spin) spin got a measure of revenge for his roughing up by Larwood by bowling Chapman for only 2. The England skipper again experienced the unfair wrath of the spectators, and needed a police escort to the dressing room.

England was forced to follow on and this time Jardine, hardened up by the unruly mob, dug in for one of his typical rearguard innings. The fans were incensed when he complained to the umpire that speedster Harry 'Bull' Alexander, who was in a belligerent mood, was scuffing up the pitch on his follow-through down the middle of the wicket. The umpire agreed and admonished the bowler. His response was to tear in around the wicket and deliver bouncers. It had no impact on the tough-minded Scot, who went on to 115 and forced a draw.

Jardine wrote a reaction to these over-boisterous crowds. 'Cricket is a game for 22 people. No game that I know of, unless community singing be a game, is improved by thirty or forty thousand people endeavouring to take part in it.'

In other words, spectators should be seen and not heard, except for polite applause.

He added, 'It will be a thousand pities if a generation is allowed to grow up in an Australia which allows a well-earned reputation for sound criticism and fair-play [presumably Jardine's reputation], to be discounted by unintelligent barracking.'

Perhaps a few Latin quotations from spectators would have drawn him out. If not, he preferred not to 'jest' with the barrackers, but to ignore them.

Jardine disagreed with the way Chapman handled the crowds, saying he should have been more disciplined rather than playing to the gallery. Jardine later told others that if he'd had 'a gun I would have shot him'. He was also unhappy with Chapman's excessive drinking.

18

MATCH-WINNER

England had to replace Sutcliffe (injured) and Chapman for the final Test. The selection committee voted the skipper out. His form had been poor with an average of 23.57 from seven innings. He had also disturbed the tour management by drinking too much, sometimes disappearing during a session for a quiet top-up of whisky in the dressing room, away from prying eyes. It was hypocritical, given that he had ordered Larwood, who thought he was putting his boozing to good use, not to over-imbibe, which caused him to drink on the sly in his hotel room. He could have a beer or two at lunch and after the game, but that was it. This added to the paceman's disgruntlement. Larwood, like other team members, knew Chapman was an alcoholic and was breaking the rules he and the committee had imposed.

In true cover-up style, the selection committee gave the captain the excuse of the flu. His replacement, young

Maurice Leyland, was a better bet to make much-needed runs to aid the fatigued Hammond. White became captain.

Had it not been for these two changes, Larwood, dispirited and homesick, would also have been left out. It had been a long trip, and all up he would be eight months away from the comforts and security of his home in Nottingham. Chapman had not been as inspiring and supportive as Arthur Carr, who knew how to lift Larwood.

White won the toss on 8 March, batted, and by the first session of day three, England had piled on 519. Hobbs 142, in another grand show of batsmanship, and Leyland 137, were the pick of the batsmen.

Australia replied and Woodfull—a rock as usual in front of his home crowd—was only removed by Larwood when he'd made 102. The strict Methodist and teetotaller had scored three centuries for the series, and continued his solid rise in Australian cricket.

At 3 for 203, Bradman was into the fray for the second session on day four. This was after days of soporific play, when even hard-hitting Ryder, with 30 in 125 balls, caught plodder's disease. Bradman immediately looked livelier, despite Fairfax at the other end giving the impression of an artist's still-life subject.

The sun was beating down mid-afternoon and the small crowd began to sit up in their seats and pay attention. More people trickled in from the city.

Larwood had just come on. In an unusual moment, fans wondered if the new captain, White, would take him off after the beatings he'd had from Bradman inside and outside the series. He was left on.

Larwood began spraying the ball as if uncertain how to bowl to his tormentor. Bradman used his feet with whatever leather missile was coming at him and cut, hooked and drove. Larwood could not find a length.

After three overs White surrendered and took the outstanding yet mercurial Nottinghamshire man off. He was banished to the covers, which at that moment was Coventry for him. There was nowhere to hide in the vast stadium, which had doubled in numbers to more than 10,000 fans. Larwood muttered to himself as unsympathetic comments were hurled at him for his capitulation to Bradman.

White brought himself on. Bradman played him to fine leg and mid-wicket with the odd contortionist's shot of unorthodoxy as he slid balls past fielders that the laws of physics said were impossible. This made him look risky. Fender in the press box raved over his brilliance but moaned about his adventurism, warning it would never work on English wickets.

White rang the changes, bringing on the genial Maurice Tate and George Geary. Undeterred, Bradman moved steadily to 50, giving one hot catching chance en route. It had taken 71 minutes, the fastest half-century of the series.

The crowd grew larger.

Bradman was 62 not out at tea, with Fairfax on 23.

Vice-captain Woodfull instructed the young batsmen to put their heads down for the last session. There were still another 200 needed to reach England's score. It was a timeless final Test. The weather was good.

White, showing more leadership initiative, kept ringing the changes. After even Maurice Leyland was tried, the skipper threw the ball to Larwood, for the first time at the members' end. With the crowd howling behind, the speedster tore in as if he had been given something stronger than beer at the drinks break in the extreme heat. Carr would have given him champagne. If White condoned a stimulant it was not obvious, except for Larwood's run to the wicket. He had morphed into the Nottingham Express.

Bradman cut his first ball for four. The members puffed their cigars and cigarettes with gusto, and applauded. They loved Larwood's scowl. He asked White for a deep backward point. Challenged, the batsman cut again to nearly the same spot and ran two.

Larwood was steaming. Everyone, including Bradman, felt they knew what was coming. Larwood ran in, bent his back and delivered a bouncer directed at the batsman's throat. Bradman slid his back foot back and across, and pulled it hard and deep to cow corner, rolling his wrists to keep it down. His timing had not been quite right, and he took an easy three. Nine runs had come from the first three deliveries of the Larwood over.

The bowler made eye contact with the batsman.

There was no leer from the striker, just the *grin*.

Larwood remarked to a reporter, 'He seemed not to notice us. But he really seemed to enjoy his batting.'

In private he expressed something harsher, suggesting Bradman was not now smug or arrogant but 'conceited'. Whereas the other younger Australians, such as Jackson, displayed deference and humility, Bradman was cool, determined-looking and competitive. What the English players did not realise was that Bradman behaved the same way to all *Australian* competitors, in everything from cricket and tennis to billiards and golf. His psyche did not contemplate defeat. He only wished to win.

In this mini two-man battle on day four, Larwood resorted to an old trick, with three vicious bouncers that had Bradman ducking. Then he delivered a yorker. Bradman moved into it, making it a full toss.

Geary bottled up Fairfax at the other end for a maiden. Larwood came on again and moved two players close on the leg side. The members mumbled dissent. A few in the 25,000 crowd voiced their disapproval and booed.

At full gallop, he started his next over with another bouncer. Bradman moved to the off and hooked it hard for four. Jardine, at square leg for the skied catch, could only watch the ball flash past. He had hardly moved when it crashed into the pickets in front of the scoreboard. Larwood sent three further balls lifting down the leg side. Bradman ignored them. He defended for the rest of the over.

In Larwood's next over, Bradman reached 98. Two more bouncers sailed over his head. The crowd hushed. Larwood delivered a very fast ball on leg stump. Bradman drove it wide of mid-on and ran two to reach his second century of the series.

The crowd reacted a little less boisterously than they did for his first ton, holding up play for just two minutes.

Larwood was spent and retired to the covers yet again.

Australia went to early stumps after a light appeal at 4 for 367.

Rain intervened, making the pitch sticky the next day and Bradman was caught popping up a catch off Geary for 123. The same bowler trapped Fairfax LBW and Australia reached 491, 28 short of England.

In England's second innings, Jardine was caught behind for a first ball duck. Perhaps he'd had enough of the continued abuse. He reminded Chapman and White that he had a boat to catch from Perth at the end of day five (when it would go on for another three). He promptly took a train and disappeared for a vacation in India. Only an amateur, and an imperious one at that, would be so contemptuous of his teammates.

Jardine was keen to put the Australian experience behind him but this was an inharmonious gesture too far that no professional would have dared. Chapman would dearly have enjoyed taking off for New Zealand (which he did at the end of the Test), but instead he did the right thing by the team by replacing Jardine in the field. A sober or otherwise Chapman was a superb infielder. Woodfull only agreed to the replacement if Chapman stayed in the outfield.

Hammond was caught for 16. He was not sick of batting, but perhaps he was fatigued from scoring and concentrating under the harsh Australian sun for so long. He had accumulated the highest number of runs ever in a Test series: 905. His average was 113.12.

England clawed its way to 257, its worst effort for the series, leaving the home team 286 for a win.

Doing its version of the Australian crawl on day seven, it reached 2 for 107 at tea. It ground its way to 3 for 166 at another early stumps. On day eight, Ryder and Kippax edged the score up to 204 before the latter was run out going for an ambitious fourth run.

Bradman entered the arena with still 82 to get. Ryder, upset by his part in Kippax's end, seemed to run himself out in a very close call, but the unsighted umpire ruled that he had made his ground, perhaps mindful of the bad decision for Bradman in the previous Test.

Ryder settled down and Bradman settled in. They moved the score on, taking their time and no risks. White, anxious now, moved his fielders often and gave his bowlers short bursts. Larwood, who'd troubled all earlier bats, was brought on after a long rest. Bradman opened up with his key adversary bursting for at least one wicket, and especially that of his persecutor, whom he failed to dismiss in the series.

But it wasn't to be.

The runs came quickly in another little victory for the Australian as they reached the target for a Test win. Ryder 57 not out and Bradman 37 not out had done the job with sensible batting, concentration and no panic.

Larwood took 1 for 83 and 1 for 80 in the Fifth Test, giving him eighteen wickets at 40.22 for the series, his figures bloated by the Australian youth he'd come to loathe. Taking his 8 for 62 First Test out of the analysis, his returns for the last four Tests saw his statistics read ten wickets at 66.20.

His series demonstrated a slide to impotency, mainly caused by Bradman going after him and sapping his confidence until he had nothing left in the tank. Not even a beer boost before bowling was enough to lift him but for a few demonic, sometimes erratic efforts. Fast leg theory had been used a few times yet it had been counter-attacked and rendered pointless.

Part of the problem was that Larwood had been over-bowled for the season on hard Australian pitches. He had been chosen for thirteen of the seventeen first-class matches. Arthur Carr had advised that Larwood should be primed for the Tests, and left out of many of the other games. He was ignored.

Chapman's mismanagement of England's finest pace bowler was camouflaged by England's 4:1 series dominance.

He would go down as the luckiest ever skipper in Test cricket. He had taken the accolades for a series win in 1928 when Carr had been unfairly dumped. Now he would return a hero as the Ashes-winning captain. His own woeful form and the running of Larwood into the bone-hard ground would be glossed over by the press and therefore in the public mind.

Bradman's final figures for the series were a strong 468 runs at 66.85. His first-class average for the season was 93.88, helped by his 148.83 average for New South Wales (he also topped St George's list at 65.25).

It meant little to most observers but he actually did better for the first-class 1928–29 season than Wally Hammond, who averaged 92.06. Yet it was *something* to statistically minded Bradman.

He loved the numbers, and to do better than England's superstar, then regarded as the world's greatest batsman, meant a further confidence boost.

19

1929:
BODYLINE BEGINS

The MCC selectors were looking ahead to the Ashes in 1930 when they observed the Tests versus South Africa in 1929. On the agenda was the leadership. White was doing a satisfactory job against the below par tourists. Percy Chapman, acting like a true amateur, had put himself out of contention after an extended holiday with his wife in New Zealand and Canada after the Australian tour. This brought him back to England on 16 July 1929, about four months too late if he wished to get his captaincy back. He put more score in socialising away from the public eye when he had only to endure admonishment from his wife, New Zealander Gertrude Lowry, who disapproved of his over-imbibing and the resultant behaviour.

Less flamboyant and more determined, Carr blasted back into calculations with a mighty innings of 194 at Trent Bridge for Nottinghamshire against South Africa. He hit 7 sixes and 20 fours in a four-hour batting display of power over technique. The selectors, making up for their hasty decision to dump him in 1926, shocked the cricket world by reinstating him for the Fourth and Fifth Tests. They liked his aggression, and he had always been a risk-taker, and also a cunning tactician for Nottinghamshire, which was top of the county table in 1929.

Carr had mixed success. England won the Fourth Test at Old Trafford and drew the Fifth at The Oval, but he only scored 10 and 15 in his two knocks. It was unfair to judge his first score when he had to push runs along. But he failed to produce the powerhouse innings expected of him. A score of even a third of his Trent Bridge performance with the same intent would have multiplied his chances of maintaining his place and position in the national team.

The MCC Committee was left in a quandary over the captaincy for the 1930 Ashes. They weren't going to retain White, and would most likely have to choose between Cavalier Carr, the binge drinker, who nevertheless mainly confined his drunkenness to after play, and 'Percy Pisspot' Chapman (so named by Carr), whom no one could trust to be sober, even on the field.

Carr was an alcoholic in the technical sense; Chapman was a chronic alcoholic in any sense. Carr was an aggressive match-winner on his day with Nottinghamshire, which was often in the decade after the war; Chapman was more reckless but also more gifted in his stroke play. The selectors could not make up their minds. Chapman didn't help himself by turning up mid-season and not applying himself with the bat for Kent, managing 1 and 9.

*

Carr focused on the last two Nottinghamshire matches of the 1929 season, which would determine if it won the county championship for the first time since 1907. Short of leading England in an Ashes series, this was the next best moment in his career as captain. Nottinghamshire had to beat Northamptonshire away in a three-day game beginning 28 August.

Carr was pleased. Larwood had overcome injury, mixed success in the Tests and a lack of confidence. Carr, with whom he felt most comfortable as a leader, was working him sparingly, and successfully. There was a strong symbiosis between the two. This was boosted by twenty-year-old Bill Voce, who had developed in three years to a fine left-arm speedster and a superb combatant in combination with his hero, Larwood.

Carr managed them shrewdly. Every now and again through the season, he directed them to use fast leg theory from both ends. The Larwood–Voce left-right combination when using this method, or 'normal' deliveries with slips, caused havoc among opposition batsmen. The fast leg stuff was often deployed to shock and hurt batsmen who were doing well. A broken wrist, a bruise that would not heal for months, smashed teeth and other injuries were the results of the bowling that was aimed as much at the body as it was in taking a wicket.

The captain had got away with it for most of the season by having the bowlers deliver it in short bursts. It was not a method that could be in play for long. For one thing, the speedsters would find it hard to sustain with much banging of the ball into their half of the pitch. In addition, there was always reaction from fans when Nottinghamshire was playing away from Trent Bridge. Carr and Nottingham-shire did not want to attract attention for the fast leg theory, claiming that the injuries were caused by the sheer pace of his two stars.

But the Northamptonshire game was at the season's pointy end. More was at stake. Nottinghamshire had to win.

Fast leg theory was on the menu.

The home team won the toss and batted. After only four overs, Carr had Larwood and Voce on bowling the 'theory'. Northampton was 5 for 39 inside the first hour, with Larwood picking up three, and Voce one. Carr then switched the field to a normal, attacking setting. The pacemen were rested.

One of the middle order facing the ordeal was Victor Rothschild, the tall, handsome aristocrat and eighteen-year-old Harrow schoolboy. The future Third Baron looked confident and at ease. He reached 8 without trouble. Carr clapped his hands. The field changed for the two quicks to four players close on the leg side in an arc from leg slip to silly mid-on. Three men were placed on the leg-side fence.

'It was the theatrical non-verbal announcement of the reversion that held our attention,' Rothschild told his elder sister (and future Dame) Miriam, who attended the match. 'Of course, we [he and his batting partner] had witnessed the devastation of our early batting order, and we braced for what was to come.'

And it came in waves of short pitches aimed at the batsmen. Rothschild was a fine stroke maker forward and back. He had a sound defence. But nothing at Harrow—or anything he had seen—prepared him for this onslaught. His feet movements were outstanding in schoolboy cricket, but not in this game. He froze and stubbornly took blows all

115

over the body. With that failing, he moved inside the flight to the leg side and cut, picking up 7 fours on the unguarded off side. He compiled 36 in an hour under perpetual fire. Fred Barratt, another Yorkshire miner who delivered with pace and swerve, had him caught.

Miriam saw him after he had showered and sat with him in the pavilion.

'What do you think of this fast leg theory?' she asked. 'It looked awful, and painful from here.'

Rothschild opened his shirt to show a rainbow of bruises on his torso and arms. They looked like the yellow and purple mosaic of some tropical disease. 'You mean fast leg, chest and head theory, don't you?' he replied with a rueful look. 'At least those two bastards didn't get me out!' He paused and added, 'They gave me some verballing when I arrived at the wicket.'

'What did they say?'

'Something unfunny about giving the Harrow schoolboy a harrowing time. They also had a bet for a beer about who would first "knock off the Toff".' He paused. 'They didn't direct their comments to me, but raised their voices.'

Miriam asked what he would do about the bowling.

'I'll try to get it banned. I'll write to the MCC.'

His many bruises were still hurting and cramping him up in his second innings, and he lasted a few overs only, making 5 before Voce uprooted his leg stump.

He wrote to the MCC saying that the Nottinghamshire tactics would ruin the game if it were not stopped. It may have been the first letter of complaint, unofficial and private, concerning the tactic. He said that if fast leg theory were not stamped out, he would stop playing cricket, which he did after one more game. Rothschild sagely also said that the decision about unfair bowling could not be left to umpires. The rules must restrict field placings on the leg side.

It was hardly a ground-shaking moment. The MCC would have slipped the letter into its complaints file for 'no action required'. Nottinghamshire was not notified and would have brushed it off anyway.

Winning this game by ten wickets was uppermost in Carr's mind. He had the satisfaction of leading the team to a victory in the 1929 county championship.

It was a sweet compensation for his rebuff in 1928, and he remained hopeful of a return for the 1930 Ashes.

PART FOUR

1930–1932

20

1930:
BRADMAN'S YEAR

All the stars were aligned for 21-year-old Don Bradman at the beginning of 1930. He had a job in a Sydney retail sports store, after the real estate company for which he'd worked closed its doors due to the Depression. There was stability in his private life with the beautiful Jessie Menzies, his childhood sweetheart. Bradman's confidence was sky-high in the first game of the year against Queensland on the SCG. On Saturday 4 January after making just 3 in the first innings, he batted a second time and inspired the 25,000-strong crowd with 205 not out in 195 minutes. Sunday was a rest day. On Monday, unfettered by serious failure in any part of his short life to that point, Bradman was thinking big as he resumed his innings.

'I felt everything was just right,' he said, 'the state of the wicket, the state of the game, the state of my health. Also, I was in the mood for runs.'

Bradman was aware of the world record of 437 set by Ponsford two years earlier. He decided that the first aim was a triple hundred, which was not foreign territory. He reached that after a pre-lunch century and was 310 in 301 minutes. His run rate had remained at a steady high in which he continued to beat the clock.

Over a light lunch, Bradman thought of the 400 milestone and beyond it. His captain had said nothing to him, not even a word of praise, which he assumed meant he could go on until stumps—another two sessions. At an accelerated rate, he believed he would be well over 500 by stumps.

Even 600 was not out of the question.

That number was on his supernumerate mind.

He passed 400 in 76 minutes of the second session. He broke the world record and was 452 not out at tea with a first-class world record of 49 fours. New South Wales was 8 for 761, and any game result was purely academic. There was no rational reason why Kippax could not let the innings go on with Bradman looking at 550 or his outside aim of 600. New South Wales would have a day to remove Queensland on day four of a deteriorating wicket (which it did).

But Kippax declared at tea, surprising the rest of the team. Bradman was not even given time to shower. Kippax took no moment to congratulate the young star, and journalists speculated on his attitude. His own highest score of 315 not out had been eclipsed, as had his public image. Kippax would always be appreciated for his elegance at the crease that matched his sartorial splendour as a dresser, and his personal charm. The emergence of the mannered and modest country star with the innovative, sometimes rustic approach to batting, would not have been easy to digest. If not for Bradman, Kippax would have been the one receiving most media attention in Sydney. Not only that, Bradman's employment at Mick Simmons' sports store had made it number one, ahead of Kippax's own retail outlet in Martin Place.

Kippax was eleven years older than Bradman and he would not have been human if he had not been envious. He had been overshadowed in batting achievement and public adulation by the young man. He was just another individual now put out by Bradman's sudden and all-encompassing ascendancy.

As his reputation built, the Bowral Boy with the permanent half-grin at the wicket was making adversaries he wasn't even aware of.

*

Bradman began in England in 1930 as he had left off in Australia earlier in the year—intent on scoring runs to the point where only his captains' declarations could stop his onslaughts. It began at a cold Worcestershire at the end of April under the majestic cathedral on the ground ringed by great elms. Bradman was 236 not out when the new Australian skipper Bill Woodfull called a halt at 8 for 492. It was the highest first-up score by a tourist in England since Hugh Massie reached 206 in 1882.

Australia won by an innings and 165 runs in an early boost to morale. Critics praised Bradman's effort but always added a levelling assessment by saying the county side's bowling was weak, or that his occasional unorthodoxy would cause him trouble. But Bradman appreciated the slower, grassier wickets and adjusted by playing shots off the back foot.

He continued scoring well until the 24 May game against Surrey at The Oval. Percy Fender was the skipper and the team included Jardine, who was distracted by business commitments. Had he been playing a full season most good judges suggested he could have captained both Surrey and even England. He was offered the vice-captaincy of Surrey, at the instigation of his good friend Fender, but turned it down. He just wouldn't be around the county enough.

He played only eight games at the start of the 1930 county season, scoring 402 at an average of 36.54 with one century. He then dropped out of the running for a Test place. England's batting line-up was strong, but there was always a place for a fighter in the top six with a determination not to lose his wicket.

Jardine also offered an unwavering strength as a leader, disciplinarian and tactician. No one denied his unpopularity as a captain but he was respected for his sometimes grim but determined approach. Many at the MCC had in mind how tough the Australians were to beat. The fact they had lost the last two successive Ashes series was no guarantee of England's success in 1930. Had they lost the recent series, there would have been attempts to cajole Jardine into making a bid for selection. But while not complacent, the establishment felt they had enough talent to defeat a weak-looking Australian squad, who, after all, had been thrashed in its own vast backyard only eighteen months earlier.

Jardine was prepared to turn up and play against Australia for Surrey (and later the MCC) to get a close-up look at what the tourists had to offer. He wanted to blunt Bradman's rapid advance and was keen to offer advice to Fender.

Bradman had read the Surrey captain's comments that he was 'brilliant but unsound'. The young Australian had remained mute to any criticism, his inner confidence telling him to let his bat do the talking. So far it spoke volumes and did not need any verbal platitudes of endorsement.

Surrey was his first big examination.

'I was determined not to make any mistakes,' Bradman said in private. He wanted a giant innings to make a point. Fender, who was good at cricket's mental tactics, took his time moving fielders when Bradman first came to the wicket, including two men close on the leg side. He and Jardine had a long chat in the hope of unsettling the batsman. When they had finished, their 198-centimetre-tall (6 foot 6 inch) speedster Maurice Allom began his run in. Bradman stepped away from the wicket, forcing the bowler to return to his mark. Bradman may have been new to the scene, but he was prepared to play mind games as much as these wily, experienced amateurs.

Surrey vice-captain Allom had him playing and missing early. Bradman claimed, credibly, that he never had nerves before and during an innings, but he was human and sometimes took time to calibrate his skills.

He was 28 not out at lunch after an hour and was playing in a way that would keep his errors to a minimum.

Bradman continued in this restrained vein until he reached 50, in 90 minutes, which reflected his more circumspect approach. Fender himself came on to bowl. The lean, curly-haired leg spinner with the modest moustache had played Tests and was one of county cricket's best all-rounders. He was the shrewdest captain in the county championship and his writing showed an incisive cricket brain. Fender was quick to remove Woodfull, who was deceived by a wrong 'un and caught.

The main interest around the packed Oval was the Fender–Bradman contest, with fans aware of Fender's prediction that the Australian would fail in English conditions. Bradman remained watchful, pushing him for a couple of twos—a beautiful late cut with the spin and a push to mid-wicket—in the first three balls.

Then the wily bowler delivered a ball that was the first examination of his views versus the batman's rare skills and unorthodoxy. The ball landed wide of Bradman's off stump and spun away. Until that moment, he had left such temptations alone, but mindful of the criticism, he used his wizard footwork to haul the ball, against the spin, to the square-leg fence for four. The crowd reacted with awe at such an audacious stroke, that might be expected from an adventurous number 9. Then it applauded.

Fender felt Bradman had taken the bait.

He dished up a slightly straighter ball which still drifted and spun across the batsman. Bradman this time hooked the ball deep and square for two. With a bemused look, Fender took his sweater from the umpire. Ten had come from his first over to the player he had dubbed as special but flawed.

Fender bowled another over, from which Bradman took another 8.

The Surrey captain removed himself from the attack. Bradman eased forward at his unhurried yet consistent rate. Fender consulted with Jardine often. There was a desperation in Fender's step. They did not want Bradman to get a hundred. Cricket was a game of psychological moments, where mental acuity and strength of mind were paramount. This was one. To break the young Australian and keep him down at such a moment would be important for the Tests.

Bradman reached 90. Fender made a double bowling change, bringing on Allom to attack him with short pitches, and the economical medium-pacer Tom Shepherd to bottle up one end. Bradman saw through the tactics and pushed singles to keep his score ticking over. At 99 he nudged a single to mid-wicket of Allom.

His century had taken 145 minutes, with his last 50 taking just 55 minutes.

The big Oval crowd got to its feet to applaud. Fender and Jardine did not clap. Allom waited a half-minute and returned to the top of his mark. He turned and stopped. The umpire's arm was out. Bradman was taking block again. The 21 year old was letting Fender, the 37 year old, know who was in charge on the field, without a word being spoken, or a glance exchanged.

Australian wickets fell steadily—Jackson, Woodfull, Richardson, Ponsford and Stan McCabe came and went—while Bradman lifted his scoring rate.

Fender brought himself on again. Bradman slapped him both sides of the wicket for fours, and the captain, defeated once more, took himself off.

Bradman made 114 between lunch and tea, leaving him at 142 not out. Australia was 5 for 240.

Bradman had won the day and settled a few arguments, including about his ability and temperament. Yet there was one more dimension to him that he wished to display after tea—his killer instinct. This went beyond recrimination or atonement for Fender.

Bradman wanted to go on and crush the opposition. He began cutting like a master surgeon in a hurry yet somehow still with clinical control. Fender kept ringing the changes, but Bradman was in his special zone of the very large score, which already in just a few years of first-class cricket he had made his own. Not one ball was let through to the keeper as Bradman proceeded to shred the attack.

The skies were darkening. Rain threatened and may have caused Bradman to accelerate. He seemed to deliberately slide shots past Fender, making him chase and chase. Some commentators saw it as pay-back time. Bradman denied it, and suggested it was an optical illusion, given Fender's attitude to him. But despite ruining the captain's bowling figures, Bradman was not there to spite the Surrey skipper. That would have been wasted energy.

He did target the opposition's top bowlers, as he did with Larwood in the 1928–29 season. But in this case, all bowlers were in his gunsights. Bradman added another century in just 80 minutes, leaving Fender and Surrey in disarray and looking ragged and second-rate.

His 200 was posted in 225 minutes. Cheek-upon-cheek, the young star took block once more, signalling he was going on. At one point he scored 51 to his partner Fairfax's 1. He hammered 29 fours and his rate overall was 52 runs an hour.

Australia was 5 for 379, Bradman on 252 not out with Fairfax on 28, when the rain came down half an hour before stumps. Fender's humiliation was over.

He and Jardine hurried from the field, making no effort to congratulate Bradman, although thousands in the crowd did as he left to wild applause. The generous English fans were demonstrating that they had seen something special in a performance of near-perfection under pressure in tough conditions; theatre that they might not witness again.

Certainly not in this game. The rain kept coming, washing the match out. Bradman was disappointed. He was in the groove to go on to 400. He also wanted to bring up 1000 before the end of May in this game but was 76 short. He achieved that milestone in the last minutes of play on the last day of the month, in a game against Lord Tennyson's Hampshire at Southampton.

21

AN INNINGS
OF RESISTANCE

Since the Surrey game, many observers had put forward theories on how to combat this new batting phenomenon from down under. Arthur Carr suggested that a speed battery led by Larwood and Voce would be the answer. Jardine, in private, thought the best swing bowlers, such as Maurice Tate, could make use of English conditions to defeat him. Others claimed a strong spin combination could do the trick. The restored England captain Percy Chapman spoke in guarded platitudes about plans but said nothing about a specific strategy.

No one thought of praying for rain, which was Bradman's undoing in his first-ever innings in an Ashes Test in England. It was at Trent Bridge. England had struggled to 270. Rain on day one created a greasy, wet and difficult wicket. Bradman looked out of touch and was bowled by Tate for 8. It was a case of déjà vu from his first Test innings in Australia in 1928, when Tate snared him LBW for 18.

Australia could only manage 144, thanks largely to a fighting innings of 64 not out by Kippax. England replied with 302, with only Grimmett standing in its way for a huge lead. He took five wickets in each innings and was the dominant bowler of the Test. As it was, Australia had a target of 429 to win, a total never before surmounted in an Ashes Test.

Australia began the chase poorly with Larwood generating serious pace after a steady but not penetrating effort in the first innings. He had Woodfull caught in slips by Chapman. This brought Bradman to the wicket to a big ovation and with even bigger expectations. He already had the reputation as a run scorer unmatched in first-class history. Yet a double hundred, which would be needed now, had been beyond him so far in nine Test innings.

At stumps, Bradman was still in. Anyone looking at the scoreboard was surprised to see he was on 31 not out in 35 minutes.

Neville Cardus, the outstanding and eloquent journalist and critic, had always been a closet propagandist for the England cause, and in a moment of unvarnished, premature jingoism remarked, 'Neither Bradman nor Ponsford exactly looked to be great batsmen. Yet both of them are beaters of MacLaren's highest [first-class] score.' He added with a touch of uncharacteristic arrogance, 'From this morning I concluded their superiority with MacLaren is strictly statistical.'

The Australians moved cautiously forward until the score was 93, when Tate bowled Ponsford for 39.

Larwood could not play on because of gastritis and this increased Australia's chances for he had troubled all batsmen, except Bradman, with his pace.

After lunch, Bradman brought up his century and took block again, a sign that he was confident of winning the match for his country. It had taken 215 minutes.

Fairfax didn't last long, with Tate doing more damage, and Australia was 4 for 229. There were still 200 to get with six wickets in hand. McCabe joined Bradman and was a little too adventurous in racing to 49 before Tate dismissed him also.

The score edged up to 316, when leg spinner Walter Robins produced a fabulous wrong 'un to bowl Bradman for 131. He had batted 267 minutes with 10 fours. It was a blow he would never forget and have nightmares about for life.

'I could have won that Test for my country,' he said by way of explanation for his torment over the next seven decades. Australia collapsed to be all out for 335, the highest score ever in the fourth innings of a Test to that point, but still 93 runs behind.

The *Daily Mail* looked past the England win and noted, 'The youthful Bradman showed nerves of iron and the poise of a veteran.'

22

LORD OF LORD'S

Kumar Shri (K. S.) Duleepsinhji, aged 25, held England's first innings together at Lord's on the opening day of the Second Test beginning 27 June. It was his first-ever Test and he hit a magnificent century in 130 minutes. His natural gifts of eye, wrist and footwork—characteristics of the best of India—were evident as he elegantly carved up the Australian attack on his way to 173 out of England's 425.

On day two, Bradman entered this most famous cricket arena at 1 for 162, with Ponsford, relieved that Larwood was still ill and not playing, dismissed for a solid 81.

It was 3.30 p.m. The crowd gave the new man in a rousing reception.

It was a critical moment. England held the Ashes. It was up 1:0 in the series and had a handy 425 on the board, which normally would ensure it could not lose. But Bradman's intervention held the hope for all Australians that he would smash normalcy to oblivion.

He was in with Woodfull, who was batting 'so finely' Bradman noted, 'that I could afford to go for the bowling'.

And go he did. Inspired by Duleepsinhji's example, Bradman began with a gentle yet confident push to mid-off for a single. There was no hurry, no urgency and no apparent nerves. He just wanted to get off the dreaded duck as if it were a rite of passage on a path to something bigger and more profound.

There was power in his early shots and yet his calm and poise were evident. He had some scintillating innings behind him, and he held the world-record score, but this was a challenging step up. He didn't care if his main target, Larwood, was there or not. He went after all the bowlers. His disrespect for the well-known stinginess of White's spin had the always respectful Lord's spectators gasping, then clapping. He played Tate, who had been a problem for him, with ease; Robins and Hammond were treated with thinly veiled contempt. They were all dispatched to the fence as he stroked his first 50 in just 45 minutes.

He was 54 not out at tea with Woodfull on 90 not out and looking like the Rock of Gibraltar.

After the break, Woodfull stepped up his rate and swooped on to 155 before being dismissed. Bradman nearly caught up to his skipper despite him giving him a 78-run and 170-minute head start. Their partnership was 231. Woodfull's steadiness was becoming legendary. He had a small back lift, which earnt the sobriquet 'worm killer', but he was giving his team backbone in tough conditions.

Bradman stroked through a century, hardly reacting to the crowd apart from a touch of his cap. He was so much in form that he didn't bother to take block at 100. It took just

105 minutes. This was his third successive century in Tests. He hooked and drove on to 155 not out at stumps, having stroked 101 in the final day's session.

The witnesses to Bradman's batting revelations were astonished, realising as they headed out into St John's Wood that they had beheld a new champion. England's 425 was an easy task at stumps. How far could he go? They now had a superficial insight to his number-crunching brain. What score, statistic or historical cricket achievement was beyond him?

Bradman cleared his uncluttered mind and relaxed on the rest day, Sunday, by playing golf with Stan McCabe. On Monday, he fronted up for the 32,000 fans who had come to see more or get a first look at this phenomenon of the national sport. They had read all the superlatives from the most famous names and observers of the game in the Sunday papers. There was no room for mealy-mouthed commentary or attempts at psychological warfare. For the moment, this cricketer had transcended all that.

Bradman continued on, marginally subdued, and despite the day's break, a little stiffly. He patted back a maiden from Tate, that drew applause for the bowler.

At 198 he cut a four to reach his first double hundred in Tests. It took 245 minutes. His sights were now set on the highest Test score of 287 set in Sydney in 1903 by England's R. E. Foster, and the crowd sensed it. At lunch, he was 231, having scored a modest, for him, 76 in the pre-lunch session. It was already the highest score by an Australian in Tests. Kippax, his state skipper and very much in his shadow now, was on a well-compiled 50.

They plundered on after lunch until the score was 585 and Bradman was on 254. He launched into a superb cover drive. Chapman threw himself left and caught it. Bradman had hit 25 fours in the highest score ever in a Lord's Test or anywhere else in England. It took him 325 minutes. He would later say without equivocation that this was his finest-ever batting performance. His reasoning was simple. He had made almost no technical error. Bradman's judgement came from his own inner monitor, a mechanism as near to perfection in the sport as possible.

Australia declared at a whopping 6 for 729. England followed up with 375, Chapman firing at last in a Test with an attacking, sometimes reckless 121. Australia had only 72 to make and won by seven wickets.

*

Fender and Jardine watched the entire game together and remained circumspect about what they had seen. Fender took his criticism underground. He had been so smartly slapped around on the field by Bradman it would have been churlish to attack him in public anymore.

Perhaps they had been stunned into silence; maybe they were cogitating how to stop this force of nature who had rounded out his skills beyond what they had seen in Australia in the previous Ashes. No one in the press bemoaned the absence of Larwood, given Bradman's dominance of England's finest and fastest paceman in every encounter to date. Fender, Jardine and others talked in private about his awesome power as a cricketer. It had dawned on them that his perceived weaknesses—the odd cross-bat shot, for instance—were actually strengths. He had the eye, forearm power and bat speed to combat any kind of bowling. His struggle on sticky wickets was obvious, but the critics with perspicacity could see that this young man would work his way around that with more experience.

Fender and Jardine were top cricketers from privileged backgrounds. They could not get their heads around Bradman's composure and self-assurance, more in their minds associated with Oxbridge. They may well have asked what was in the water in the backwater of Bowral in country New South Wales.

Despite playing against him, they had not met him. They were amateurs. They did not fraternise with professionals, let alone foreigners. Where did this quiet confidence that only manifested with his half-grin, which his jealous rivals (and later enemies) would call 'twisted', come from?

Above all, this 21 year old, who conducted himself like someone ten to twenty years older, had the 'X factor', an inner, unshakeable belief in himself in any competition against any other person in any sport.

*

Arthur Carr was at Lord's too and in admiration. He was no longer sure that even his dynamic pair of pacemen, Larwood and Voce, could do anything to stop the young Australian. Carr's own career seemed in decline at worst and stagnant at best. His batting average had dropped, although his leadership had remained effective despite his spasmodic appearances for Nottinghamshire. In 1930, stories about him being replaced as captain surfaced, but they had become an annual event to fill newspapers' rumour mills. Walter Robins had been suggested as taking over the leadership soon after he bowled Bradman for 131 in the First Test at Trent Bridge. The Nottinghamshire members got excited about his ability and the talk began and spread like a virus in the pavilion and the Tavern Bar afterwards.

Carr rebuked them from the song sheet he had used before, 'It's all bosh, I have no intention of giving up the captaincy.'

He had not even abandoned the possibility of leading England in the current or future Ashes. Chapman appeared to have sealed his spot for the moment with his daring hundred at Lord's. But England had lost. Considering the MCC Committee's consistent inconsistency, and apparent whimsicality, if England were to lose the next Test, and Chapman were to fail, then the issue of leadership could be revised.

23

ONWARD,
EVER UPWARD

Two weeks after his triumph at Lord's, Bradman strolled out to bat on the first day of the Third Test, at Headingley, Leeds, in the grey, thin July light. Archie Jackson had just been dismissed by Tate for 1. The score was 1 for 2. The knowledgeable Yorkshire fans had seen him before early in May when he scored a respectable 78 in a game at Bramall Lane, Sheffield, that had been dominated by Grimmett, who took all ten of the county wickets for 37 and broke many records himself. Despite Bradman's achievement so far in the season, the Yorkshire public had yet to make their own judgement.

Larwood was back after injury and pawing the ground. Tate was eager, having dismissed Bradman early in two Tests. The impressive George Geary was in too, and his pace and accuracy were expected to restrict him. The first opportunity was in those early overs when even someone with this player's skills would be vulnerable to the right delivery. The fans had read the papers in the morning where they were reminded the Australian had now scored four centuries in his last five Ashes Tests, scoring even higher in each innings when he passed a hundred—112, 123, 131 and 254.

Bradman joined Woodfull and began in what was now typical fashion with a casual clip to the on side for 2 against Tate. The bowler nearly had his moment when he got one through Bradman two balls later and just missed the stumps. The batsman did not react. He just leant on his bat as if he'd just leg glanced a four and waited for the next ball.

He had 18 on the board with 3 fours in as many minutes. He accumulated runs with such style and grace that he had beaten the clock to 50 without any fuss or loose, lucky flashes. His 'wagon wheel', the sketch of every shot, already showed every major stroke in the book of orthodoxy, and some that were not. Yet not once did he lose control in execution; always keeping the ball down.

Larwood was bowling with all his force, and Bradman thrived on the speed, cutting and driving him in an unhurried manner. Once more the Nottinghamshire star was pushed aside and out of the attack—no doubt wishing he had not recovered from illness. Bradman's unerring capacity to pierce the field was Larwood's undoing. It frustrated him into spraying the ball and offering up a few extra cuts and hooks.

Chapman took Larwood off for almost the rest of the pre-lunch session then brought him back to block Bradman's attempt to score a century before lunch. He greeted the bowler with a full-blooded drive for four. He became the third person to reach a hundred in the morning session after Australian greats Victor Trumper and Charlie Macartney, and in the fastest time. He was 105 not out at the big break, having stroked 16 fours.

Post-lunch, Chapman soon had Larwood, ignited with beers, on for another burst. But apart from troubling Woodfull and hitting him once, he was manhandled by Bradman with several more delightfully struck fours—two cuts and two pulls. On numerous occasions Chapman pulled a player from one position only for Bradman to punch the next delivery through the position from which the player had just come.

Larwood asked for field changes, Bradman responded by again placing the ball in the position just vacated. Larwood would stand mid-pitch, hands on hips and scowling. He scratched his head, mumbled something under his breath and plodded back to his mark before running in for more punishment.

The bowler let go a ball directed at Bradman's throat. He moved with lightning footwork and pulled the ball through mid-wicket.

The Yorkshire fans loved brilliant bats and fighters, and to observe one possessing both qualities was a treat, even if he was embarrassing England. After all, it wasn't *Yorkshire* that was left floundering.

They clapped all Bradman's shots. They were so precise that no matter what the captain or bowlers tried, he could not be drawn into a false stroke. There was no rush of blood, no injudicious, pompous or ego-driven shots.

Larwood tried fast leg theory, but in his enthusiasm to generate the pace that had battered and bruised many a county opposition, he strayed *too much* down the leg side. Bradman responded by hooking and pulling him straight to earth so that no chance was given. He was too set to be intimidated by balls directed at his ribcage.

Chapman had no choice but to banish Larwood to the outfield for the third time. As the afternoon wore on, Larwood was forced into more running the boundary than he would ever have liked, which added to his humiliation and inner hostility.

Woodfull had been up the other end with a ringside seat of England's destruction until Hammond came on and bowled him for 50. The score was 194. Kippax joined Bradman.

Bradman went to tea at 220, after hitting another century in the session. His double had taken 214 minutes, then the fastest double hundred in Test history. He had sinned by his own assessment by miscuing two shots that were not near catching fielders. When he compared this innings with his idea of perfection, as at Lord's, that was two too many. He was already downgrading this superb performance in his rankings of personal efforts at the crease, even though the attack he faced was stronger.

Refreshed by a cup of tea and a foot massage during the short break, he and Kippax (77) indulged in a 229-run stand, a second-wicket record. Bradman was conscious of his failure so far to break R. E. Foster's record of 287.

Chapman had run out of options, and had to bring on a reluctant Larwood for more scoring abuse, and he was humbled once more. But this applied to all the bowlers: Bradman had fun picking out the elderly Jack Hobbs, and the rotund Dick Tyldesley for long chases.

At 5.57 p.m. Bradman, who was on 273, gave his first real chance of the innings, flashing at a faster ball from Geary outside the off stump. He nicked it and keeper George Duckworth dived, got a glove to it, but dropped it. Bradman nodded to the keeper with a consoling look, a minor departure from his usually relaxed expression.

Bradman had given three chances in the three Tests, which had seen him at the crease for fifteen hours. On average you had one chance every day he batted. If you missed it you suffered.

Bradman cruised past Foster's record with a drive for three, without any fuss or demonstration. He raised his baggy green, waved his bat perfunctorily to the applause. His humble consolation for this performance was a wider, still boyish grin. Hammond, England's top scorer, came and shook his hand, as did Chapman, followed by Hobbs and then the rest of the England team, including Larwood who flapped Bradman's palm briefly and kept his eyes down. The paceman was still smarting from the day's humiliation, where he had been thumped for a hundred for the return of one wicket—Stan McCabe whom he bowled for 30.

Australia reached 3 for 458 at stumps.

Larwood had been given a tough time by Bradman on the pitches around the vast, hot continent of Australia in front of sometimes hostile crowds. But the experience at Headingley was the worst he'd had in his sporting life. Home crowds cheering an Australian for belting him around the park was dispiriting, especially a Nottinghamshire-rival Yorkshire crowd. He had felled more than a few of the county's batsmen over the years. There was an element of revenge in the spectators' reaction, although he was not booed or jeered.

The crowd mobbed Bradman as he strode from the field on 309 not out, the highest one-day Test batting score ever (a record that still stood 91 years on in 2021). They ignored

Larwood. The fans waited outside for Bradman to come onto the pavilion balcony.

Larwood could hear the chant of the Australian's name as he showered and dressed. He wanted to disappear from the scene of his shame and join teammates for beers of consolation. Even as he walked from the ground, Bradman, the reluctant hero, was being cheered as he emerged, shy, footsore and fatigued to wave to several thousand in front of the pavilion.

*

At 334 the next day, Saturday, Bradman succumbed to Tate (who took five wickets), caught behind. Australia reached 566. Bradman had now scored five centuries in six Tests and had kept his sequence of ever higher scores going.

England replied with 391 (Hammond 113, in a long, slow innings), and its bowling 'problem' Grimmett captured 5 for 135. England followed on and was 3 for 95 when the weather closed in and the final day, four, was a washout.

The series was locked at one win each.

*

Douglas Jardine was away on business for Barings and missed the Headingley Test. Percy Fender covered the entire game for the newspapers, and Arthur Carr saw all of Bradman's innings. They were yet to detect any serious weakness in the Australian's play or character.

24

DECIDER
AT THE OVAL

A dejected Larwood told Arthur Carr he expected to be dropped for the Fourth Test at Manchester after his hammering by Bradman at Leeds, and he was, joining Tyldesley and Geary on the sidelines. They were replaced by speedster Morris 'Stan' Nichols, off spinner Tom Goddard and Scottish leggie Ian Peebles. The game was a disappointing washout with Australia scoring 345 (Bradman caught off Peebles for 14) and England replying with 8 for 251.

Three weeks later on 16 August, the Fifth Test began at The Oval, with its ugly yet imposing Victorian steel gasholder dominating the view. It was to be a timeless match to make sure someone won the Ashes, which decided the fate of captain Percy Chapman. He was allegedly dumped because of his sometimes reckless batting and his attitude that would be unsuitable for a long game of patience—a similar excuse to Carr's sacking in the Fifth Test of 1926.

It was the second time Chapman had been dropped in the final game of an Ashes series, although this time there was a logic of sorts to his ousting. He was replaced by the solid all-rounder, 29-year-old Bob Wyatt of Warwickshire, known for his steady batting and serviceable medium-pace bowling. In keeping with this selectorial choice of timeless endurance, reliable Nottinghamshire opening bat Dodger Whysall also got the nod. His score of 120 against the Australians in his county game helped his cause.

Larwood was restored to the national team after a run of good performances over the last month. Out went Nichols and Goddard.

For Australia, Archie Jackson came in after his exclusion from the previous game, and replaced vice-captain Vic Richardson.

Wyatt won the toss and batted. Thanks to a dependable, if slow 161 from Herbert Sutcliffe, a dashing 50 in 50 minutes from refined Duleepsinhji, and a stolid but important 64 from Wyatt, England made 405 in 171.2 overs, a plod of just more than 2 an over, but an understandable crawl given the Ashes were at stake. Grimmett (4 for 135) was outstanding as he had been all series by taking wickets steadily and blunting Hammond's performance.

England's score of more than 400 would have appeared a bridge too far near the end of a long tour for any visiting team, except for one factor: Bradman. He had lost none of his lust for runs, and he was very keen for an Ashes win after his experience in the 1928–29 series.

Australia batted on day two just before lunch in front of a packed Oval crowd. Inspired by Bradman's methods, Ponsford went after Larwood from the first over, bearing in mind that the Nottinghamshire champion had troubled him in every way, particularly in crashing lifting balls into his rump and back when the gutsy opening batsman had turned away, not being fast enough to avoid deliveries. He made a classic 110, before Peebles had him caught behind.

It was tea. Australia was 1 for 159.

Rain came and held up play for an hour after tea before Woodfull walked out with Bradman, the man of the moment, and already, the season. The conditions were not ideal as they had been at Leeds and Lord's. The wicket was damp; the light was indifferent. Peebles had two men in close on the leg side. There was tension. Silence reigned for a second or two as Peebles wheeled in with his leg spinners. Bradman cut him for a single.

Tate was on and the crowd was hoping he would work his swing magic in the humid atmosphere. He did, beating the bat outside the off stump twice. This young new star, on whose performance the Ashes would probably be decided, took precious minutes to calibrate everything—the light, the swing, the pace, the variation on the damp pitch.

Bradman pushed for ones and twos, refusing to be bogged down as Wyatt worked his bowling changes. Bradman made one rare swipe over the annoying close-in men for three, and the crowd gasped at him going airborne.

Peebles broke through with the score at 194, having the Australian captain caught behind for 54. Rain stopped play with Bradman on 28 not out and Kippax on 8. Australia was 2 for 208, with the match and the series in the balance.

*

The weather forecast for day three, Tuesday, was not promising although the game began on time and in sunshine. Bradman settled in again—his third start in the innings. He saw off Peebles after a long duel, which for the moment put paid to the argument that Bradman was susceptible to leg spin.

Wyatt tried Larwood. He began with a head-high, accurate bouncer. Bradman swayed under it, eyes on the ball. Larwood threw everything at both batsmen, but they coped well, with Bradman restraining the urge to stroke him out of the attack. Seeing this, Wyatt kept Larwood on as a stock bowler delivering line and length, and brought Peebles back on to relieve Tate.

Peebles had Kippax (28) caught brilliantly by Wyatt in the leg trap. Australia was 3 for 263, still 138 in arrears, with Bradman on 68 not out, and looking comfortable, if watchful. He was joined by his good friend Jackson who had instructions from Woodfull to play defensively and let 'Don take control'. This was not Jackson's style but he was in no position to defy his skipper. The young, frail and potentially great player had had just one Test innings on the tour for 1 run. An unknown illness had kept him underweight and struggling. But with a dictate within his capacities, he was able to stay in and let Bradman step up his rate.

Wyatt used Hammond and Peebles in tandem and Bradman hit them to the fence. They were followed by Wyatt himself and Tate, which had no impact. When Bradman was on 99, Wyatt brought Larwood back, almost as if it were his duty to deliver Bradman another century. The batsman duly obliged and drove him for four to record his fourth century in the series in five Tests and sixth in eight Tests against England.

Larwood did not shake his hand, but he did make a congratulatory remark which Bradman acknowledged.

He raised his baggy green to the crowd and his half-grin once more developed into a full smile, however briefly. He had enjoyed the challenge and achievement but there was still much work to do. Australia was still a hundred behind. Unlike at Leeds, where he had batted unfettered, Bradman took block again, motioning to himself, if not the opposition, that he wanted at least another hundred.

Bradman told Jackson, mid-pitch, that they had to climb well above England's score. 'The wicket is sure to be even more trouble in a day or two,' he said. 'We don't want to bat on it again.'

This was a confidence boost for Jackson. Bradman was set on scoring so big that Australia would not have a second innings. This was not bombast but his little mate speaking pragmatically and within the scope of his, and Jackson's, capabilities. Like him or not, this was Bradman's way of leading from the front. There was no 'gee up' of platitudes, not even a pat on the bum. Instead he was demonstrating a belief in himself, Jackson and the rest of the team. This was why Bradman inspired respect and awe. His character had an unshakeable gravitas. Without a word being spoken, everyone in the team, the opposition and even the spectators were aware of his personal will to win, and more.

It was an obsession.

Bradman moved on into his second hundred with ease. He always learnt by doing and he was now picking Peebles' good wrong 'un. It held no more terrors for him and he was skipping down the wicket to score off it.

At lunch Australia was 3 for 371—just 34 short and closing on England. Bradman was on 112 not out, having scored 86 before lunch. His display was tenacious and a fraction understated compared to his punch and power at Leeds and Lord's; more like his fighting 131 in the First Test at Trent Bridge.

It rained during the long break when the debonair Prince of Wales met the two teams in the members' stand under-cover. King George V had met Bradman at Lord's and was keeping a file on him, as he did with all 'famous' members of the Empire from Lawrence of Arabia to Australia's General John Monash. Now it was the opportunity too for his son, Prince Edward. He had even less interest in cricket than his father, and would rather be at Ascot, or Wimbledon or the Chelsea Flower Show. Yet a photo opportunity with the most popular young man from the dominions, who was taking the 1930 summer by storm, was important for his public image.

Bradman was no small-talking champion. He would rather avoid such moments but he would never let such an 'event' distract him from the task ahead. Not even the weather, which interrupted the day and made him start his innings for the sixth and seventh time, could frustrate him into error.

He reached 130 not out at stumps and Australia was 3 for 403, two runs short of England's tally.

The next morning the papers were pessimistic about England's chances with Bradman at the wicket. Many uncon-vincing ideas, mainly negative about England's players, were proffered. Some of the press played down the game. The *Daily Mail* editorial said, 'There is nothing to say about the match except that Bradman is a menace to English cricket.'

Again, he had developed during the game, turning an alleged weakness—inexperience on wet English wickets—into an asset in one long stay as the rain continued to unsettle the pitch conditions.

25

THE LAST BARRAGE

On day four, Wednesday 20 August, the wicket was firmer, yet more uncertain and dangerous. The unassuming and surprisingly quiet Larwood, backed up by the always noncha-lant and loose-limbed Hammond, now had their chance to break through. The ball was darting and lifting off a good length. Hammond caught Jackson in the midriff, winding him and holding up play. Then Larwood hit Bradman on the upper right shoulder. The crowd reacted. Bradman flexed his arm an over later, showing the first signs of discomfort. Larwood with a dressing-room beer in him was electrified. His wonderfully smooth run to the wicket seemed quicker and his deliveries more deadly. He was accurate too, and his desire to collect Bradman on the body was satisfied.

But one would not be enough.

The batsman took one on the sternum. It hurt and caused him to hold up play for a few seconds. His foot movements were so quick that he had rarely, if ever, been hit in top cricket.

The little win for Larwood demonstrated his pace and the difficult nature of the pitch. The bowler found the sweet spot again. This time the ball crashed into Bradman's fingers. He removed his flimsy glove and examined the digits. Umpire Parry moved from square leg to apply a bandage. Bradman flexed his hand several times, pushing blood into the affected area, and faced up again. Larwood was back at his mark. He had Bradman on the defensive for the first time in a score of encounters. He ran in, dropping the ball shorter than the deliveries that had struck home and aiming higher, at the head. Bradman used his back foot for perfect positioning and crashed it through mid-wicket for four.

Larwood stood hands on hips mid-wicket, and then strolled back to his mark. Instead of trying to knock off his cap again, he delivered a beautiful away swinger. Bradman moved onto his back foot just enough to effect a cut to the fence. He had counter-attacked and given Larwood that old sinking feeling once more.

Wyatt kept him on and bowled the next over at Jackson, who could not manoeuvre away from a lifter that struck him on the hip bone as he jumped in the air to defend. It was a stinger. Jackson took a few moments to recover.

Larwood's tail was up.

He was doing what he loved—second only to hitting wickets.

He was pummelling bodies.

Jackson took another delivery in the ribs and was forced away from the wicket. The fielders and umpires crowded around him. Larwood stood by, not even bothering to feign concern. His position in the Test team was on the line and he had seen this many times in his career. It was part of the first-class game, accentuated at Test level. He had softening-up, bone-crunching power and had used it ever since his Nottinghamshire captain Carr had urged him to in his first full season for the county.

Bradman trotted over to console Jackson, pulling him aside and telling him he would take the bowling for a few overs. He was keen for Jackson to stay at the wicket. He did not wish England to break into the middle order, and he wanted the psychological advantage of letting the opposition know blasting them out was not an option.

Hammond saw Jackson faltering and went in for the kill. But Bradman had the strike and hooked him to the fence. He then cut him for three to reach 182. This left a shaky Jackson facing one delivery. Hammond dropped it short. The batsman half-turned and was collected on the elbow. Jackson's eyes were watering as he rubbed the swelling bruise. He had been struck in the ribs, chest, hip and elbow.

Bradman went over to him for the second time, knowing that his mate was ailing even without the bone-crunchers. But he did not suggest he go off. Instead, he encouraged him to go on. Stoic beyond the call, Jackson took some deep breaths and faced up.

Victor Rothschild, now a nineteen-year-old microbiology student at Cambridge, was at the game, riveted. He wrote in his diary, 'It [the physical attack on Bradman and Jackson] was not fast leg theory, with only two or three men in close on the leg side. But it was effective in its damage. I felt for Jackson. I know how he felt . . . Bradman was intent on counter-attack . . .'

Larwood continued with thunderbolts and Bradman took most of the strike while Jackson regained his composure.

At 196, Bradman drove Tate straight for four. His double century had taken 383 minutes. Jackson walked up the wicket as the applause lingered and shook Bradman's hand a little too enthusiastically. His fingers were still sore after the earlier Larwood knock.

Wyatt signalled another win to Bradman by taking a flat and dejected Larwood out of the attack. This hurt the bowler more than any other belting. Australia was taking a grip of the Ashes urn. Wyatt brought himself on. Jackson, after riding and colliding with bounce and bump for most of the morning, was relieved.

He struck out at the England skipper and was caught for 73.

Australia was now 4 for 506, a lead of 101. The most critical partnership of the summer had produced 243 runs. Jackson had scored at half his partner's rate, but the important fact was that he done exactly as the captain ordered and let Bradman take control.

McCabe joined Bradman as he pounded towards a century before lunch. He fell 2 short and was 228 not out at the main break. After it, McCabe had most of the strike for the first twenty minutes before a refreshed Larwood came on. Bradman advanced to 232. The bowler produced a fast, lifting ball that swung away. Bradman noticed the movement and turned his bat at the last split second. The ball flew harmlessly through to Duckworth. Larwood appealed, more it seemed to say that he had beaten the bat. Duckworth didn't even hold the ball up, or throw it high, which he did when he thought he had a catch. Hammond at slip did not appeal. He looked up, wondering if the bowler's appeal meant he had missed something. But the umpire upheld the solitary appeal.

Bradman said, decades later, that he did not get near the ball. But he was on his way, with Australia at 5 for 570.

His Lord's innings was his technically most perfect exhibition; the effort at Leeds was the most scintillating and the performance at Trent Bridge was determined. But The Oval innings was the most important of the series. The wicket was physically dangerous and the Ashes were at stake. Bradman batted with grit, drive and skill against the hostile attack that would have been satisfied to get him out any way possible.

Australia scurried up to 695, thanks to Woodfull's tight, disciplined leadership, Bradman's great batting, and outstanding middle and late order Test performances from McCabe (54), Fairfax (53 not out) and Oldfield (34).

Peebles took 6 for 204 with a marathon 71 overs, while Larwood was the most expensive with 1 for 132 from 48 overs. In the last two bowling stints against Australia he had taken 2 (really just 1) wicket for 271 off 81 overs. His series record was 4 for 292 off 101 overs at an average of 73 runs a wicket. Most of these runs had come from Bradman's flashing blade. Larwood delivered 147 balls to him and Bradman had taken 137 runs off them, which was a rate of 93.21 runs per 100 deliveries.

There had been no more-decisive winner in the battle of two Titans in the history of Test cricket.

Bradman had made 974 runs for the series at an average of 139.14, eclipsing Hammond in Australia in the previous series.

Neville Cardus noted, 'We have now seen Bradman the brilliant and Bradman the shrewd . . . his versatility is astonishing and he is indeed a great batsman.'

*

Tall, long-limbed Queenslander Percy Hornibrook, on a wicket conducive to his slow-medium, left-arm, 'dibbly-dobbly' bowling, delivered the performance of his life, taking 7 for 92, and doing most to fell England for 251. The difficult wicket was the same for both teams on the last two days, but the Australians, led by Bradman, played the conditions with more skill and spine against a better bowling attack.

Australia won by an innings and 39 runs, which gave them the 1930 Ashes 2:1, thanks mainly to Bradman with the bat, and Grimmett with the ball. The latter took 29 wickets at 31.89 and limited his main quarry, Hammond, to 306 runs at 34.00, which was one-third of his 1928–29 batting record.

Arthur Carr and Jardine were at The Oval and witnessed England's humiliation. They did not discuss it then, but they were both cogitating how to curtail or defeat the immense talent who had crushed the might of their country.

*

There was one more encounter between Bradman and Larwood at the HDG Leveson-Gower v Australia match at Scarborough on 10 to 12 September. It was billed as a 'festival' match, but the stacking of the England team with Test players made it more like a Test. Naturally, the English wanted to send the Australians off with a defeat.

The English team batted first and Hornibrook finished where he left off at The Oval, taking 5 for 69 from a total of 9 declared for 218. Australia responded and was all out for 238. Bradman took to Larwood for the final contest and drove him from the attack on the way to the game's highest score of 96.

It was a less-than-gentle reminder of the Test series' pattern.

Woodfull's team played 33 tour matches, won twelve, lost one (the First Test at Trent Bridge), tied one and drew nineteen.

It restored Australia's dominance in world cricket.

26

JARDINE'S RISE

Bradman was happy to move through all the celebrations for him and Woodfull's team and get down to cricket against a West Indian team making its inaugural tour of Australia. Yet he was distracted by fundamentals in life, such as looking for more sustained employment beyond his impermanent work in a sports store, and finding the right time to marry Jessie Menzies.

He played only six Test innings against the tourists, scoring 447 at an average of 74.50, and was just pipped by Ponsford, who had seven innings for 467 runs at 77.83. Bradman's run of Test scores against an inexperienced West Indies were 4, 25, 223, 152, 43 and 0. The opposition was not the easy-beats expected. They boasted the polished stylist George Headley, dubbed by the press 'the black Bradman', fast bowler and brilliant fielder Learie Constantine, along with pacemen Herman Griffith and George Francis.

The West Indies lost the series 4:1 but shocked Australia, and themselves, by beating the home team in the Fifth Test in Sydney.

Overall, Bradman was about half as effective, statistically, as he had been in England in 1930, but he was still the dominant batsman in the nation for the third successive season, scoring 1422 first-class runs at an average of 79. Yet his desire for runs was undiminished. He scored 2679 runs in all games, with twelve centuries, including four doubles. Observers such as A. G. Johnny Moyes felt Bradman could score at will when his mind was settled. He had been distracted by battles with the Australian Cricket Board over it telling him he could not earn money from print journalism while playing for Australia.

Bradman badly sprained an ankle at the end of the season, which put him in hospital for eighteen days. It gave him time to think.

'The enforced convalescence may have been a blessing,' he noted. 'It certainly gave me a rest . . . and provided a tonic for a constitution somewhat jaded by concentrated cricket and publicity.'

*

Many cricket administrators in England were watching Bradman's progress. No commentary they had read or letters they had received could pinpoint any new or obvious weakness. He handled speed with counter-attacks and with a range of shots, especially the hook and pull. His footwork against spin was second to none, and he used this to drive spinners out of attacks, and refused to be pinned down.

In early 1931, the MCC Committee was already looking ahead to the next Ashes tour to Australia scheduled to leave by boat in late August 1932, less than twenty months away. England's cricket supremo and MCC Chairman Pelham Francis (Plum) Warner, of Oxford, Middlesex and England, was more concerned about preparation than most. He had toured Australia twice, bringing back the Ashes with a 3:2 victory in 1903–04 and also being part of the 1911–12 tour. Warner knew well the demands of the long trip of up to three months of sea voyages and then travel by boat and train around and across the vast continent. That was the easy part. There was also the most intense and skilled opposition, and jingoistic crowds, whom he appreciated had become more vocal and demonstrative than when he played, although he had experienced mob attitudes of wrath as well.

World War I, and Australia's significant part in it on the Western Front and Middle East, had developed a certain independence of mind. Australia, once a group of basically subservient British colonies, had become a dominion, hardened by mind and keenness to break away from dependence on the 'Mother Country', but bound to it by tradition, values, race and trade.

Sport, especially cricket, had created the battlefield where differences could be fought over in 'friendly' rivalry on the pitch, and similarities of sportsmanship could be displayed. The seat of Empire did not wish to be beaten by a far-flung fledgling nation of misplaced Europeans at the bottom of Asia. Australia, now aware of the British attitude to it in war—as expendable front-line shock troops—was equally keen to upset the Empire's sense of dominance, where it had rarely been challenged in 400 years.

Leadership was seen as important, in fact, vital. It stemmed from the establishment's appreciation of discipline and control, instituted in the public schools, with its prefect system and the choice of team 'captains'. It was imperative to choose the right man for the down-under tour. Yes, there would be carnal temptations everywhere, but knowledge of such issues was hidden or ignored. Partying and drinking would be tolerated to a point. The leader had to balance discipline with common sense. Yet this tour in general and the 1932–33 tour in particular had endless demands that had to be coped with. If they weren't, teams could fall apart even in the initial weeks.

The Australians were no longer the easy-beats they were in 1928–29. Since then Bradman had developed into the greatest batsman yet to be seen in the game. He had dominated the 1930 series, and pulverised England's finest pacemen. On top of that, Australia had the best bowler of 1930 in Clarrie Grimmett. He had subdued England's best batsman, Hammond.

Warner had not been content with the performances of skippers chosen in recent years. Carr had not done *badly*. He had the right look and attacking mentality and had proved it over and over, but not in Tests where he had been unlucky in limited opportunities. Warner knew of his, at times, irresponsible behaviour off the pitch with women, drinking and driving. Carr was popular with the troops and the spectators. He had squeezed the brutal best out of Larwood and now Voce that had kept Nottinghamshire at the top—or near the top—of the county table for many seasons. How would he handle abusive crowds? Probably with his usual aplomb mixed with some mischief.

Warner had no answers.

He had dumped Carr for the Fifth Test in 1926 and the move had made Warner appear a sage. Carr's replacement, Percy Chapman, had done the job then and in Australia in 1928–29. When he had been dumped for Jack 'Farmer' White in the final Test, England had lost the game, which may have embarrassed the tour selectors. But they had their reasons. Some in the team, including Jardine, had frowned at his clowning at the wicket, when he wore a cap designating a 'pair' at Cambridge. Jardine saw it as mocking Oxford and the harlequin cap, and it rankled with him. There had always been a healthy rivalry between the two leading universities in academic and sporting life, which was as strong as the Eton versus Winchester competition. Old boys at these institutions always had grudging respect for each other, but the adversarial attitude, even if expressed jocularly, was for life.

Jardine also thought Chapman's antics in joking with the crowd unacceptable for an England captain and he let everyone including Chapman, but excluding the press, know it.

No one minded someone who liked a drink. England players tended to scoff, behind the scenes, at the Australians being mainly teetotallers. Warner loved a gin and tonic after play or when watching the game. Yet the stories about Chapman's penchant for booze were disconcerting. They worked against him in 1929, and again in 1930 when solemnity ruled, if not sobriety. He had not quite delivered with the bat except for his superb hundred at Lord's in 1930, that had been overshadowed by Duleepsinhji and totally eclipsed by Bradman.

Bob Wyatt had handled his leadership well enough, but he had not inspired selectors beyond his solidity. It seemed almost certain he would be chosen in the squad for the 1932–33 tour, and possibly as leader.

There were no other serious contenders, except for one: Douglas Jardine. He had the right amateur pedigree, especially being an Oxford man like Warner. He was also unscarred from captaining against Australia and Bradman. He had all the necessary characteristics for being a general in a long war of attrition against the Australians. Jardine also had the necessary 'dignity' for the job and was a careful drinker. No one had ever seen him drunk. He would be expected to manage the crowds and press, even if he simply ignored them, or gave them very little. He had the upright look of a focused leader. He would not be overly popular within the squad but the contest was not about being the 'best chap'.

It was about coming back with the Ashes.

Warner invited Jardine for a drink and a chat at Lord's and to meet the MCC Committee in mid-February 1931. He behaved perfectly. At the end of the discussion, Warner took Jardine aside and asked if he would consider captaining England in the one Test scheduled against New Zealand.

Jardine said 'yes'.

What about Australia for the 1932–33 Ashes?

Jardine demurred. He wanted to take it one season at a time. They discussed the 1928–29 tour and Jardine spoke of his dislike of the local crowds. Warner mentioned the lack of discipline under Chapman and Jardine agreed that this had to change, and would if he were captain. But he would not commit himself beyond the 1931 season, saying his own form would be a factor, as would his business commitments. This was a vague yet acceptable response to Warner's feeler about leading in Australia.

The appointment to lead against the Kiwis was announced a few months into the 1931 season on 10 June. It received a lukewarm response. Jardine was unknown as a captain, not having been a skipper at his county. Yet it was accepted that his batting would add backbone to the national team. Commentators wondered if this appointment presaged the next Ashes tour.

Warner refused to comment beyond 'looking forward' to the New Zealand Test.

The game drew out issues from the first day and a stark look at the Jardine style, hitherto unknown. He lost the toss at Lord's and was understandably nervous. It was not his style to curry favour with the troops. Rather, he wanted to dictate and show who was boss early with the professionals, which he did too eagerly, like a school prefect giving out a detention to a pupil soon after receiving his badge.

Early in the innings, Jardine placed Frank Woolley at fine leg instead of his usual place of slip. Woolley misread his positioning in front of the alphabet letters clearly marked on placards. Hammond ran in to bowl. Jardine held up play. He called out in a loud voice, heard by sections of the quiet crowd, 'I said "B", Woolley, not "C".'

Woolley held up his arms, confused. He looked to Hammond for explanation. Hammond pointed in different directions. This elicited much mirth from the younger members of the team, including Ian Peebles.

Jardine was not amused and Woolley was humiliated in front of the big Lord's crowd, some of whom laughed at his predicament.

New Zealand was all out for a modest 224.

According to the then 23-year-old Ian Peebles, also a Scot who'd graduated from Oxford, Jardine didn't help his first-up cause for discipline when he entered the separate professional dressing room to dictate the batting order. 'Woolley, you will bat at number five and I shall bat at six. But if there is a crisis, I shall be at five, and you, six.'

Woolley felt set upon with Jardine's stark words indicating that Woolley was not a man for a difficult situation.

England wickets did fall quickly and it was soon 3 for 31 with both Jardine and Woolley padded up. Jardine indicated he would go in at five.

'It's a bloody crisis!' Woolley said, annoyed.

He was soon in at 4 for 62, and built recovery partnership with the captain of 67 before Jardine was out for 38. Woolley blazed his way to a run-a-minute 80 and had the last laugh, but not in front of the captain.

Jardine sent Peebles in as night watchman with the score at 6 for 188. Hammond and Walter Robins made some amusing remarks about his ability as he went out to bat. He was promptly stumped for a duck and received some good-natured derision from Robins, who laughed and joked at Peebles' embarrassing performance.

The next morning in the dressing room, Jardine was annoyed. He became head prefect and gave Robins a dressing-down saying that his behaviour was 'rather fourth form'.

Peebles and the other amateurs made it worse for Robins by pulling faces through the glass door behind Jardine's back.

When Jardine was out of earshot, Robins was reminded his acts were 'rather fourth form'.

He quipped, 'And you were rather *first form*.'

*

Jardine didn't have a chance to show much with the bat, scoring 38, 7 not out and 28 not out in the three Kiwi Tests won 1:0 by the home team. His captaincy was satisfactory, once he settled down and the team got used to his stentorian demands and strict disciplines. Whatever his ranking as a leader, he was not short of tactics, and well-articulated reasoning if he had to give answers for his decisions to anyone, including the press.

At The Oval, Jardine strengthened his claims to the top job in a September final game of the season captaining The Rest v Yorkshire, the county champions, which Warner hoped would sort out some selection issues for both bat and ball.

Yorkshire bowled first and Bill Bowes and Hedley Verity put in claims for notice, with 4 for 16 and 3 for 49 respectively. Twenty-three-year-old Bowes was a tall, at 193 centimetres (6 foot 4 inches), raw-boned and bespectacled fast bowler with a prodigious inswinger, who troubled all batsmen with his dangerous lift. Verity, aged 26, was already judged as the best left-arm orthodox spinner in the UK.

All eyes were on Jardine when The Rest batted and collapsed for a disappointing 124. He was stoic in his 26 resisting Bowes and keeping out Verity, who were out to impress, aware that it was possible he would be skipper for the prized tour down under. Bowes tried to ruffle Jardine with short pitches, but the batsman played front on, left elbow held high to counter the lifters.

Yorkshire replied with 209, Maurice Leyland top scoring with 96. In The Rest's second effort, Jardine (104) and Bob Wyatt (57), had an important partnership, both being removed by Verity (4 for 48) who all but sealed his selection for Australia.

Bowes clashed with Jardine, hitting him in the shoulder and arm, and breaking a bone in Wyatt's hand. The latter refused to retire hurt, and batted on effectively one-handed, impressing Jardine with his courage.

At one point, Jardine gestured to Bowes, walked down the wicket and patted a spot well inside Bowes' half of the wicket, indicating he was overdoing the short stuff. Bowes responded with two good bouncers. No one knew how his defiance of the current England skipper would be taken. Jardine, in typical fashion, ignored press queries and remained silent after the game.

Warner, however, did comment, saying that the strength of England lay with its young spin bowlers. He had Verity, Freddie Brown and Peebles in mind. No mention was made of England's speedsters, but unless Larwood broke down, as he was apt to do, he would probably tour. He tended to be pessimistic and needed bolstering by beer and his supporters.

After 1930, where he said he had been 'pasted mercilessly' by Bradman, he was not confident about selection despite having topped the domestic bowling averages in 1931. Voce was a likely starter also, as were George 'Gubby' Allen and Bowes, although selections would not be announced until mid-1932 at the earliest.

27

A NORTH AMERICAN STAR

At the start of the 1931–32 season, Don Bradman toured country New South Wales. Playing for the Blue Mountains combined team against the Lithgow Pottery Cricket Club, he created another batting record that may never be beaten.

Blackheath Council was opening a new ground and testing a new 'malthoid' wicket—a rubberised tar surface that didn't need matting—and a crowd of about 7000 people packed in and around the oval. Bradman came in at 1 for 16. He stepped straight into the second-class bowling, scoring 54 in 25 minutes. Unusually for him, he was hitting up and under the ball, collecting 3 sixes. The captain brought on an off spinner, Bill Black.

'What's this fellow bowl?' Bradman asked the keeper, Leo Waters, as Black placed his field.

'Don't you remember?' Waters said. 'He bowled you in that Lithgow match [on another Kippax-led tour] a few weeks ago. He's been boasting about it ever since!'

Bradman didn't react. He glanced around at Black's ambitious field and faced up. The first ball was walloped for six over the tall Monterey Pines at the side of the ground. The second went straighter for six more. A boy retrieved the ball in a street near the ground.

Black asked his captain if he could have two more men in the deep. His third ball was straight-driven along the ground for four. Bradman proceeded to take 33 from the eight-ball over and ended with a single, which saw him retain the strike. He was in a particular type of zone. He was not going to throw his wicket away, but he seemed to want to make a competitive statement. The next bowler was hit for 40—6, 4, 4, 6, 6, 4, 6, 4—in another four minutes, making 73 in eight minutes' batting. His score was 127. Black came on for his second over and a chance for glory. Bradman clobbered him for another 27 runs, meaning he had scored 100 in just twelve minutes. It was the fastest hundred ever recorded in cricketing history. Black had the ignominious figures of 0 for 62 (Bradman's partner, Wendell Bill, having scored two singles in Black's second over).

Now Black was part of history and had a form of backhanded glory for his bowling that he could dine out on for the rest of his life.

Bradman went on to score 256.

The innings indicated he had lost none of his indiscriminate lust to compete and score big. He was aged 23 years, in peak physical condition and match hardened. His mind was at ease too, having secured a two-year contract with Frank Packer's Sydney Newspapers Ltd. It published the Sydney *Sun* and owned radio station 2UE, and Bradman would work for both as a journalist. It also meant he could be with Jessie Menzies. They announced their engagement at this time and that they planned to marry at the end of the 1931–32 season.

Bradman's peace of mind allowed him to focus more on his game than in the previous season. His scores in five Tests against South Africa were 226, 112, 2, 167 and 299 not out. In five innings only, he had amassed 806 at an average of 201.5. He had a bumper season scoring 4053 runs in all cricket at a 98.8 average.

If Warner, Jardine and Larwood were looking for a drop in Bradman's prolific scoring they were disappointed. The England tour of Australia in 1932–33 was less than a year away. Bradman's Test aggregate and average from just five innings was even more chilling than his 1930 Ashes figures.

Some serious planning would have to go into how to combat him otherwise his figures could assume astronomical proportions. The numbers for his career so far were already well ahead of anyone else in the history of the game.

*

Don Bradman married Jessie Menzies on 30 April 1932 and they drove on a short honeymoon to Melbourne. Apart from the bliss of marriage to his long-term sweetheart there was the joy of getting away from the prying press of Sydney. In addition, the chance to visit Canada and the US during the Australian winter months soon presented itself. The break would have been as good as a holiday—except for him having to play cricket all the way.

The trip was organised by the enterprising ex–Test player Arthur Mailey. With the backing of the Canadian Pacific Railway, Mailey arranged for a team to play a series of exhibition cricket matches across baseball-loving North America.

Even a busman's holiday would have been fine, but the success of the tour depended on Bradman, the drawcard. He told Mailey he would not go without Jessie, and so it was agreed she could go too, all expenses paid. Overseas travel was a luxury afforded to a select few, particularly given the effects of the Great Depression. The newlyweds viewed the trip as an extended honeymoon.

The major problem for Bradman was his heroic reputation throughout the Commonwealth. In the US he was a curio and dubbed the 'Babe Ruth of Cricket' in advertising, and extra burdens were laid on him to turn up and perform. He met with Ruth, known as the 'Sultan of Swat', in New York. The American was surprised at Bradman's knowledge of baseball, which he had played in some winters.

Beginning on 17 June 1932, the touring party was expected to play an exhausting 51 matches in ten weeks, a challenge far greater than the comparatively leisurely tour of England with 30-odd matches in 26 weeks.

If anything, the same pressures he faced all year, every year, were evident in the US as much as anywhere. Aubrey Smith, a British actor, former Test player, and permanent Hollywood resident, organised several games for the Australians. The Bradmans were treated like visiting royalty. Instead of them wanting to meet such notable expatriate British actors as Cary Grant, Ronald Colman, David Niven and William Pratt (aka Boris Karloff), the stars came out to see the Australian couple and watch Bradman play.

In reality they were simply screen actors. Bradman was to them a superstar who performed live 'theatre' in front of massive crowds in Australia and England, and now more modest events in the US. How he achieved his 'shows' and his general demeanour added to his attraction.

As usual, Bradman did as well in the matches as was humanly possible, scoring just under 3800 runs at an average of 102. His ego wasn't going to let the spectators down, no matter how social and pointless the cricket was. Another factor was Bradman's sense of contractual obligation. He had signed on for Jessie and himself, not realising that he would be such a drawcard. But he was a stickler for a written agreement being a bond not to be broken without an extraordinary cause. His signature was his word that he would meet the commitments expected.

The whole experience took its toll. When he arrived back in Australia in mid-September he was suffering from fatigue and nervous exhaustion, not a fit state for facing an England team incandescent with determination to win back the Ashes.

28

SURREY WITH
JARDINE ON TOP

Douglas Jardine took over as captain of Surrey at the beginning of 1932 when Percy Fender stepped down. It was an action meant to be for the 'good of English cricket'. Jardine was captain of England, but a man without broad leadership experience. He had been the national team's skipper in four Tests, including one international Test against India. It was the first Test series for India, and expected to be a pushover, but they had a strong bowling line-up that surprised England and the counties. Jardine stepped up with the bat scoring 79 and 85 not out, the only England player to score more than 30 in both innings.

He remained the disciplined, well-researched captain, but let the head prefect approach slip a little. Players still had to act like obedient soldiers, but he listened, occasionally, to arguments about tactics, while never admitting he had not been right. Jardine essentially was a 'my way or the highway' leader, who wanted the players to behave like gentlemen representing their country.

The captaincy of Surrey was a master stroke, which gave him a full season of dealing with a varying bunch of first-class cricketers, and the sometimes ignorant hoi polloi in the stands. He made errors and overreacted, and was too caustic in remarks for several players' comfort zones. Yet he was getting used to being a leader in often trying conditions over a full season. He had experienced a tough environment in Australia but that was not as captain. Now a full team was dependent on him for everything from personal problems with wives and girlfriends to whether they could go to the toilet in the middle of a game. He had to find the right balance for drinkers and how much they should imbibe during play. Jardine had to adjudicate over team members' squabbles and select or drop players based on his assessments and instincts.

Surrey provided a crash course in captaincy. It was one thing to have the right pedigree; it was another to have the persuasive skills that would make a team a winning one. Jardine was not above praising players, but he was not one for cajolery or psychological boosting. Cricketers had to have backbone or they were no use to him.

He wanted batsmen in his own image; he wanted bowlers who would plough on even through injuries. Most of all he desired to mould a team that would do his bidding without querying his methods. Jardine did not care to be liked or loved, or a crowd favourite. He wanted to win above all else within the rules, like any conscientious lawyer. He cared little for the 'spirit of the game', which was indefinable. If such a thing were laid out in defined rules, clause by clause, then he would adhere to it.

An instance of this occurred in the Indian Test at Lord's when the Indian batsmen were having trouble picking up the ball against the crowd.

Jardine pulled aside Bowes and Voce, both in their first Tests, and said, 'I want you to bowl one full toss an over to each of them.'

Bowes and Voce locked eyes for a split second but did not react. They felt such a tactic was wrong, but said nothing. They wished to keep their hard-earnt Test spots.

Bowes bowled only one full ball, which was more of a yorker than a full toss. Voce did the same. Jardine waited until the tea break to upbraid them both.

Voce remained mute, but Bowes answered back.

'It's unfair, skipper,' he said. 'Could lead to repercussions.'

'You'll do what I say,' Jardine shot back. 'There is no law against bowling a full toss!'

Full tosses that were hard to pick up against crowds, and in poor light, would have been considered against the 'spirit of the game'. But Jardine was technically correct. Nothing in the *laws* of the game prohibited such a practice.

Bowes believed his speaking up, or answering back, had cost him a tour of Australia. He was right. He was not initially in the seventeen players selected.

*

Jardine performed well with the bat for the season, making 1464 runs at an average of 52.28, enough to justify Warner and the MCC Committee inviting him to captain England to Australia for the 1932–33 Ashes series. They believed they needed a leader unscathed by Bradman. Chapman may not have been up to the task, and Wyatt, although a much-admired character for his grit and stickability, had also been defeated by Bradman at The Oval.

Jardine wavered over the offer. He was not sure he could endure another six months of abuse which was sure to come from the crowds he hated. As skipper, he would be even more the focus for invective and insults from 'uneducated, deplorable' Australians and merciless critics.

Not even appeals to his patriotism could sway him. Warner became concerned. He wanted to make the announcement soon after the Test against India. He decided to ask Jardine's father, 63-year-old Malcolm, who was now living in England, for help. Warner was four years younger and had been a contemporary of Malcolm's at Oxford and represented the university with him in first-class matches. There was a mutual respect, along with the Oxonian link. Malcolm, similar to son Douglas, was sharp-eyed, thin-lipped and ram-rod straight in bearing. He had retained a stronger Scots accent, despite a twenty-year stay in India as a judge and barrister.

Malcolm Jardine had a minor claim to fame in his final game for Oxford, against Cambridge, scoring a match-winning 140 in 285 minutes. His stock stroke to bowlers delivering to the orthodox off-side field was to leg glance. At the time, top public schools and Oxbridge players con-sidered it was 'outside the spirit of the game' to hit the ball on the leg side. Nevertheless, it was *inside* the rules. Warner and all Oxonians considered Malcolm's approach innovative and heroic, mostly because it won. Leg-side play became 'normal' soon afterwards. Warner was in admiration of him. A strong first-class career beckoned Malcolm but he chose to develop his legal skills in India instead.

Plum Warner explained the situation about Australia. Unsaid would have been an indelible belief by both men that all dominions and colonies had to be 'kept in line' for the prestige of the seat of Empire.

Could he help persuade his son to tour? That amused Malcolm who had a similarly stubborn streak. Douglas had complained to his father about 'the heat, flies and crowds' in Australia. Malcolm sympathised; he had a disdain for such things in India.

But he said he would have a chat with him.

A week later, Douglas Jardine agreed in writing to captain England, subject to meeting the MCC Committee.

*

Jardine wanted to win. It would justify his sacrifice for England. He long ago had decided on defeating Bradman. He was an obsession. He had to find *something* with which to target the Australian. Jardine had discussions with Percy Fender, who had been so humiliated by Bradman. Fender suggested he should work on any vulnerability to fast bowling, especially with fast leg theory. Jardine was said to have watched footage of Bradman in his 232 at The Oval. He had watched the game closely on the spot and had not noticed anything beyond normal reaction to the speedy bowling on a dangerous, wet wicket. Bradman had played one of the great double hundred innings of all time, scoring 98 in a pre-lunch session and mastering all bowlers, especially his main competitor, Larwood. It had won the Test and the 1930 Ashes.

He had been hit a couple of times and flinched, a common reaction in batsmen with no extra padding on the arms and chest. But he had shown exceptional courage in batting on and getting on top. Jardine decided it would be useful to suggest that Bradman was 'yellow' or cowardly. The fake label for someone regarded as the best hooker in Test cricket was as specious as it was devoid of credibility. Yet he needed a raison d'être to justify his plans.

Jardine also went through the motions of consulting Frank Foster, who had toured Australia in 1911–12 and bowled leg theory, as opposed to the fast variety. Jardine was careful not to mention his plan for Bradman. This 'research' was to make out he had done studious homework on the leg theory, a quaint cover for what he planned to unleash.

It would all suit the propaganda when fronting the MCC Committee.

Before he did that, he wanted to meet Arthur Carr, whom he knew had used the aggressive tactics with Larwood and Voce. Jardine had faced them himself. The main point of consulting the trio was to get the bowlers to agree to fast leg theory, directed at the batsmen, not all the time, but enough to hurt, dislodge, frighten and defeat the opposition.

They met for dinner in the grill room of the Piccadilly Hotel in London's West End. Larwood and Voce were intimidated by the setting of white high ceiling, gold inlaid Corinthian columns and white-clothed tables weighed down with silverware and cut glass. The two former Nottingham-shire miners liked to label any such place, and the people in it, as 'posh'. They were also a little uncomfortable with waiters in starched collars and black jackets swooping around them and not making eye contact.

Carr said he had to ply the two speedsters with beer to get them to loosen up and discuss the subject of Bradman with 'Mr Jardine'.

Jardine, looking like Shakespearean actor Basil Rathbone, with blade nose and pipe, was his formal, yet seemingly retiring self. 'Do you think you can bowl on the leg stump, making the ball come up into the body all the time so that Bradman has to play his shots to leg?' he asked. Larwood wasn't sure this could curb him, but if he were going to tour he wanted a plan to stop the batsman. He, like Jardine, had no love for the gruelling Australian conditions, unless they could compete and win.

Another issue for Jardine was Voce's acquiescence. The captain needed at least two bowlers who could turn on the theory in tandem when directed. All heads turned to the laconic left-armer. It was all a bit daunting for the soon-to-be 23 year old. He had heard all the 'horror' stories about Australians and the tour from Larwood and Carr. The latter had never been there and had made the acquaintance of very few Australians apart from four Tests in the 1926 Ashes. His autobiography, *Cricket with the Lid Off*, demonstrated a dislike for them, especially Bradman, without any specifics, despite his stated passion to lead an England team in victory in an Ashes contest.

Voce nodded his agreement to bowling fast leg theory. He would do it with his good mate Harold.

It was a significant moment for Jardine, although he didn't let it show, except for ordering champagne. He needed Voce. It would be too much for Larwood to carry on his own. He had seen him tire against Bradman so many times; on this occasion the pressure had to be concentrated over the entire series. The implication was clear to Carr, Larwood and Voce. There was no way Bradman could be stopped unless he was battered into submission.

Larwood wanted to know if any others would be asked to bowl this way.

'No, not Hedley Verity,' Jardine said with a smile. He was evasive, not having consulted the other speedsters to be chosen.

'What about Big Bill Bowes?'

'He won't be touring,' Jardine said, crisply.

But the Surrey v Yorkshire match beginning 20 August at The Oval changed Jardine's mind. Through an intermediary, Jardine suggested that Bowes bowl fast leg theory, which was an obvious hint that he might get selected for the Ashes tour. Bowes obliged and gave both Jack Hobbs and Jardine a severe working-over with short-pitched deliveries. He took ten wickets in the game and was in good touch. Hobbs was most upset by the attack. On his way to 90 in the first innings, he confronted Bowes and remonstrated with him mid-pitch at the end of a torrid over.

'If this goes on,' Hobbs said, pointing at Bowes, 'someone will get killed.'

The Surrey supporters roundly booed Bowes and kept up a barrage of abuse during the game, which reached a peak when he bowled Hobbs for just 1 in Surrey's second innings. Bowes was chastened and had never received such a negative reaction before.

Jardine quietly acknowledged the bowler's performance.

Bowes was selected three days before the boat sailed.

Jardine presented his plan to Warner and the MCC Committee, watering down the impact by calling it a 'variation on leg theory', with no specifics and cunning language that avoided saying he intended to blast Bradman out. The committee had no idea if it would work, but Jardine was very impressive for his knowledge of cricket history, tactics and strategy. He was a lawyer and their verbal agreement was the next best thing to writing down his plans and having the committee sign off on them.

Jardine now could always say he had the complete endorsement for his use of leg theory if matters went awry, which he feared they could.

Jardine and Lord Hawke as chairman of selectors, along with the committee, had chosen a team that was strong on paper. Jardine would be captain and Bob Wyatt would be his deputy. Then there was Hammond, Sutcliffe, Verity, Voce, Bowes, Eddie Paynter, Les Ames (keeper), Brown, T. B. Mitchell, the Nawab of Pataudi (K. S. Duleepsinhji), Leyland, Tate, Duckworth (keeper) and Gubby Allen, a fourth speedster.

It was a well-balanced side with a powerful batting line-up, excellent pace and spin. Ames would be Jardine's keeper of choice, primarily because of his batting. Duckworth was a better keeper to spin, and here was a small window into the captain's thinking. He expected pace to be used much more than spin, despite press talk of playing two, even three spinners.

Jardine did not bother to consult Allen on using the fast leg theory. He was certain to reject it as unsportsmanlike. Allen would bowl bouncers and was not against intimidation or unintentionally hurting batsmen. But a team of bowlers deliberately trying to blast out the opposition, causing some to be maimed along the way, was against his principles. He happened to have been born in Australia. At age six his family moved to England. He was educated at Eton and Cambridge and had become more British than the British in his manner. He knew how the countrymen of the land of his birth would react to Jardine's methods.

He understood the potential for ill-will. By virtue of his establishment background, Allen would not be afraid to stand up to Jardine on any issue.

Hammond too, was not consulted. He was very aware that a bumper war would be sure to backfire on him, the number one England bat. Jardine would worry later about last man chosen Bowes, whom he did not foresee playing in all the Tests.

*

Jardine kept away from his team, staying in his first-class cabin on the ship, SS *Orantes*, dining most nights alone or with the ship's captain. Reading and also working on his plan to defeat Bradman took up much time. Jardine gave out some instructions about the team's behaviour on board. They were allowed to drink alcohol but had to keep their fitness levels up with daily exercises on the deck, but before the sun was up to avoid skin problems. Jardine also told them to restrict their autograph giving.

He called for meetings with Larwood, Voce and Bowes to discuss bowling tactics against specific batsmen. Bowes did not say he was against fast leg theory, which he had used on odd occasions in the past, such as against Surrey, but he did say, when alone with Jardine, he would set his own fields and bowl the way he wanted to. Jardine tried to lay down the law, but Bowes stayed with his original attitude. He had been put off badly by Hobbs, Surrey supporters and a few mentions in the press which was not impressed by his barrage of bumpers in the Surrey v Yorkshire game.

Jardine explained to Hammond that Larwood and Voce would use fast leg theory. Hammond's response was non-committal. He would bowl when required but again, like Bowes, with his field and his way.

Jardine was very keen on Verity's role, explaining he was to be a foil to the fast men. He expected batsmen to be softened up before Verity came on, and it would be up to the spinner to take advantage of that, without being specific. Jardine had faith in his left-armer's bowling skills and expected him to do well and add variety to his attack, that would look a little 'one note' without spin.

Plum Warner was the main team manager and spokesman for the tour. Within days of the trip, he was concerned with Jardine's solitary, often aloof behaviour. He had been amused by Jardine's old Winchester coach joking just before the tour group left England that Jardine as captain 'will win the Ashes but lose a Dominion'.

Warner was already realising the line might not be that funny.

He was not happy with Jardine telling each team member to refer to Bradman as 'the little bastard'. Like a military martinet, the captain was demonising the enemy and one person in particular. It was not really in the 'spirit of the game', yet there was no rule against such propaganda.

Disquieted, Warner let it go through to the keeper.

29

BEFORE THE STORM

Bradman's song 'Every Day is a Rainbow Day for Me' had been a hit in Australia but he was beginning to doubt its veracity soon after he sailed from the US into Sydney on the steamer *Monowai*. The squabble with the Board of Control had reared as a troublesome issue again. He was set to honour the contract with Frank Packer, which, he threatened, would mean he would stand out of the Ashes series to fulfil it. The press was hounding him and Jessie. After the relative freedom of the US trip, it was a return to an even greater invasion of their privacy. He went to the trouble of obtaining a private telephone number, and he and Jessie were forced to find ways to disappear from their home without the press knowing their whereabouts.

He said that he would not write anything about the First Test, and if agreement could be reached with the Board, he would continue with his journalism after that. If not, he would sit out the series.

Bradman began the 1932–33 season with dashing centuries for St George in a trial game as if he were carrying on with his form in the US. He agreed to play in a Combined Australian XI against the MCC in Perth but thought it may have been a mistake as he took the arduous five-day journey across the country. He had not recovered fully from his American trip, and the tedious train ride brought back feelings of fatigue. On top of that, his teeth were giving him trouble, and he decided to consult a dental surgeon. But Bradman was not the type to complain and make excuses. He did not wish to give the visiting tourists any ammunition.

More than 20,000 spectators, huge then for Perth, turned up for the first day of the game for the rare event of seeing Bradman bat in the west. Jardine won the toss and deprived them of the chance by batting. Much to the crowd's disappointment, the MCC batted on for two days compiling 7 for 583 against a weak Combined attack. It was so light on that Bradman had his longest spell of bowling at the first-class level of 19 overs, in which he took 2 for 106 with his not unworthy leg spinners. The crowd gave a big cheer when he had Jardine caught for 98 going for a first-up tour century. There was unfortunate booing as the England captain reached the pavilion, yet something he had expected from the 'plebeian' spectators from the vast, hot continent.

Jardine had left his trio of pacemen out of the team, not yet ready to unleash fast leg theory on the opposition. More importantly, he did not want the opprobrium of the press from the very first match. He had already planned the theory to be implemented further into the tour, *when he was not present.*

It rained and Australia batted on a sticky wicket. Bradman was in with the score at 61. When on 3, he pushed at a good length ball from Verity and edged it to slip where Hammond threw out a hand and snaffled a fine catch. Verity then ran through the Australian line-up, taking 7 for 37, from the team score of 159.

Jardine was quietly thrilled with the first-up early dismissal of Bradman and Verity's form. He enforced the follow-on in the afternoon of day three. Bradman came in this time at 1 for 0. Allen had him struggling with his zip off the wicket, and got one delivery to lift into the ribcage. Bradman was caught for just 10 at leg slip, but without a fast leg theory field.

Jardine was all smiles. Without saying anything to Allen, and without the theory being employed, Bradman had shown vulnerability to the lifting chest-high ball, or had he? Was it an early hopeful aberration? Apart from when not out, he would have to fall in one or two innings in any match he played. This was just one innings against speed on a conducive wicket, which left the Australian XI battling for a draw at 4 for 139.

Bradman took the train back across the country to Sydney having been dismissed twice for very little in the one day. He was puzzled by Jardine's withholding of his pace attack after having read the British and local press, which played up England's unusual five-strong (if Hammond was included after his 1930 Ashes effort) speed battery. There was no holding back on journalistic analysis of the expected target of a barrage on Australia's fast wickets. No one knew of the fast leg theory plan, but there were queries about Jardine's approach. He gave nothing away to reporters, except to utter the clever deflection that 'Hedley Verity was his secret weapon' for the Ashes.

One local, intrepid reporter asked him as he was leaving the ground what he looked forward to most on the tour.

'Trout fishing in the bush,' was his reply with a tight smile.

'Not an Ashes win?'

'That too.'

Bradman's competitive juices were flowing in the next game when New South Wales played Victoria at the SCG. Ponsford scored a double hundred, his ninth, drawing him level with Bradman, who responded with a murderous 238 in just 210 minutes, his fastest double to that point. The performance salved his conscience after his double failure in Perth. He thrashed everyone, including Len Darling (pace), Alexander (pace), Ironmonger, Blackie, and the newcomer, left-armer wrong 'un bowler, Chuck Fleetwood-Smith, to whom he deliberately donated his wicket by lofting several chances into the outfield.

There was no doubt about his form, and Australian journalists went into overdrive, to counter English reporting, by comparing Bradman favourably to the late Victor Trumper in all respects and particularly footwork to the three spinners. Bradman scored 52 not out in the second innings, when he would sometimes lapse when a game was all but won, and New South Wales were victors by nine wickets.

This was useful and confidence-building for the next match, again in a Combined XI against the MCC at Melbourne. This time Larwood, Voce, Bowes and Allen were chosen for an all-out pace attack. Jardine's fast men had been drilled about the line—the leg stump or just outside, length (short), and field placings which were strictly marked for certain fielders. Six, sometimes seven men would be on the leg side, five in close-catching positions. This was the first sight of fast leg theory, Jardine-style. It was to be used in bursts that would shock the opposition.

Jardine then confused everyone, including all but a few in the touring party, by going trout fishing on the Kiewa River, not far from Albury on the NSW border, with his old schoolmate from Winchester days, who had taken him to the Penstock River in Tasmania on the previous tour. He could hardly have chosen a more remote place to disappear from the MCG, which was then seven hours away by road.

PART FIVE

1932 – 1934

30

THE STORM BEGINS

England's stalwart vice-captain Bob Wyatt was left in charge of the match beginning 18 November. He won the toss, batted and his side made a patient 282. Bradman came in on the second afternoon with the score at 1 for 51. For the first time on tour, Larwood had seven on the leg side with five men close in. The crowd reacted at this astonishing field arrangement, which it soon realised was not defensive leg theory, which had been tried over the years.

This was something else: an all-out attack.

Leo O'Brien, a solid Victorian opening batsman, was up the other end and noted, 'The atmosphere was electric as Bradman strode in. Here was the man England most feared. They were prepared to get stuck into him. There was a lot of action, a lot of chit-chat, not "tally-ho!" or anything like that, but more, "C'mon chaps, let's do this!" They all seemed to be up on their toes, and getting ready. They attacked him remorselessly. The wicket was a little on the green side.

Larwood and Allen [using a normal field] had him in a bit of trouble.'

Bradman did much bobbing and weaving as if in a boxing match, which it was. Larwood was bowling more at his head and chest than the wicket. It was a torrid time but Bradman moved at his usual good rate to 36. Larwood delivered a ball that was swinging way down the leg side and hit him in the pads. Larwood went up but no one supported him with any heart.

The umpire hesitated then put up his finger.

'It was a rough decision,' O'Brien said. 'It would have missed another set of stumps.'

Bradman's score was second only to that of O'Brien (46) of the Australian XI's meagre 218 total. Bradman had had two poor decisions in two innings (including the 1930 Oval decision) facing Larwood, who was pleased. After so many beltings from his persecutor, this was a sweet moment regardless of the decision's merit.

Retired Australian Test player Hunter Hendry noted, 'They had adopted the tactics that "if we can't bowl 'em out, we'll knock 'em out!"'

Jack Hobbs was covering the tour as a journalist. He'd been known to avoid matches against Nottinghamshire when Larwood and Voce were playing and he'd had a brutal experience when Bowes went after him in Surrey v Yorkshire two months earlier.

'I felt a lot safer in the press box,' he said, 'for the bowling looked very dangerous stuff.'

Rain intervened and England made just 60 on a difficult wicket with 198 centimetre (6 foot 6 inch) medium-pacer Lisle Nagel taking 8 for 32.

Bradman had to meet the barrage again. He had decided to try to counter the bowling with attempts to hit the ball on the vacant off side, which meant him pulling away to leg. Until then in history this was always frowned upon as a sin against orthodoxy and the courage to face up. Tailenders could be forgiven for doing it, but not top-line batsmen, and certainly not the greatest batsman in the world.

But as every cricketer knew it was actually more dangerous to pull away, if it were intentional or unintentional. The ball tended to follow the batsman and corner him far more than if he played in an orthodox way.

Bradman cared not a whit for how it looked and knew he would be branded a coward for not standing up to it. But he was short of stature and square-on, back-foot play would see him struck. He was determined not to get hit, which he knew Larwood loved to do, especially with him. There was a long list of county and Test players who had been debilitated in body and mind by Larwood. Several times struck, meant many times shy, and Bradman did not want to be one of those so bruised they could not bat properly, or without fear.

He was soon in for a second time when Woodfull was removed for a duck and the Australians needing just 125 for victory on a nasty track. Bradman tried his cross-bat, stepping-away tactic on the wrong wicket. The ball was coming through, skidding sometimes and lifting on other occasions. Larwood bowled him for just 13.

This dismissal excited Larwood more than anything he'd achieved in his career. He knew he had not got Bradman out at The Oval and in any case Bradman had long before won the dual in that match. He knew also that the LBW in the first innings of this game had been a very lucky decision.

But when he spreadeagled the stumps, there was no disputing his small personal victory against the player who had humiliated him so many times and nearly ruined his career. In addition, he suddenly viewed his skipper as a very shrewd tactician and strategist. This moment had been planned for months, and drilled into him and Voce. For the first time Larwood believed it could actually work and allow him to get on top. Until this match, all Larwood had been left with for so many encounters was that little half-grin from his number-one opponent. He did not see it in this game. That was almost satisfaction in itself.

He was quick to suggest Bradman had been frightened, unaware that the Australian had decided on a counter-attack to pull away. In that moment of barely containable joy for Larwood, the Jardine-inspired propaganda that Bradman was a coward seemed more than myth and gained fake currency in the British press and with those, such as former Australian captain Warwick Armstrong, who disliked Bradman for one reason or another.

Tall poppy syndrome and jealousy were just a couple.

*

Jardine had a lovely time fishing on the Kiewa, and an even more joyous time when he learnt of the double blow to his obsession, 'the little bastard'.

It was only round one, but the plan had started far better than expected.

Bradman read the papers and understood the tactics perfectly now. Journalists had dubbed the method of bowling at the batsman's head or upper-body, with a stacked close on-side field, as 'bodyline'. It stuck and was more to the point than 'fast leg theory', which was now exposed as a fake cover.

The vision for the Ashes was clear. Jardine viewed the series as a battle that had to be won without regard for what it would mean for the game.

Bradman, in private and aware he could be branded a squealer, complained to Australian Cricket Board members. But he was ignored.

He didn't have time to reflect much before he was in facing the rough stuff in Sydney for New South Wales. Jardine, handling Larwood with sense and cunning, left him out of the game and instructed Voce to go after Bradman 'with everything' using the stacked leg-side field. Voce was more erratic than Larwood as he delivered three or four body-directed bouncers an over. But he was still unsettling for all batsmen. Bradman, naturally, was discomforted and in two minds about using his counter tactics with tennis shots. When facing Allen, who was in fine form delivering to his off-side field, Bradman reverted to normal shots but looked uncertain as he reached 18 in 41 minutes. On came medium-pacer Maurice Tate, whom Bradman had conquered in English conditions.

Bradman was trapped LBW for just 18. New South Wales reached 273, and Allen, revelling in the conditions, took 5 for 69. He was not going to deliver the way Jardine had divined, but he would be hard to leave out of the First Test.

The MCC compiled 530 in two days. Jardine was caught for just 4. He was given a nasty crowd send-off with catcalls and invective as he walked to the pavilion, harlequin cap in hand. It was a building hate, and a justification for all he planned. But the proud Scot was hurt.

Just after the NSW game on 29 November, the tourists were entertained at a home overlooking the Sydney Harbour Bridge, which had been opened eight months earlier and was the pride of the city. As a squadron of RAAF aircraft flew over, an embittered Jardine said to Warner, 'I wish they were Japs, and I wish they'd bomb that bridge into their harbour.'

The Japanese had been attacking Manchuria since the previous year, 1931. The comment chilled Warner and revealed much about the captain's feelings.

In a letter to his wife, Agnes, on the day the NSW game finished, Warner let his growing frustration with Jardine surface. 'He is a very difficult fellow—such a queer nature—rather cruel in some ways. Hates Australians and his special hate is for Bradman.'

Allen added, 'I am terrified of Douglas. For all his education, he is easily the stupidest man I know and conceited.'

But it was early in the tour before Jardine's plans could really breathe and be appreciated, or not.

Warner was aware of 'the little bastard' label for Bradman but he would never use the term in a letter to Agnes. He went on as if he were trying to distance himself from the decision to push for Jardine as skipper, 'He is not the right fellow to be captain.' This was a telling comment for a fellow Oxonian. 'He says cruel things of people and his language is poor at times. He is conceited—only he knows—and arrogant.'

But both manager, and vice-captain Bob Wyatt, who also had misgivings about Jardine, kept their counsel for the sake of team harmony and unity in the 'quest' for the Ashes, in which Jardine had invested almost a crusader's religious zeal.

*

Bradman contracted the flu and missed a day's play in the MCC v New South Wales game but still batted on the last day. Despite a severe sore throat, and increased pain from his teeth, he was in good touch against all bowlers with Voce, under instructions to go after him again, delivering an inordinate number of short pitches. Bradman was bounding to the on and off to play shots or avoid collision with the leather missile. He moved to the off for one expected lifter and shouldered arms. The ball came through low and clipped his off bail.

Bradman was on his way for 23. His competitive desire, as strong as anyone's in sport, had led him to playing when he should have been in bed.

There was rejoicing in the England camp. Verity, Allen, Larwood, Tate and Voce had all now dismissed him in six innings, in which he had scored just 103 runs.

The momentum was with the tourists with the First Test at Sydney on 2 December. Then there was a bombshell on the day before the game.

The team doctor ruled Bradman unfit to play.

He still had the flu and was generally run down. The doctor recommended that he have his troublesome teeth attended to. On top of all this, his mental state was not the best. His ongoing dispute with the Board, Jardine's tactics to get rid of him one way or another, and the expectations of a nation desperate for a repeat of the 1930 Ashes, were all taking a toll.

Still, Bradman, looking gaunt, turned up at the First Test to report for 2UE, determined to honour his contract with Packer.

*

Bradman's health and form were of concern to the entire nation. The population had experienced a long-running malaise which had begun during World War I, and afterwards when the volunteer armed services survivors had returned from fighting in Europe and the Middle East. There was a limited appreciation of what they had been through and the successes they had attained. The ex-soldiers faced depression, alcohol and drug dependence and poor employment opportunities as they reintegrated with the rest of the country while the economy struggled through the 1920s and fell into the abyss of the Great Depression in 1929. There were few heroes who could unite Australia. Bradman was the most celebrated of all, especially after his 1930 Ashes performances. His insatiable appetite for runs and winning were unmatched. He had entered with force the collective psyche of Australians and represented more than hope. The young Bradman's unassuming yet deftly confident manner and utterances had an enduring air.

His travails were a worry, and the creation of potentially huge theatre that would be played out around the nation in front of hundreds of thousands of people, and in the media, was now in jeopardy.

Could 'our Don' prevail over those who would bring him down by fair means or foul?

The negative attitude to the touring MCC team—the 'villains' in the developing drama—was exacerbated by the belief that British owners of Australian bonds were being harsh in demanding that interest payments from state governments be made as agreed, and not relaxed during stringent economic times.

The stage was set for an epic showdown.

31

ALLEN DEFIANT, LARWOOD RELIANT

Just before the First Test, Jardine told Allen he had to bowl fast leg theory, with more bouncers and the fielders close in on the leg side.

'I'm not going to play cricket like that,' Allen of Eton and Cambridge told Jardine of Winchester and Oxford.

'Larwood and Voce will be.'

'I won't. If you are not happy leave me out [of the team].'

Allen was chosen.

It became Larwood's Test. He began with a fearful blow over Woodfull's heart before Voce had him caught behind by Ames. At the first drinks break, Jardine wondered why Larwood would not drink the orange juice on offer.

'I couldn't drink that muck,' he said. 'I want my half-pint.'

'You can't drink beer on the cricket field,' Jardine said with mock disdain. 'What would Lord's say to that?'

Jardine arranged that at every ensuing drinks break there would be a glass of beer hidden among the orange juices.

'Grog' consumption was not restricted to the visitors. Despite being a non-drinker, Woodfull was generous and understanding enough to let his men drink at lunchtime if they wished, and after the game. He was following the fashion that beer was a good thirst-quencher and useful, as the wisdom at the time went, for energy and to allow his players to sweat 'better'.

It certainly refreshed Larwood enough to help him take 5 for 96 in Australia's first innings. Stan McCabe told his father before the game, 'If I get hit, stop Mum jumping the fence!'

Mrs McCabe was sorely tempted to make the leap as her son was thumped by three lifting deliveries. But she was restrained and very proud as her son played a great, fortunate innings of 187. He was dropped twice and lobbed several other shots that fell safely.

Voce had Richardson caught by Hammond for a dogged 49 in two hours of determined batting in which he took several hits, mainly from Voce. The bowler said to Richardson, a moment after he was dismissed, 'If we don't beat you, we'll knock your bloody blocks off!'

It was the type of threat county batsmen had heard often enough. Now Australians were receiving physical and verbal attacks. Larwood and Voce were making a mockery of their own claims that they never aimed at the batsmen. Most Test sides had bowlers who could 'soften up' batsmen as part of a tactic to take a wicket.

The Nottinghamshire pair had taken it to a pitiless art form.

Larwood hit all of the top seven, with Ponsford, Woodfull, and Jack Fingleton, all gutsy but not quick enough on their feet, being struck often. Fingleton took eight blows, Ponsford four, and Woodfull three. A battered McCabe played bravely in his second knock but the bruises he collected in his first innings retarded him. He was LBW to Hammond for 32.

Voce backed up his hero with six wickets and England won easily by ten wickets.

The tourists had two notable batting performances with tenacious Yorkshireman Herbert Sutcliffe on a long but effective plod of 194, and Duleepsinhji scoring a most stylish, 'cultured' 102, but which had patches of inertia. So much so that at one point, 'Yabba', the famous fan on the Sydney Hill, was prompted to call out to the umpire, 'Put a penny in 'im, George! He's stopped registerin'.'

*

Before the end of the game, the press and public were talking about Bradman and the necessity of his return. He saw a dentist, who removed an infected tooth. Then he and Jessie took off for a secret location on the NSW coast for a period of mental and physical recovery.

They went on long beach walks and he had time to reset his mind on tactics to counter the theory that everyone, except England's team members, were calling 'Bodyline'. There was no way of countering it by conventional means. He had watched, with some anguish, his slower-footed teammates getting hit multiple times. Even Stan McCabe, whose footwork was outstanding, had been reduced to near-immobility after facing Larwood and company twice. Bradman knew the mood in the dressing room. It was both sombre and fearful. The tailenders were petrified. It did not augur well for the rest of the series or holding the Ashes.

The leg-side crowding meant a defensive push would pop up a catch. There was no better hooker than Bradman, but he would have to put that shot in the locker for the series. McCabe had got away with it but was lucky not to have been caught in the deep on the leg side, which would be the fate of many a happy hooker. A Bradman specialty—the pull shot past mid-on—would also be put asunder for the series. It was too awkward to play with Larwood lifting the ball on or outside the leg stump into the ribcage.

The Nottinghamshire express was already established as the most effective deliverer of Bodyline. No one else could regularly lift the ball from a good length. Voce was a useful support, but not as consistent. His left-armers were important in tandem with his Nottinghamshire partner, keeping the pressure on from a different angle; something Carr had capitalised on for many seasons. Now Jardine was perfecting the attack with serious backup.

Unlike Larwood, Voce and Bowes relied on banging the ball into their half of the pitch. Allen, in the form of his life, was nearly as effective as Larwood in getting the ball to rear up off a length.

The time away from the madding crowd—and the maddening press—was allowing Bradman to ponder it all coolly. While the press was rampant with reports about his state of mind, and whether he had the courage to face this new weapon, Bradman was using his intellect, a gift well above the average, in search of a rational response. He was a true pragmatist who could cut to the core of an issue, not just in cricket, but anything he encountered in life.

He discussed it with Jessie, whose knowledge of the game he regarded highly. While distressed with what Jardine was doing to Don and our boys', she knew she could not prevent her husband from staying in the fight and following any course he chose. Jessie hated what was happening but in typical fashion said she backed him in any decision. He said early in the marriage, with an allusion to batting, she was the best partner he'd ever had in life. This was the most important problem he'd face on and off the pitch, right in the middle of his dispute with the Board. Had he not had Jessie, it's doubtful he would have been able to tackle the crisis.

Bradman's solution was to take block on leg stump. He would then make the decision on which shot to play depending on what Larwood delivered. If it was Bodyline, he would put his body out of the ball's direction by slipping back outside the stumps and swing a cross-bat shot, aiming the ball into the vacant off side.

'If this method worked,' Bradman surmised, 'the bowler would be forced to revert to the conventional off-side field, when the batsman would return to his normal range of orthodox and unorthodox shots.'

Bradman was confident he could counter-attack this way. He had outplayed Larwood before by going after him and forcing captains to take him off. That would be the aim again. Bradman would be relying on his unmatched combination of eye, bat speed, fast footwork and forearm strength. He saw it as inculcating his outstanding capacity as a tennis player with the use of the backhand smash. He had given away the game officially to concentrate on cricket, but he had kept playing, often against Wimbledon stars who challenged him to games. At age 24, he had defeated every Australian tennis star of the day with his usual relish and drive to compete. He had a most polished range of tennis shots.

Now he had to implement a couple of them, with the very occasional, breathtaking and risky overhead smash, to take on the Bodyline challenge.

Bradman always consulted or tested his ideas with others he respected for their comprehension of cricket. In this case, one was Jessie; the other was A. G. Johnny Moyes, aged 39, a sports journalist, former state cricketer, and sometime Bradman mentor. Moyes was a World War I Military Cross winner, and a rounded character with a cheerful outlook on life. He had supported the younger man at the selection table when assessing him for the state team in 1926–27.

Moyes said of Bradman then, 'He was always quick to learn. He already had a firm grasp on the game for the history to the laws, and of course, he could rightly be called a genius of the game. He had the weight of the world on his shoulders [at that time], not the least reason being the former Prime Minister Billy Hughes calling him "the greatest Australian ever born". Quite a label for one so young!'

Bradman appreciated Moyes' articulation on cricket and life, and his thoughtful approach. Like his protégé, Moyes had a shrewd, quick brain. He was outspoken and fearless in his appraisals. He was also known to be fair and impartial in his analysis. For these reasons, Bradman wanted his opinion on what he was scheming to defeat Bodyline.

He met him back in Sydney after the break on the coast.

Moyes' response was to point out that Larwood would counter by bowling fast yorkers, leaving Bradman stranded and backing away to leg. Bradman said he would be relying on his speedy feet. He had the quickness of everything needed to wait until Larwood had let the ball go, and then react accordingly. This was in contrast to the trend in Australia to move across the stumps as the bowler was running in or about to deliver. That method was giving all the fast men and medium-pacers, including Allen, Bowes, Hammond and Tate, split-second opportunities to change the delivery of pitch, pace and swing.

Bradman also expressed to Moyes and Jessie that he felt an obligation to make runs and fulfil spectators' expectations.

Moyes asked him how he felt about the perception of him running away from Bodyline, and that he would be seen by some as letting the team down by being so individualistic and risky. Moyes said Bradman was so self-contained and invulnerable to criticism that he never even considered such reactions. There had to be a plan. It had become a battle of wits and tactics against Jardine and his force.

Bradman saw it as a challenge, and that he was up to it.

32

CRACKS IN THE JARDINE SHIELD

Jardine could not have been happier with the team performance in Sydney and Bradman's sudden disappearance. Instead of relaxing, he wished to tighten the discipline in the squad by ensuring Bodyline tactics were adhered to. He feared Bradman, despite his travails, would come back for the Second Test in Melbourne in a fortnight's time. It was imperative in Jardine's mind that he reinforce the new 'weapon'. He wanted Bowes in to make it a four-man speed quartet, and was planning to drop Verity, and re-jig the batting order. But before final decisions were made, he would insist on Bodyline, which Allen had had strong feelings about. He had rejected it to Jardine's face before the First Test, but had not performed that well with bat or ball, making just 19 and taking 1 for 68 for the match.

Jardine took him aside at net practice, and tried a new ploy.

'Larwood and Voce want you to bowl theory,' he said in an attempt to goad Allen.

'Not going to do it, Douglas, sorry.'

'They think you only refused before because you wanted to remain popular here.'

'That's all very well for gutless, uneducated miners!' Allen said. 'They have to grovel to you for their place in the team, and to fucking Carr for selection at Notts. Otherwise it's back to the bloody pits for them!'

'Your form wasn't too good at Sydney,' Jardine replied. 'It might be an idea for you to try theory.'

'Fuck you and it, Douglas!'

'Might be an idea for you to step aside from the team.'

'Drop me, and I'll go back to England and tell the press about everything on the tour and your approach to smashing Bradman.'

Jardine didn't pursue the matter.

He tried big Bill Bowes.

The Yorkshireman had had a strong county season, knocking over team after team. He was not inclined to change his methods or field placings for anyone, despite taking ten wickets in the August game against Surrey using Bodyline. Jardine thought him obstinate.

In the MCC game against South Australia, Vic Richardson had laid into him. Bowes had asked for an extra man on the leg side to counter the hooking and pulling.

'No,' Jardine replied, 'but you can have five [extra men on the leg].'

This indicated he should bowl theory.

Later the two chatted alone.

'I'll bowl short, Mr Jardine,' Bowes said, 'but not with the leg theory all the time.'

'You object to it?'

'No, skipper. But it's just not my way all the time. I like to bowl with my field and change it when I want to. I received a lot of bad comment at The Oval.'

'We'll be a long way from Kennington . . .'

'Jack Hobbs will be in the press box. He is dead against leg theory. Mr Jardine, I'll be more use to you with an off field.'

'If you want to have any chance of selection, you'll obey my instructions. Is that understood? Otherwise you go home.'

'Right, I go home!'

Jardine was surprised to see that Bowes meant what he said. The captain then set about explaining what he had planned and why Bowes could not spread the field in this series. It had to be either an off- or leg-side field. It was so Jardine could manipulate the bowling quickly and without hesitation. There was a psychological element to his method. Bowes was impressed and from that moment a convert to Jardine's plan. He decided not to return to England and was surprised to be selected for the Melbourne Test.

Hammond had again refused to bowl Bodyline, saying that he would not be as effective as Larwood and Voce, which Jardine accepted. If England were to win the Ashes, Hammond would be more useful for his batting, which had slipped from the standard he had set on the 1928–29 Ashes tour, and his backup, stock bowling of medium-pace swing.

Jardine was unhappy with some reactions, but reasoned that Allen and Bowes in form would help make up a formidable foursome of speed to an already shaken Australian line-up.

Another character discontented with Bodyline was Duleepsinhji. He was ambivalent about the method and being part of the leg trap, and did his best to avoid taking a position close to the wicket in the game against Victoria in the lead-up to the Second Test in Melbourne. He told Jardine he preferred to field in the deep. Jardine did not argue, telling him the experience in front of the outer MCG crowd would be useful for him. Unsaid was that his nationality would undoubtedly elicit some pithy remarks.

He had only been on the fence for less than an over when a spectator called, 'Hey, Gandhi! Where's ya goat?' That induced guffaws from the crowd within earshot.

Duleepsinhji took a couple of steps towards where he thought the comment had come from. He nodded at the possible culprit, smiled and said, 'There you are! Could somebody lend me a piece of rope?'

Spectators clapped and cheered.

The Nawab in a flash had won over the crowd.

33

THE SHOCK

Packer's company released Bradman from his obligation to write for the Sydney *Sun*, which had been the hang-up from the Australian Cricket Board. He celebrated this freedom by playing at the MCG in the return Shield match between Victoria and New South Wales, scoring 157 at about a run a minute. He looked in deft touch. The more observant in the crowd noticed how he was pulling away from his leg stump to play shots into the off, regardless of the pitch of the ball. Bradman was both unorthodox and audacious, and this was his dress rehearsal for taking on Larwood and company at the same ground in a week's time. The big Melbourne crowd loved his every move and had adopted him even more than his home Sydney supporters.

The Australian selectors dropped the talented Alan Kippax, who had been more than uncomfortable against Bodyline, and brought in Leo O'Brien, the Victorian left-hander. Grit had replaced grace; the stroke player had been shoved aside for the solid defender. It was a technical blow for the tourists, with Kippax being a victim of Jardine's methods.

The build-up to the Second Test was so big that a world record crowd of 63,993 packed the MCG under a hot sun on day one, 30 December 1932. Cricket fans sat with those with scant interest in the sport, most of them there just to see Bradman and his titanic struggle with those who would destroy him, or his game, or both. Two thirteen-year-old schoolboys, born on the same day, Keith Miller and Trevor Perry, were there. Miller, who would go on to become a great Test all-rounder, wanted to watch his hero, Bill Ponsford. Perry had never seen a big game before and was only interested in the theatre around Bradman versus Larwood and Bodyline.

Jack Hobbs, in the press box, was in awe of the crowd's size, observing 'one huge bowl of staring faces'.

Larwood and company were billed as the 'villains', and Jardine was their unpopular leader. He had been dubbed the 'Iron Duke' in the press and the more the spectators booed and heckled him, the more entrenched he became in what he was doing.

It was building his justification.

Yet had the Australians sat and clapped tamely as was the custom at Lord's, he still would have presented steel towards Bradman. The Australian had humiliated the seat of Empire. Jardine was going to do everything in his considerable power to make sure the Empire fought back—and won. For Jardine, if nothing else, was a true Empire man. A Scot, born in India to a father whose family ties to the so-called 'Jewel in the Crown' had disparate links within the Empire. The features were Scottish in outlook, English in educational approach and Indian by family interests, which made him the right sort of mixed mind and figure to run the show. Although born into the Edwardian era, the Indian connection made him more Victorian in outlook. There was an attitude, more inbred than spoken in public at least: the Empire's seat had to be seen as superior to its dominions and colonies.

Before the Melbourne Test, there was much talk about Australian retaliation using Bodyline. The moral Woodfull, whose father was a Methodist minister, said he would not captain the side if speedster Tim Wall was expected by the Board to copy England's methods. Woodfull said he would 'not adopt such tactics, which bring such discredit to the game. I know Tim could do it but I am not going to participate in actions that could only hurt the game.'

With that, Woodfull won the toss and batted. He, Fingleton and O'Brien chuffed along at a snail's pace, until Australia was 2 for 67 in the second session. The captain had held Bradman back, thinking it might be a fraction better for him if those three attack blunters were at the wicket before him. Bradman did not agree with the logic. In his mind, it was better to get out there and take charge rather than wait.

A massive single roar went up when he entered the colosseum, for Melbourne fittingly in this case, with its huge stands gorged with fans, was an appropriate stage. The crowd wished to give the thumbs up for Bradman and the thumbs down for the visitors.

They had been taunting Bob Wyatt, fielding near the fence, with calls of 'wait till our Don comes in'.

A few metres onto the field he passed the imperturbable Sutcliffe, who remarked, 'Wonderful reception, Don.'

'Yes, Herbert,' Bradman replied, 'but will it be so good when I'm coming back?'

Young Don Bradman with his first bat in 1926.

Arthur Carr as Nottinghamshire captain.

Douglas Jardine wearing his Harlequin cap from Oxford that attracted the ire of Australia's crowds.

Harold Larwood: 'quick, accurate, deadly'.

Harold Larwood, as batsmen saw him, bowling for Nottinghamshire in 1932.

Above: Sir Julien Cahn, Harold Larwood's benefactor.

Right: Percy Fender, captain of Surrey and Bradman's most vocal critic.

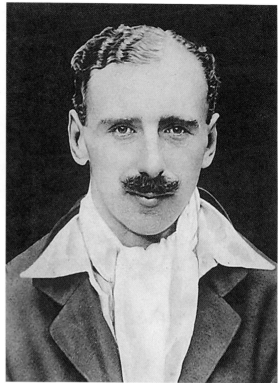

British establishment figure Sir Pelham 'Plum' Warner. The former England captain was Chairman of the MCC during the Bodyline saga and would eventually turn against Jardine.

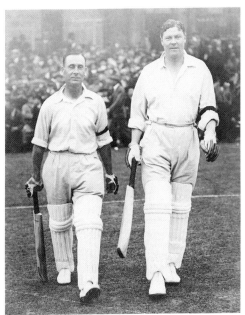

Jack Hobbs pictured with Percy Chapman, Carr's successor as England captain, in 1930.

Bill Voce, the left-arm complement to Larwood for both Nottinghamshire and England.

Clarrie Grimmett—the Australian was the world's finest pure leg spinner of the era.

Victor Rothschild experienced 'leg, chest and head theory' in 1929.

Wally Hammond, England's greatest batsman between the wars.

Prolific Ponsford. Larwood had broken his wrist in the Second Test of the 1928–29 Ashes series.

Laurie Nash, the 'best exponent of intimidatory fast bowling in Australia'.

Queensland speedster Eddie Gilbert floors Don Bradman, and he hurt Jardine with his pace. Would he be Australia's answer to Larwood?

An England cricket tour attracted enormous attention around Australia. The Sydney Cricket Ground was packed for the MCC versus New South Wales in 1928. *State Library of NSW*

Bradman on the drive against the MCC at Trent Bridge in 1930. His dominance over England's bowlers was becoming embarrassing—they needed a plan to contain him.

Don Bradman and wife Jessie on their extended North American 'honeymoon' in 1932.

Bradman meets US baseball champion Babe Ruth in New York.

Australia's two top batsmen of the Bodyline series, Don Bradman and Stan McCabe, take the field at the Sydney Cricket Ground in 1932.
State Library of NSW

The talented 1932 Australia team pictured not long before the Bodyline series against England. Front row, from left to right: Clarrie Grimmett, Alan Kippax, Bill Woodfull (captain), Don Bradman, Bert Oldfield. Back row: Stan McCabe, Jack Fingleton, Keith Rigg, Bill O'Reilly, Bert Ironmonger, Laurie Nash, Len Darling (twelfth man).

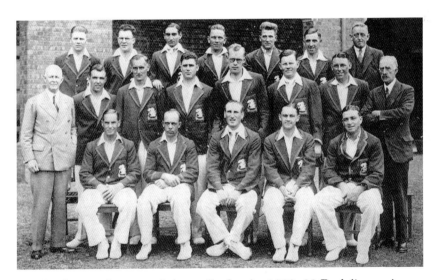

The England team that toured Australia for the 1932–33 Bodyline series oozed batting class and had a fearsome bowling attack, but could they beat Bradman? Back row: George Duckworth, Tommy Mitchell, Nawab of Pataudi, Maurice Leyland, Harold Larwood, Eddie Paynter, W. Ferguson (scorer). Middle row: Pelham Warner (co-manager), Les Ames, Hedley Verity, Bill Voce, Bill Bowes, Freddie Brown, Maurice Tate, R.C.N. Palairet (co-manager). Front row: Herbert Sutcliffe, Bob Wyatt, Douglas Jardine, Gubby Allen, Wally Hammond.

Jardine, wearing his trademark silk choker, leads the England team onto the Sydney Cricket Ground on the first day of the First Test of the Bodyline series. From left to right: Bob Wyatt, Douglas Jardine, Bill Voce, Hedley Verity, Maurice Leyland, George 'Gubby' Allen. *State Library of NSW*

A world-record crowd of 63,993 filled the Melbourne Cricket Ground on the first day of the Second Test in the 1932–33 Bodyline series.

Big Bill Bowes bowls Bradman first ball in
the Second Test.

Bill Woodfull struck above
the heart by Larwood in the
Third Test in Adelaide.

Bert Oldfield struck on the skull by a Larwood bouncer later in the same Test.

A more-relaxed Douglas Jardine on tour in India a year after Bodyline.

Australian Captain Bill Woodfull with King George V during Australia's Ashes tour to England in 1934. Woodfull led his team admirably and was widely respected for his conduct as captain during the uniquely stressful and physically parlous Bodyline series.

The new captains: Don Bradman and Gubby Allen, successors to Woodfull and Jardine, at the first coin toss in Brisbane in the 1936–37 Ashes. Never again would relations between the two sides sink to the levels seen in the Bodyline series.

Don Bradman's skills and reputation only grew after Bodyline. Here he is being mobbed by English autograph hunters as he goes out to bat in the Fourth Test at Leeds in 1938. Over his career he made two triple hundreds and a century at Headingley.

Don Bradman answering one of the millions of letters he received over 73 years.

Prime Minister Robert Menzies with Douglas Jardine in 1954. It took a cricket-loving, high-powered Imperialist to draw out a small concession of regret over Bodyline from the former England captain.

Bradman and Jardine in 1954 'seeing things differently'.

Sir Donald Bradman (left) interviewed by author Roland Perry about Bodyline.
© *Dean Golja*

During the interview Sir Donald demonstrated the problem with fending off a fast ball lifting into the ribcage with six fielders close on the leg side waiting for a catch. © *Dean Golja*

It was the sort of feet-on-the-ground riposte expected from a realist untouched by the noise. He had a premonition that the first ball he would face, from Bowes, would be a bouncer. The bowler had a six-three field—four close to the bat on the leg side, two in the deep on the leg, and three on the off side.

Bradman surveyed the placings, took block on leg stump as planned and settled in over his bat. Bowes took a few steps forward on his run, then stopped. He looked over at Jardine at mid-on. Hammond was moved from mid-off to the leg trap. Bowes, despite his objections, had been manipulated into delivering to a near-Bodyline field.

Now it was full on.

Bradman settled again after this staged delay intended to put extra pressure on him. Bowes stopped at the top of his run again. This time he motioned for Larwood at fine leg to go finer. This was all indicating, as Bradman had imagined, the ball would be pitched short, to draw a hook shot.

The crowd sensed this was all Jardine-directed theatrics. They roared their disapproval, not for Bowes, but for the England captain.

In steamed Bowes for a third time and let loose a chest-high half-volley. Bradman swivelled into the position, his back foot sliding back and across in the accepted orthodox manner. He took a tremendous swing at the ball expecting it to spear through mid-wicket to the fence.

Instead it hit the bottom edge of the bat and cannoned into the base of his leg stump.

Don Bradman was out for a first ball duck.

'Well, I'll be fooked!' Bowes said. His captain, normally sphinx-like, even when a wicket fell, let his emotions go for the first time in his cricketing life. He clasped his hands above his head and jigged around doing a war dance.

'I could have tried to hit the ball that way for 50 years and would have failed,' Bradman said. 'I walked past Herbert again. The crowd was completely silent.'

Bob Wyatt, smirking, turned to the crowd and said, 'When's *your Don* coming in, then?'

It hardly earnt a riposte from the stunned fans.

Bradman was not one to fret, throw down his bat in the dressing room, hide in the toilet and cry. He was far too phlegmatic and pragmatic for such histrionics. He had now been out to six different England bowlers for still only 103 runs.

Leo O'Brien came out of the shower and was stunned to see Bradman taking his pads off.

'What the devil happened to you?' he asked.

'I got bowled.'

Typically, he did not bother to say 'I played on'. It was down in the scorebook as 'Bradman Bowled Bowes, 0' forever. He'd been in the game long enough to know there were good and bad umpiring decisions, and lucky and unlucky moments. One day you'd be dropped, the next you would be snaffled by a near-impossible catch. To Bradman, it was a waste of time dwelling on a mishit. His basic plan of counter-attack was not shaken by a false start, even if it were in front of a record cricket crowd.

Australia's morale was down. Only Fingleton, stoic and trussed up in protective gear, was able to stay at the wicket for just under four hours scoring 86 before Allen bowled him. No one else managed to reach 35. Voce was the pick of the bowlers with 3 for 54. Larwood's normally dead-eye calibration of line and length was off, and he only picked up tailenders O'Reilly and Ironmonger. Yet his stalking presence unsettled all batsmen. His battering of most of them in the First Test had left scars. He had still added several bruises to four of the batsmen.

Australia only reached 228.

Jardine was satisfied with his pace attack and had no misgivings about not having Verity's spin after telling the press that he was his secret weapon. This was now seen as a red herring. Jardine didn't say much to journalists, but every utterance was tactical and within the overall strategy of bringing down Bradman and Australia.

He thought differently when O'Reilly ran through England taking 5 for 63 and reducing them to 169. Only Sutcliffe reached 50. South Australian quick Tim Wall on debut created the biggest two crowd roars of the day, New Year's Eve, when he bowled Hammond for 8 and had Jardine caught behind for 1.

The MCG rocked with derision for the England captain's walk back to the pavilion. Some members even stood and clapped. Jardine thought this was most ungracious but remained implacable. The crowd reaction continued to reinforce his attitudes. It also galvanised some of his team members. They may have had mixed feelings about him and even the use of Bodyline, but such 'mob' behaviour caused them to fall in behind the skipper.

National pride was at stake.

The series had become combative and the atmosphere so electric that Plum Warner was again having second thoughts about Jardine's fitness to lead in an Ashes competition. His plans were working but Warner had already almost given up on Jardine's lack of diplomacy.

34

THE COMEBACK

New Year's Day 1933 started badly for Australia in front of an even bigger record crowd than on day one. Allen, who'd batted well for 30, had Fingleton on his way for 1, and Larwood bowled O'Brien for 11. This brought Bradman to the wicket at 2 for 27 to face Bowes in an identical situation to his first innings. The Bodyline set-up was in place again. The crowd went silent as the gangling Bowes ran in and delivered the exact same ball, a lifter at chest height. This time Bradman made the same orthodox movement back and across. But instead of crashing into his stumps, the ball was sent to earth, bisecting short leg and mid-on.

It raced to the boundary and the crowd reacted as if he had reached a hundred.

Jardine took Bowes off and replaced him with Larwood. With Voce on at the other end, the crowd and members were on the edge of their seats. The two Nottinghamshire demons began with orthodox fields. Larwood sent two balls to Bradman with the off-side configuration. Jardine did his head-high, double-clap of the hands. The fielders walked snappily into the Bodyline set-up.

Bradman on 8 watched. The crowd booed. When they quietened down, he faced up.

Larwood made his rhythmic, ghostly run to the wicket and heaved down a bumper. Bradman ducked. The ball sailed through where his head had been. The crowd let out a long 'oooh'. Larwood stepped up again and delivered a fuller ball on leg stump. The crowd gasped as Bradman pulled away to leg to give himself room and lashed the ball through the vacant cover field to the longest boundary and ran three.

Bradman set the pattern and the pace of the game, either ducking or pulling away to leg to nudge or drive into the empty off side. Larwood and Voce began to leak runs. No one at the county level or anywhere else had used this counter so systematically. The bowlers became frustrated.

But Larwood was also relieved for the first time in a Test bowling to Bradman. The Australian was not giving him a pasting and forcing him out of the attack.

Woodfull (26) fell to the dreaded leg trap, caught by Allen off Larwood. The score was 3 for 70. Allen was now the only one of the four pacemen not delivering Bodyline but with some contradiction, he was fielding in the trap. However, Duleepsinhji, a Cambridge man, refused to move there when Jardine clapped his hands.

Duleepsinhji stood still at point.

'I'm not going there,' he said with a defiant, hands-on-hips, tea-pot stance and glared at the skipper.

'I see His Highness is a conscientious objector,' Jardine said, loud enough for the rest of the close fielders to hear.

It was Duleepsinhji's official princely title and the remark had a cynical undertone that may have flown over the heads of some. His antecedents had been warriors alongside the army of the British East India Company early in the nineteenth century fighting the Maratha Empire. Jardine added, 'You can do that for the next Test as well, if you wish.'

Duleepsinhji did not budge.

'Very well,' Jardine snarled, 'you won't be fielding at all.'

This was a threat he would be dropped for the Third Test.

Jardine had a quick word to Voce at the top of the mark. The Bodyline field was set for McCabe, and he was given a torrid time with three successive bouncers, one of which ricocheted off his back. Bradman walked down the pitch to enquire how he was. McCabe, clearly shaken and annoyed, shook his head.

Three balls later, Allen bowled him for a duck.

Larwood's impact was as an invisible wicket taker.

Richardson joined Bradman and the two withstood everything thrown at them by Voce and Larwood, forcing Jardine to rest Larwood and bring on Hammond, who was meant to act as a stock bowler, plugging one end with medium pace, but he trapped Richardson (32) LBW. The partnership had been 54.

Australia had five wickets left with a lead of 197, not enough for the home team to be comfortable.

Bradman was batting with confidence and was implementing his plan of tennis shots into the off from Bodyline to keep the scoreboard ticking over. He reached 50 in 93 minutes in a performance that had as much attraction as an innings of twice that rate. The spectators were fully aware of the battle: Bradman versus Bodyline. Jardine was using it in shrewd bursts, but the shock tactic was wearing off. The fans could now comprehend Bradman's method. It was not cowardly but courageous, although risky. He was preserving his physical condition by not getting struck, while scoring runs. It was the only way to have a chance of winning. The alternatives were not promising. All bats could have a bash, which would net a low score. Or they could rely on defence. This led nowhere except to incapacitation.

Jardine was ignoring Bowes after he had argued about field placings, with the bowler wanting a more conventional arrangement. Larwood had become frustrated with Bradman's defiance, which left Voce to do the damage. He stepped up, delivering two extra-quick balls to bowl Oldfield (6) and Grimmett (0).

The MCG crowd became anxious as Australia went to tea at 7 for 156, with Bradman on top with 77 not out. The discussion in the stands during the break was whether he could reach a century.

After tea, Tim Wall was plucky for half an hour before Hammond trapped him LBW for 3. That brought Bill O'Reilly to the wicket. He had made clear his hate for and fear of Bodyline. He stayed three overs while Bradman kept on scoring. Knowing O'Reilly's attitude, Jardine brought back Larwood.

Bradman went on the attack and took 9 off his over, which had him moving into the 90s, much to the crowd's rapture. Jardine, his face dark yet inscrutable, took Larwood off in the smallest mini-victory for Bradman over the England express. Hammond removed O'Reilly (0), caught behind.

The score was 9 for 186. Bradman was 98 not out.

Ironmonger, a rabbit's rabbit, moved slowly to the wicket as fans bit their nails. He had to face two balls from

Hammond. Bradman walked over to offer a few words of encouragement. They were needed. Ironmonger had scored five runs in his last five Shield innings. He was old enough to be Bradman's father.

He responded with, 'Don't worry, son, I won't let you down.'

Hammond bowled and just missed the off stump twice. That left Bradman to deal with Voce, who was bowling at his peak for the tour. Jardine abandoned the Bodyline setting for the moment. Voce had a normal off-side field, which allowed Bradman to return to orthodoxy. He defended four deliveries on his stumps and let a flyer wing over his head.

The crowd was more restless with every delivery.

What was 'our Don' doing? Why didn't he belt one? The ground fell eerily silent as Voce loped in. The ball streaked down leg side. Bradman leapt on it with a stroke behind square leg. The noise was deafening as the batsmen ran three.

Bradman had become the first Australian to score seven centuries against England. It had taken him 185 minutes of chanceless batting, but given the strength of the opposition and Bodyline, it ranked with the great innings, even the doubles, and triple he had made before.

The crowd was ecstatic. They were on their feet cheering and clapping for three minutes.

Soon afterwards Ironmonger (0) was run out, with Bradman 103 not out and the tally at a meagre 191. He had faced 146 balls, 83 of them from Larwood and Voce. Most deliveries were with the Bodyline field, from which he scored just over half his runs.

The fans realised he had given the Australians a fighting chance. England had to get 250 for victory. This was a fair challenge on the fourth day of a tight Test but England's strong batting line-up made them favourites with the bookies. Their assessment looked right when England's opening stand reached 53 with Sutcliffe making the pace as if he intended to wipe the deficit quickly. But then O'Reilly, at his peak, bowled him for 33. Leyland (19) fell at the same score, bowled by a Wall fast ball.

The scales were even once more, but not for long as O'Reilly (5 for 66, following his 5 for 63 in the first innings) and Ironmonger (4 for 26) ran through England for 139, which lost 10 for 86. Australia had won by 111 runs, thanks to Bradman with the bat and O'Reilly with the ball.

The series was level at 1:1.

Hammond's disappointing run continued when O'Reilly had him caught for 23. His form was a far cry from his 905 aggregate of the previous tour.

The biggest roar of the Test came when Ironmonger had Jardine caught for a duck after facing just three balls. His tally for the match was 1 run. The crowd gave him a vociferous send-off similar to that of the raucous, insulting fans on the Sydney Hill on the last tour. He had then spat in their direction but was not about to do that as captain. Jardine realised the crowd's reaction was a backhanded compliment. He was seen as the dangerous bogeyman who was a threat to the crowd favourite, whom he continued to disparage inside the English dressing room.

When Bradman was informed by a journalist about this unflattering 'bastard' epithet, he smiled and said, 'I can produce my parents' marriage certificate and my birth certificate that prove he is wrong.'

35

A PERSPICACIOUS
COMPLAINT, IN PRIVATE

Bradman, with his exceptional perspicacity on the game
and its history, foresaw the problems that would emerge
if Bodyline worked. Opposition teams would be forced to
use similar tactics in retaliation. Lower grades of cricket,
with less adept batsmen, would see all sorts of injuries,
even death. He again spoke in private to the Australian
Cricket Board about the problem. His timing was
perfect—both he and Australia were back on top. Com-
plaining when Australia was down would have appeared
like squealing.

Bradman's skills had allowed him to avoid hits on the
body but all his teammates, bar a couple of tailenders, had
suffered with bruises on limbs and torsos that would linger
all summer. The atmosphere in the dressing room was one
of relief rather than elation at the Melbourne win. There
were still three matches to go, and there were no signs that
Jardine would stop using Bodyline.

Bradman speared right to the heart of the issue when he said, 'Sooner or later someone will receive serious injury, not necessarily from an erratic ball, *but from the very nature of the bowling* [author's italics].'

In other words, Bodyline would do real harm, which at best would be incidental, and at worst, intentional.

In response, the Board noted that both Bradman and McCabe had scored great centuries, and no one had been badly hurt.

'If they hadn't faced it,' Bradman reflected, 'they didn't appreciate the problem. Even the opposition players were indifferent until they later had to face it.'

The Board was deaf to any argument. Money talked. Record crowds were filling the stadiums to see the combat. The English tourists' games were raking in revenues never seen before.

Bradman argued further that the future of the game as an attractive sport was in jeopardy. Bodyline restricted many shots. It was negative in every respect. He said the Board should protest to the MCC now, but it did nothing. The Board had been unhappy with his public rebuking of them in recent months over his contracts. Its members were not going to jump when he asked them to.

They wanted to know if he could handle the attack.

Did he believe Australia could win the Ashes?

Bradman's answers were both in the affirmative. But he was frustrated by their indifference. The Board was confident that Bodyline would be overcome and Australia would retain the Ashes.

Australia's win in Melbourne camouflaged the problem for the MCC. Warner was not going to tell them of his fears about the bitterness and conflict that Bodyline caused. MCC Committee members would have read the newspaper reports but not appreciated the feeling. Australia was back on the winning list, and this was more of a worry for them than the ramifications of Bodyline.

Warner felt impotent. He could only complain in confidential letters to his wife about Jardine's behaviour, and hope the tour would turn out fine in the end.

36

ADELAIDE CRUNCH

Jardine's fervour for a series win had moved from obsessive to fanatical by the time of the Third Test in Adelaide. Driven by criticism of his leadership style, he was determined to double down on his methods, including Bodyline. In ruthless moves, he dropped Duleepsinhji for refusing to crouch in the Bodyline trap, although the official 'leak' was that he was too adventurous with the bat when Jardine wanted players who would not give their wickets away easily. This was after his fine century in the First Test. It was harsh, even vindictive, given that he had made the only score of three figures for England in its two Tests. His replacement was Eddie Paynter. Duleepsinhji felt sure he would not be reselected while Jardine was captain although nothing was said to his face. Instead he was treated as if he didn't exist, or with the captain's infamous icy contempt.

Bowes felt a little differently. He had not played his best in a squad bursting with pacemen who were in top form, with Allen being the big surprise for the tour. Bowes believed Allen, rather than any ambivalence towards Bodyline, had edged him out of contention. Allen had taken just one wicket, but it would give him a reputation for life. He was the man who had dismissed Bradman for a duck in an Ashes Test in front of a record crowd.

Verity was his replacement. Jardine knew he needed balance in the attack, and the Yorkshire left-armer had no peer in his field.

Australia brought back Ponsford and left out Leo O'Brien.

*

Jardine won the toss on Friday 13 January, batted and opened himself in order to get a better start. But the move was an early failure when home-town boy Wall bowled him for 3, making the England skipper's tally 31 from four innings. The Adelaide crowd cheered Wall, but there was still room for residual, unnecessary booing and jeers for Jardine. At one point England was 4 for 31 but its strong line-up recovered to be all out for 341, thanks to left-handed Yorkshireman Maurice Leyland (83); Wyatt (78); and Paynter (77). Wall was at his best in front of his supporters, taking 5 for 72.

Australia batted and was soon in trouble when Allen justified his position over Bowes by having Fingleton caught behind for a duck.

Bradman came onto the field just as police began to circle the ground. They had been kept out of sight on the number 2 oval until now. The press had suggested there could be trouble, even riots, if Bodyline got out of hand, and mounted troopers were ready.

Bradman was greeted with gusto all the way to the wicket. He saw out the Allen over. Duleepsinhji was running onto the field often between overs to give Larwood and Voce a sip of beer, and later in the day, champagne, disguised as bottles of water. Larwood also liked snuff, a smokeless tobacco, which was inhaled up the nose for a swift hit of nicotine at the top of his run.

It all helped him, especially when he was bowling downwind, his speed building.

Woodfull defended grimly, his backlift shorter than ever. Next over from Allen, Bradman nudged a single to mid-on. The fans reacted as if he'd hit a straight six. In Larwood's next over to Woodfull with an orthodox field, a ball reared off a good length and crashed into the Australian skipper's chest, just above the heart. He staggered from the wicket, dropped his bat and clutched his chest.

Jardine called to Larwood, 'Well bowled, Harold!'

He could have been yelling the family motto, *Beware, I am here*. Bradman heard the remark as he walked to sympathise with Woodfull. Play was held up. Stunned silence was followed by anger. Abuse was hurled at Larwood. Bradman thought the spectators might invade the ground as more police, thinking the same, moved into position. Concerned for Woodfull's pale look, Gubby Allen ran to the pavilion to get a glass of water. Jeering continued from all sections, including the members. Hammond could see Larwood's concern and called to him, 'Take no notice of them!'

Woodfull was not acting. He was hurt. Players had been killed by such blows. Reporters scrambled for the record books.

An unsteady Australian skipper faced up again and saw out the next few balls. Bradman took a few runs off Allen before Larwood bowled again. Woodfull was facing. Larwood had begun his run to the wicket when Jardine stopped him and clapped his hands. Fielders, like a squad of robots, moved into the Bodyline set-up, leaving only Voce on the off side.

Everyone at the ground other than the England team saw it as a callous attempt to get rid of the Australian captain. Larwood was counted out. Normally placid supporters in even the members' stand were apoplectic. Matters didn't improve as a Larwood stinger knocked the bat from Woodfull's hand.

Allen, in the leg trap, asked umpire George Hele to leave him a stump with which to defend himself.

'Not on your life!' Hele replied. 'I'll need all three myself.'

Jardine had Allen on instead of Voce. Allen's refusal to use the Bodyline field lowered the spectators' collective angst just enough for a funny man in the crowd to point at Jardine and yell as a flock of seagulls flew over the ground, 'There he is at mid-off!'

With Larwood and Bodyline on at the other end the temperature rose again. There was baying for his blood.

Woodfull managed to get off strike with a single. Bradman on 8 now faced Harold 'Thor' Larwood hurling his accurate thunderbolts.

He seemed to have left his anti-Bodyline shots in the locker, or perhaps he was intent on getting his eye in against this intense bowling before opening up with shots so successful in Melbourne. Then he tried one, slicing Larwood into the off for two. Next ball he tried a leg glance and spooned an easy catch to Allen at short leg. Larwood jumped in the air with clenched fists. Jardine allowed a grin to pierce his grey face shroud.

The crowd was stunned. The national hero had been removed for a mere 8 runs with a tame shot off an innocuous ball.

Bradman's departure signalled a strong chance of defeat. Jardine and the team were thrilled. Larwood had won a legitimate victory over his tormentor for the first time in a score of Test innings. The bowler would not, however, be satisfied with getting him once. He wanted to get him over and over. Larwood also fervently desired to strike Bradman and make him suffer, as he had, for all the humiliation in two Ashes series. The fact that he had only managed bruises at The Oval in 1930 rankled with the Nottinghamshire star, especially when no other batsman had treated him so roughly without paying a price.

'Bowling to Australia's batsmen was like potting pheasants on the wing,' his ghostwriter said in Larwood's 'autobiography'. 'But with Bradman it was like trying to trap a wild-duck, his movements were so swift.'

The clumsy shooting, maiming or killing analogy was apt.

Bodyline, seven innings into the series, had succeeded in its aim. It was having consequences for the rest of the Australian batsmen. They were unsettled and taxed about how to combat it. Some went into their shells with little capacity to fight back. Most defended. There were only sporadic attempts to counter-attack. McCabe (8), a shadow of himself in Sydney, was unsettled by Larwood's deliveries lifting into his chest. He too soon succumbed to the pace and pushed a catch to Jardine at short-forward square leg.

After tea, Allen bowled Woodfull for a gutsy, painstaking 22.

37

THE WARNING
TO WARNER

Plum Warner had watched the ugly drama unfold. His fears about Jardine's approach and his 'queer' character had manifested. He made his way to the Australian dressing room where the battered Woodfull was having a rub-down after a shower. The red bulls-eye over the Australian captain's heart stood out among other red weals, and some now yellow ones after earlier hits.

'I'm very sorry, Mr Woodfull, for those terrible injuries,' Warner said with a ring of sincerity. 'I really am.'

'I don't want to see you, Mr Warner,' the Melbourne high school master said. 'There are two teams out there. One is trying to play cricket and one is not. It is too great a game for spoiling by the tactics your team is adopting. I don't approve of them. It might be better if I do not play the game.'

Woodfull was considering stopping his team from playing on. It was an amazing declaration by the highly principled and respected Australian skipper. Warner left the dressing room. He was furious and wondering how he should tackle Jardine over the matter.

Journalist Jack Fingleton heard of the confrontation and did cricket a favour by leaking the story to a fellow journalist, who had it published in the next morning's newspaper. It inflamed the situation but also brought the true feelings into the open.

On Saturday evening after the day's play, a South Australian official told Woodfull there would be no more beer delivered to the Australian dressing room. 'You've exceeded your limit,' he told the non-drinker Woodfull.

'Tomorrow's a rest day. I want the Sunday quota delivered.'

'Can't do it, Mr Woodfull.'

Woodfull was ropable. He was in no mood for anyone saying 'no' to him after what he and his team had been through on the field.

'Deliver that beer now,' he snapped, 'or no play Monday!'

The official obliged.

*

Back on the field on Monday, day three, even fearless and attacking Vic Richardson was nullified in front of his home crowd, scoring 28 off 81 deliveries in a stay of 95 minutes. Ponsford was putting his body on the line. He resisted for hours. A recovery partnership with Bert Oldfield took Australia to 5 for 185 at lunch.

After the break, Ponsford compiled a painful 85 in three and a half hours, during which he wore a dozen hits before Voce bowled him. It had been a strong innings, with cuts and drives in an intermittent counter to Larwood in another heavyweight round.

Adrenalin had sustained batsmen on the field, but at breaks, when they cooled down and the wounds hurt more, it led to their downfall. Grimmett came and went, caught off Allen for 10. Wall joined Oldfield. Australia was 7 for 212, with Oldfield fighting hard in his third hour at the wicket and on 41.

He and Ponsford had earlier seen off the Bodyline field as its exponents tired from banging the ball in hard, and running on the rock-hard ground. Larwood was bowling with an orthodox field when he bounced one at Oldfield. The keeper hooked at the head-high ball, and deflected it into his skull.

He stumbled away from the wicket, holding his head.

Players went to his aid. Woodfull, dressed in civvies, hurried onto the field and escorted him off, retired hurt.

The crowd, which had simmered since Woodfull's rough treatment a day earlier, erupted again, especially after reading in the morning paper Fingleton's leak concerning the Australian captain's rebuke of Warner. The normally sedate elderly Adelaide members were irate and on their feet, shaking fists and screaming invective they didn't know was in them, such was the rage being felt.

Bill O'Reilly came to the wicket amid a near-riotous atmosphere with even more police than the previous day circling the ground. He had never had batting pretensions and had stated his fear of Bodyline. Yet he had a sense of humour. He loved telling the story of a county batsman facing Larwood at his quickest in the 1932 season. The batsman played at a ball which flew to the keeper. A half-appeal went up. The batsman walked. The umpire said, 'Not out.' The batsman kept walking. A leg-slip fielder called out, 'The umpire says not out. You didn't hit it.'

'Yes, I bloody well did!' the batsman said, and kept walking.

Larwood knew he only had to put a fast few balls at the spinner's stumps to end his misery, which he did and bowled him for a duck. Ironmonger up the other end was relieved he didn't have to face a ball, and remained not out at 0, which did his batting average no harm.

The O'Reilly dismissal helped Larwood's figures to 3 for 55. Allen, with 4 for 71, demonstrated that even without Bodyline they could do well against the Australian batting line-up. But he admitted that Jardine's methods shocked the opposition, leading to rushed shots, errors and more fear than usual when facing it or orthodox bowling.

Australia was all out for 222, which not even a future Richie Benaud's sibilance could have brightened up, especially with Oldfield being diagnosed with a linear fracture of the right frontal lobe. A few centimetres either side, the diagnosis said, and the collision could easily have killed the plucky keeper. He showed character from his hospital bed by telling reporters, 'It was my fault, not Larwood's. I shouldn't have tried a hook to something so fast and accurate [a ball directed high over middle and leg stumps].'

The home team was 121 in arrears.

Towards the end of day three, Jardine set the lack of pace in the England second innings, ordering all bats to dig in, reminding them that every run would take them closer to victory. This was the amateur leader determined to play it like a county professional keeping his job with a stolid, long innings. It was the ominous correctness inherited from his Calvinist Scots ancestors who eschewed frivolity and 'entertainment'. It was the complete opposite of Bradman's sense of obligation to the myriad fans who came to see him and paid to do so. He was as much about winning as his nemesis, but not at any cost.

When Jardine took an hour to score a single run, a fan yelled, 'Give us one attacking stroke, you Pommie bastard. And make it sunstroke!'

The tardy performance in making 24 gave plenty of chances for more exasperated cries. At a drinks break, Woodfull offered him a glass of cordial.

'Don't give him a drink,' a barracker called. 'Let the bastard die of thirst.'

Scot R. C. Robertson-Glasgow, Jardine's fellow Oxonian, who had known him since university days, felt 'something in his temperament would not let him play free and full in the greater matches'. As 'the task grew greater, the strokes grew fewer'. Jardine just refused stubbornly to let loose and play the grand scoring strokes of which he was most capable. In this fierce competition—akin to war with Australia—he was not prepared to have a go as if on a village green in England. Jardine was against self-indulgence in the battle of his life. He liked a drink, but was never seen intoxicated, despite encouraging Larwood and Voce to dose themselves with alcohol if it helped them roll the opposition in the harsh Australian heat. Jardine's suppression and self-control diminished his record as a batsman.

Scots journalist Alex Massie wrote, 'Just as Calvinist Scotland was a dour and often joyless country, Jardine's many achievements came at a price.'

Yet his motivations were different and varied, and not about money.

The more he was booed and abused, the more he dug in.

38

CABLE CALAMITY

Two weeks after Bradman urged the Australian Cricket Board to alert the MCC to Bodyline, its members were stunned into action. Everything Bradman had predicted had come true. His fellow batsmen had been bruised into submission. His words that 'sooner or later someone would receive serious injury' were proven correct with Woodfull's hit over the heart and Oldfield's bash on the skull. That it had not been directly due to Bodyline was irrelevant. The tactic of using it had caused anxiety and rash decision-making, which was leading to injury. Bradman was right in suggesting that Larwood in particular was hell-bent on hitting opponents. Taking away his Bodyline facility would have brought him back to orthodox field settings, where he was less potent in the mind and wicket-taking stakes. Curbing Jardine's strategy would have reduced the chance of legalised thuggery, which under the present rules it was.

Australia could take the tit-for-tat route. It could produce hits like all teams using Bodyline. They would not have been as proficient and skilled as the accurate and very fast Larwood. But if so directed, they could deliver balls that could maim, even if they were delivered at an erratic pace, which was Bradman's pragmatic crystal ball–gazing prediction.

He was also concerned about the impact on lower grades and school cricket. They all mimicked Test players. The result would surely lead to bad injuries and death, where bowlers delivered anything from throws to head-high full tosses. It would destroy the game. There was also the important aspect of cricket as entertainment. Shot selection against Bodyline had been limited. Drives either side of the wicket were drying up. Cuts and pulls square were fraught with dangers, and near impossible for head or higher bumpers, unless the batsman was proficient at the overhead tennis smash.

Bradman believed Jardine's method had to be stopped. But the less astute Board members in their ignorance—and thinking only of gate receipts—were slow in their response. They now understood Bradman's concerns. But none of them had his comprehension of the game and his exceptional sense of timing on or off the field.

Press, public and even government criticism goaded and prodded the Board into action, but it was too late and blundering, and viewed as insulting by the unwitting MCC in St John's Wood back in London. The Board held a press conference and sent a cable to the MCC:

Bodyline bowling has assumed such proportions as to menace the best interests of the game, making protection of the body by the batsman the main consideration.

> This is causing intensely bitter feelings between the players, as well as injury.

This was all true. Then came the line that was bound to cause controversy:

> In our opinion it is unsportsmanlike.

This was followed by an overreaction that was sure to call politicians, bureaucrats, diplomats, even prime ministers, into play:

> Unless stopped at once it is likely to upset friendly relations between Britain and Australia.

It caught the MCC off guard. There would be a lot of cabling, letter-writing, meetings and discussions before it would be in a position to reply.

*

Warner was thrown and in a nervous dither. At the end of the third day of the Adelaide Test, he consulted the not out Jardine, who had faith in his earlier presentation to Marylebone and was not prepared to make a press statement.

But Jardine, too, was rattled. He felt the cable had finished his career.

He confided in Allen, who had been his main influential friend on tour, despite his denigration of his captain in private letters, 'I don't think Lord's will back me.'

'You're wrong, Douglas,' Allen said. 'The Board will never get away with using the description "unsportsmanlike".

Sportsmanship and fairness are fundamental to the English mind.'

'You really believe Lord's will be in support?'

'Absolutely. The Australian Board is made up of bloody colonials!'

Jardine was bolstered by this and cheered up.

He set his jaw to the task at hand and that was winning in Adelaide. If anything, the England squad was drawn closer together. They would fall in behind what the skipper wanted. Each team member had witnessed his messianic resolve in the face of crowd opposition. He had not faltered when a pitch invasion looked likely.

More to the point, England was in a more favourable position, in other words, they were 'winning'. Now was not the time for the faint-hearted.

39

ENGLAND'S GRIND
AND BUMP

On day four of the Adelaide Test, Jardine reached 56 in more than four hours at a 21.05 strike rate that hardly justified the designation of 'strike'. His run grind was important, however, as he bored away from Australia with every beautifully correct single to mid-wicket or elegant nudge to fine leg in an 84-run snore with his dependable deputy Wyatt (49).

Almost all the England bats knuckled down and followed the captain's lead. Hammond (85) top scored but hated his dismissal when he mistimed a full toss from Bradman, the last man in cricket he wanted to get out to. It was Bradman's first Test wicket, and the England champion was one to savour and remember, even if it were off an ordinary ball.

Ames (69) justified his selection over Duckworth by partnering Verity (40) in a 98-run stand that took the game away from Australia, *unless* ... unless Bradman could do what he had done in seven previous Ashes Tests by scoring big—a double hundred at least.

England's reply was a dogged 412 at a 2.15 run rate off 191 eight-ball overs. It led by 532. On similar occasions in 1930 Bradman had scored 131, 254, 334 and 232. He had won the last Test a few weeks earlier with a century. The press and public were wondering if he could deliver another match-winner, or was Bodyline too much even for him?

*

Before Australia batted, Warner, angry with Fingleton for leaking Woodfull's comments to the press, offered Larwood a pound if he dismissed the Australian opener. He collected the money by bowling him for a duck. In came Ponsford (0) for a short stay before he back-cut a ball to Jardine. Larwood had both wickets delivering to an off-side field. Australia was 2 for 12. Bradman was in.

Larwood maintained the field. His second ball was a head-high bouncer. Bradman hooked it off his face to the square-leg boundary. The crowd roared. Next ball he late-cut for four more. The spectators loved it. It seemed Bradman had decided to hit back. Woodfull, ever watchful and intent on staying at the wicket for as long as it took, blocked Voce's over.

Larwood then charged in to Bradman and was met by a scorching cover drive for four more. The bowler had boot trouble. He left the field, returned and was promptly cover driven for *another* brilliant four that caused the fans to stand and cheer wildly.

Jardine sidled over to Larwood, asking if he wanted a leg-side (Bodyline) field. Larwood shook his head. He raced in once more, sending down two deliveries on leg stump and was pushed into the vacant leg-side field for 2 twos. Jardine spoke to him again, ordering him to change the field. Larwood looked glum. He did not want to concede another mini-defeat to 'the little bastard' who now appeared relaxed with that half-grin which had so annoyed him since 1928.

Jardine insisted on moving players over to leg, hoping Bradman would be intimidated into a false shot, given his present mood of all-out aggression. The crowd voiced huge disapproval, which may well have helped Jardine's psychological ploy. Bradman stayed in the 'normal' position and swung wildly at two balls flashing down leg side.

Bodyline was back from both ends. Bradman reverted to unorthodoxy, stepping to leg to smash Voce and Larwood into the off. It was a game of cat and mouse with Bradman waiting until the last moment to adjust to the delivery and trying not to give the bowlers an indication of his movement. His reactions were so speedy and his strokes so late that they could have been posthumous.

The crowd gasped until they grew used to this unconventional response. Only the genius of the man could have done this. He stayed with his unwritten contract with the Australian crowds to entertain and score runs, while avoiding the bowlers' attempts to hit or remove him, or both.

He kept scoring. Larwood ran out of puff and Jardine, acknowledging the setback, took him off. Allen and Hammond were tried but could not penetrate Woodfull's wall of defence and Bradman's daring enterprise.

Jardine then resorted to Verity. Bradman moved down the wicket to him and moved to 50 in just a little over an hour of scintillating batting. Woodfull had a quiet, schoolmasterly word, reminding him of the importance of a long and patient partnership.

But Bradman's blood was up. His confidence was brimming over after seeing off the Bodyliners. He swept to 60 after two terrific pulls for four. Woodfull again implored and ordered him to back off. It put Bradman in two minds. Should he bow to his captain's wishes and check his audacity, or follow his instincts and go for complete control of an opposition attack in a manner he had done in Tests and first-class games for five years?

He launched into Verity with a prodigious six over mid-on and into spectators in front of the grandstand. It was a disarming moment for a woman struck on the elbow. Woodfull made a third attempt to calm his younger, more gifted partner. The captain was concerned. Bradman had never hit a Test six before. Was he out of control?

Bradman hated Woodfull's caution. Verity dropped a ball a fraction shorter. Bradman was torn between captain and compulsion. He made a half-hearted stroke instead of launching into the deep as he had the ball before, and was caught and bowled by Verity for a dashing—but for his leader disappointing—66. (Historians had been furrow-browed for decades over why Woodfull said he was not happy with Bradman, long into retirement. The historians had grossly over-rated this moment, so important to Australian and sporting history. Woodfull longed for someone to stay at the wicket with him, particularly Bradman. Only good partnerships would win the Test and take the lead in the Ashes. He felt Bradman had let him down. For his part, Bradman had been unsettled by Woodfull's continued admonishing and blamed the captain for his mis-stroke to Verity.)

The partnership had yielded 88. Australia was 3 for 100. It folded to be 9 for 193 (Oldfield's injury kept him in hospital) with only Woodfull, who carried his bat, resistant at 73 not out. He made the case that he would be there for the duration, and it reinforced his belief that Bradman had not been patient enough.

Woodfull had watched him in England score two doubles and one triple hundred under just as much pressure as in Adelaide, and especially in his courageous Oval display on a dangerous wicket. If he had been able to reach 250 in this innings, Australia would have had a chance. But as in many Tests, there were always recriminations for failed performances with bat and ball, talk of ill-luck, and the what-might-have-beens.

The result was clear and on the scorecard forever.

*

At the end of day five an incensed Jardine knocked on the door of the Australian dressing room. Richardson answered the door.

'Vic, one of my players says one of your team called him a bastard.'

'Which player, Douglas?'

'Harold Larwood.'

'You know it's a term of endearment in this country?'

'It wasn't meant that way.'

Vic turned to the players who were changing out of their cricket gear.

'Which one of you bastards called Larwood a bastard instead of this bastard?'

'I think we all did, didn't we?' Tim Wall replied with a mock frown.

Jardine just contained himself and walked off.

He had the last laugh. England had won easily by 338 runs. It now led the Ashes contest 2:1.

40

THE EMPIRE
WRITES BACK

The MCC's reply to the Australian Cricket Board's cable came two days after the end of the Adelaide Test. It had taken the Club's luminaries, including Lord Hawke, Lord Hailsham, Lord Lewisham, Sir Kynaston Studd and secretary, William Findlay, five days of moustache-stroking and gin and tonic consumption to come up with a shrewd, direct response.

They represented the epitome of the British establishment, all having gone to Eton and Oxbridge. They were going to side with Warner and Jardine, even if the latter had attended Eton's rival school Winchester.

Before the tour, Jardine had given them a brief academic rundown on fast leg theory, but they were not told that the aim would be to blast out Bradman and the other Australians off the pitch, without regard to the dangers and the possibility of injuries.

To supplement Jardine's briefing, the committee had only the tame British reports from journalists with vested interests in playing down the Bodyline impact and endorsing Jardine's point of view. The committee, indeed the British public in general, read the bland articles in the *Evening Standard*, *The Star*, *The Times* or from Reuters and wondered what all the fuss was about. Very few, except those who followed the fortunes of Larwood and Voce at Nottinghamshire under the mercurial, hard-nut skipper Arthur Carr, could imagine what was going on in Australia. There was no TV. Cinema newsreels were either fleeting and nebulous, or edited to show only harmless wicket-taking.

Predictably, the Australian reaction was seen as 'squealing' by the ill-informed or those wishing to denigrate the dominion. This was a consequence of the Board's tardy response. But even if it had been fired off the moment Bradman alerted them to the problems that would arise over Bodyline, it would not have made any difference to the MCC's direct yet careful and subtle response.

Waiting to see the result of the Third Test allowed the committee to be on the front foot. England was likely to win the Ashes. The implication now was that Australians were poor losers. The MCC replied that it 'deplored' the Board's cable. What rankled with them most was addressed in the second sentence, 'We deprecate your opinion that there has been unsportsmanlike play.'

Their collective ignorance of events in Australia meant it saw the Board's comments as a direct dig at the integrity of the manner of play learnt at their illustrious educational institutions. The committee could not countenance that such upright characters as Warner and Jardine, both, like the committee's members, men of Oxbridge and the *right* schools, would act unscrupulously on the field. It said,

'We have fullest confidence in captain, team and managers and are convinced that they would do nothing to infringe either the laws of cricket or the spirit of the game.' Further, it 'regretted accidents' to Woodfull and Oldfield and believed that 'in neither case was the bowler to blame'.

The Board was invited to offer a new rule for the MCC's consideration. It also would agree to the cancellation of the rest of the tour 'with great reluctance' if the Board wanted it.

The tourists themselves then chimed in with the threat that unless the Board's cable was withdrawn it would not play in the Fourth Test. Wyatt and Allen organised the team members to make a declaration to the press that there was no dissension in the squad concerning Jardine. They were loyal to their captain under whom they 'hoped to achieve an honourable victory'. It was not true, of course, but those who had issues with him, such as Duleepsinhji, Tom Mitchell, and Allen—with whom he'd had blazing rows—signed off on their support.

Jardine, whose zealous approach had forsaken any sense of empathy with many of the team members in the interests of winning, was touched.

The Board was forced to back down on the 'unsportsmanlike' accusation in order that the tour went on.

Bodyline was alive and well.

41

NASH, TOO RASH?

Straight after the Third Test there was more aggravated discussion in the Australian press about 'fighting back' against Bodyline by including 22-year-old Tasmanian tear-away quick Laurie Nash. He had played one Test against South Africa in 1932 in which he had done well taking 5 for 22 over the two innings. Said to be raw and impulsive, he had not been chosen so far for the Ashes. Even at his young age, many believed he was one of the most outstanding all-round sportsmen in the nation. At just 173 centimetres (5 foot 7 inches) tall, Nash was a talented and fearless champion Australian Rules footballer. He was also as fast and dangerous as any bowler in the world, and a big-hitting, late-order batsman. Said to be too erratic in his character and his bowling, he remains one of the most mystifying non-selections in top cricket.

'He had great energy,' Bradman said, 'and was a selfless team man. He was as quick as Larwood, but not as accurate.

Remember, he was one of the youngest to ever play for his country. He needed guidance and time to develop. I think he liked his football more and that may have derailed his cricket ambitions.'

Woodfull and the selectors were under pressure now to choose Nash to counter Larwood. Vice-captain Vic Richardson was all for it, saying, 'It would give the Poms back some of their own medicine.'

However, there was a split among the players on whether Nash should be included. Fingleton thought it would work, noting, 'Nash was the best exponent of intimidatory fast bowling in Australia.'

Another name that came up was 27-year-old Queensland Aboriginal Eddie Gilbert. He became famous nationwide for bowling the fastest over ever faced by Bradman, who said, 'The keeper took the ball over his head and I reckon it was halfway to the boundary. The deliveries were faster than anything seen from Larwood, or anyone else.'

Gilbert hit Bradman in a painful blow to the midriff with one delivery. Bradman attempted a counter-attack but was caught off a top edge for a duck. Gilbert's bowling action was suspect, but he explained it was because of a most flexible wrist developed by his boomerang throwing from the age of seven. He walked to the wicket only a few paces, like a spinner, and chest-on.

Gilbert had been called by only one umpire for throwing and opinion was divided, with most commentators giving him the benefit of the doubt. Astute commentator Alan McGilvray said Gilbert whipped his right arm over so fast that it was difficult to tell. But he agreed with Bradman that he was the fastest bowler he'd ever seen.

Bringing in Nash and Gilbert would have created a sensation.

While many about him were losing their sense of perspective, Woodfull remained calm and much against bashing back, knowing that a Bodyline 'bumper war' would only exacerbate the situation.

O'Reilly backed him up. So did Bradman.

Smarter and cooler heads prevailed.

'I didn't agree with Vic [Richardson] on this,' Bradman said. 'But I had no say officially. I was not then a senior member of the team. If Laurie was to be chosen on merit, that was one thing. But if he was chosen to instigate Bodyline reprisals it would have been wrong.'

Nash himself was against Bodyline, but would have used it if so directed by Woodfull. The bowler reflected on his non-selection later, saying, 'I could have ended Bodyline in two overs without having to resort to a leg-side field. I watched them [the England batsmen] play. They couldn't hook. A few overs of sustained short pitches would have ended it.'

The retaliation was never going to happen, especially when the Board had taken the high ground on sportsmanship in its cable ping-pong with the MCC. In addition, the highly respected Woodfull was never going to buckle and select bowlers to hit back with Bodyline. He and Ponsford had been bruised more than any other batsmen. The captain, like Bradman, could easily predict the slippery slope this would lead to. The lower grades of cricket in Australia were already seeing the results of copycat Bodyline bowling (which would be repeated in England).

*

Bradman, undaunted by not scoring a double hundred in the Adelaide Test, faced the MCC again at the end of January 1933 playing for New South Wales. Derbyshire's leg spinner, and another former miner, 30-year-old Tom Mitchell, was on trial under Jardine's hawk eye. Bradman scored just one run before the wrong 'un specialist bowled him with a superb topspinner. Jardine decided that that was enough to earn a Test place. Mitchell was picked for the Fourth Test at Brisbane.

Bradman came back on a sticky wicket in his second innings and scored 71, a gem of a knock in New South Wales' paltry score of 128. So bad was the wicket that the versatile Hammond turned his hand to off spin and took 6 for 43 including the wicket of Bradman, caught behind.

Bradman followed this up with another brilliant cameo of 56 in a NSW total of 113 against South Australia, this time on a rain-free, hard and fast Sydney wicket. In New South Wales' second innings he made a rapid 97 chasing runs in a recovery for a win by 98. Bradman, literally and numerically, was the difference between the two sides.

His scores for the season read: 3, 10, 238, 52 not out, 36, 13, 18, 23, 157, 0, 103 not out, 8, 66, 1, 71, 56 and 97. His aggregate was 952 at a 63.5 average, well below his normal season of about a hundred. Bodyline had made it a 'slump' by his standards, yet he was still in better and more consistent form than anyone in the country, including the tourists.

*

In private, Douglas Jardine had been so down on his form and over the crowds hounding him at every match, that he left it to the other members of the selection committee—Wyatt, Warner and Hammond—to decide if he should be chosen. The committee supported him without equivocation. This and the team's public support for his leadership boosted his morale, although he knew he had to make runs.

With this in mind, Jardine batted twice in the MCC game against Queensland Country early in February, scoring 29 in the first innings and a graceful 77 not out in the second (while Larwood returned his best figures ever in Australia in one innings taking 8 for 28 against the terrified rural Queenslanders).

Jardine batted again in the match against Queensland two days later and wished he had not. He had to face Eddie Gilbert, who whipped up a terrific speed. As Jardine walked onto the ground, he heard a barracker scream, 'Get stuck into the Pommie bastard, Eddie! It was his mob that took the land from your mob up north years ago!'

Jardine allowed himself a fleeting grin. It was a good line he would remember. The conglomerate that had purchased tracts of land in Australia was Jardine Matheson.

Gilbert was erratic with balls flying left, right and over the top of the stumps and batsmen. He let one go that no one really could claim they saw, including Jardine. He was struck on the hip bone, which is one of the worst spots to be hit by the leather missile, alongside the elbow 'funny bone'. Neither created amusement for the receiver, except if he were a masochist.

Gilbert took a few steps towards the England captain, expecting to have to apologise. But Jardine did not rub the spot. Nor did he flex his right leg. His look was as inscrutable as ever. He faced up and batted on but was out bowled for 34 soon afterwards. He strode back to the dressing room, shut the door and collapsed onto the massage table.

'My hip is killing me!' he said through gritted teeth.

Gilbert had claimed his second greatest victim.

*

England dropped Voce and brought in Mitchell for the Fourth Test in Brisbane. Australia brought in Hampden 'Hammy' Love as a replacement keeper for Oldfield. It dropped Grimmett and Fingleton for two left-handed batsmen, Ernie Bromley and Len Darling.

After losing the toss, Jardine addressed the team as they sat under the corrugated roof that masqueraded as a dressing room. It was minutes before going out to the field 'to face the baying mob'. Some players smoked; a few, including Larwood, drank beer in preparation for a long day in extreme heat. They didn't expect a pep talk. Because of his aloofness and shyness, Jardine preferred verbal brevity. He didn't slap backs or try to excite the bowlers for an extra effort. Instead he quoted Charles Mordaunt, British officer and poet, who wrote during the Seven Years' War in the mid-eighteenth century, 'One crowded hour of glorious life is worth an age without a name.'

It was his classical way of saying now was the time to win and be forever famous as a player in a successful team reclaiming the Ashes.

Jardine then stood erect and led his team out.

*

Richardson (83) swept away to a good start before being stumped off Hammond.

Bradman joined Woodfull (67) and kept up the momentum created by Richardson, reaching his half-century in 88 minutes.

He was still there on 71 not out at stumps, including 11 slashing fours, with Australia on 3 for 251. Bradman had met orthodox fields with conventional footwork and conventional shots, and Bodyline with his 'pull away and deliver approach'. His unmatched ability allowed him to switch his methods like a modern short-game specialist and succeed. But his response had to be precise. If it were a fraction of a second out, or he misjudged the ball's bounce or length, he would fail.

The next morning Jardine brought on Larwood with Bodyline again. Bradman had not quite calibrated his skills with the ball not getting up enough to bother him. But he still went on with his method, and paid the price, bowled by Larwood for 76.

Bradman was scoring well, but not with the command, steadiness and confidence that led him on to centuries and beyond. Bodyline was quelling him, much to the continued disappointment of his legion of fans.

Australia scrambled to 340, when it needed at least a hundred more.

Jardine opened the England batting and found some form, but at a cost to the fans in the heat as he meandered to 46 in 190 minutes. He wore his harlequin cap and silk choker but despite his occasional classical attacking strokes received more abuse for his slug-like performance. His 3 fours were received with little more than a smattering of applause. Yet he was reasonably content with his 114 opening stand with Sutcliffe (86). It gave England a strong start. It reached 356, thanks to a courageous innings by Eddie Paynter. Overcome by the heat and a mild tonsillitis attack, Paynter somehow roused himself from his hospital bed and managed to notch up 83 in a four-hour stay at the wicket.

Bradman was in again at 1 for 46 and found himself immediately duelling with Larwood bowling to an off-side field. The batsman was cautious, picking up singles with his partner Woodfull again telling him to settle in. Larwood was taken off but came back after a twenty-minute break.

He immediately switched to Bodyline.

And Bradman was suddenly ferocious.

He cut Larwood for 3 fours to reach 24. In the next Larwood over, Bradman's adrenalin was pumping and he slashed a ball for an easy catch in the covers.

It was the shot of a tailender, not the greatest batsman in the world.

Australia stumbled to all out for 175. England needed 160 to win the Ashes.

Jardine scored a painfully slow 24 in 132 minutes before Ironmonger trapped him LBW. He was anxious that England got the runs and it won easily enough by six wickets.

In the dressing rooms afterwards, O'Reilly called to Jardine, 'Well batted, Douglas.'

'Really, Bill?' Jardine replied with a wry expression. 'I thought I batted like an old maid preserving her virginity.'

Jardine could afford to let his guard down. The Ashes were England's. His captaincy and the use of Bodyline had been successful. Bradman had been dismissed by Larwood three times and Verity once in scoring 8, 66, 76 and 24 in the Third and Fourth Tests. On three occasions, uncharacteristic over-aggression, brought on by his effort to counter Bodyline, had seen Bradman reduced to half his capacity.

*

England's celebrations were mild. Popular Archie Jackson, just 23, died of tuberculosis in a Brisbane hospital on 16 February. Only a few days earlier he had sent a note of encouragement to Larwood, believing he'd been harshly treated by the Australian spectators. Jackson's death upset the great bowler. During their brief encounters since 1928, the two had hit it off. Larwood would carry Jackson's note in his wallet for life.

The Australian team insisted on the sombre duty of accompanying Jackson's body back to Sydney in an express coach. It prompted O'Reilly to quote from the 1856 poem 'Maud Miller' by American Quaker, John Greenleaf Whittier, 'For all sad words of tongue or Pen, The saddest are these: "it might have been".'

He was referring to Jackson's life and career, cut tragically short, not the Ashes loss.

42

GROUNDHOG
DAY, ALMOST

The Fifth Test in Sydney was a dead rubber and England could have been excused for slackening off, but that was never going to happen under Jardine. The more press criticism and crowd abuse he received, the more he was determined to make it a 4:1 record.

England swapped Mitchell for Voce. Australia brought in Oldfield, Philip Lee (a bat from South Australia), fast bowler Harry 'Bull' Alexander from Victoria, and O'Brien. Love, Bromley and Ponsford were omitted.

Woodfull won the toss under darkening skies on 23 February 1933 and elected to bat.

Bradman came in without a run on the board when Larwood dismissed Richardson for a duck with his fifth ball. He was not greeted with the usual explosive applause, even though it was his first appearance in a Test at the SCG.

Larwood bowled four overs with an off-side field, and came back for an over of Bodyline without effect.

If anything, Bradman was in a more reckless mood than in earlier innings, almost as if he expected the inevitable and was determined to thrash as many runs as possible in a short time. The Sydney crowd was alive with Bradman on top, despite his cuts from outside the leg stump, and Larwood screaming in at top speed.

He bowled Woodfull (14) off his pads.

Bradman made 48 in 56 balls, a rate faster than anyone else in the series. He was making use of the leg side, and also moving across his stumps in attempts to slice into the heavily patrolled close-in leg trap. He played roulette with Larwood once too often, moving to the off stump to glance him. He missed and his leg stump was knocked over. It was almost Larwood's last hurrah, for he had taken all three wickets to fall.

There were jarring similarities between performances in the Fourth and Fifth Tests, except for Australia's high run rate (4.01 an over) in the first innings. It reached 435, with six batsmen from number three to eight putting in strong performances.

Jardine surprised, as was often his way, by placing Larwood as night watchman should a wicket fall close to stumps on day two. The Nottinghamshire star was unhappy about this, having delivered 32.2 overs in taking 4 for 98. The captain over-bowled him and he just wanted to put his feet up. But he was needed, coming in at 2 for 153 just before stumps.

The following day, Larwood attacked the Australian bowlers, easily outscoring his illustrious partner Hammond in a luck-riven 92-run stand. It was one of those innings where a non-recognised batsman throws everything at it and it comes off. He had nothing to lose and hammered his way to 98 in a strong display before being caught by Ironmonger off Lee.

Larwood strode from the ground to a standing ovation. It surprised him and showed a different side to the Australian psyche. The fans were not blaming him for the fiasco of Bodyline even though he was the main culprit. Instead they were acknowledging him for his greatness.

'There you are, Harold,' Jardine said, greeting him in the dressing room. 'You went for 98 runs bowling and now you've got every one of those runs back. Well done!'

Hammond was LBW to Lee for 101 in a return to good form when it didn't count, and England reached 454 (at a 2.64 rate per over), a lead of 19, as compared to 16 in the Fourth Test.

The sameness, however, didn't keep the fans from streaming into the SCG to see the final Bradman–Larwood encounter for the series.

Australia's innings began when Richardson (0) was caught brilliantly by Allen off Larwood, who had picked up the hard-hitting opener twice in seven balls for no runs.

In came Bradman. He looked confident against Bodyline, stroking Larwood into the off so often that he was forced to take a man out of the leg trap and put him on the off. The 30,000 pre-lunch crowd was wise to the significance of the move. The fans applauded as Australia made it to lunch without further loss in 25 minutes of play. Bradman was on 22.

By the time play resumed after the long interval, the spectator numbers had swollen to more than 40,000 as people clamoured to get a look at the great cricketing gladiators. The gates were shut with 8000 more fans swarming around the SCG disappointed not to get in.

Larwood smashed Woodfull on the back of the shoulder, and the gutsy Australian skipper took two minutes to recover. The Larwood versus Bradman battle resumed. The stumps seemed to be irrelevant as the bowler did his best to hit Bradman, who moved to avoid giving Larwood the satisfaction of striking him. No one had struck Bradman in the series, and he remained the only Australian batsman not to be hit, slowed down, injured or forced to miss a Test.

Then Larwood managed to get him high on the fleshy part of his left arm. It stung. Bradman flexed his arm but did not take time out. It gave Larwood extra satisfaction in potting 'the wild duck' in contradiction to obviously false declarations that this had never been Bodyline's aim. Larwood was now bowling at his fastest for the entire series. Every time a batsman scored runs off a delivery, he would send down another vicious bouncer.

Voce, who'd always taken the lead from his Nottingham-shire partner, got into the act and hurled down a fast lifter, this time into the front of Woodfull's shoulder.

However, the batsmen won through. At 2.45 p.m. Larwood was taken off after two spells of some of the most express bowling ever seen in Sydney. The crowd clapped him all the way to his fielding position, which was applause for the two batsmen too. Larwood had reached his peak in speed, direction and lift.

Bradman and Woodfull had geared their minds to the bowling after so many clashes. Their reflexes had quickened as a consequence. Neither would meet such a ferocious and brilliant opponent again. Test cricket would never be easy, but facing Larwood and combating him was the toughest task in the game.

Allen replaced Larwood and Bradman hit several fours, forcing Jardine to bring his star back. He was not happy about it. He had a bruised and swollen foot and argued that he couldn't even run up. Jardine ordered him to bowl, even if it were off a shorter run.

He stood at the wicket and rolled his arm over. Woodfull was facing. Demonstrating true sportsmanship as ever, he patted each ball back up the wicket until the end of the over. Larwood made as if to leave the field. Jardine stopped him.

'I want to go,' an anguished Larwood said.

'Not as long as that little bastard is still in.'

Bradman smote Verity for a couple of fours.

But then on 71, he helped his rival out by playing over a surprise yorker from Verity and was bowled.

'You may go now, Harold,' Jardine called.

Larwood and Bradman left the field a few metres apart without acknowledging each other. They received a standing ovation, such was the spectacle these two had performed over several months, and before that in two earlier Ashes.

The England bowlers then ran through the rest of the Australian batting line-up for 182, with Woodfull (67) the rock once more. Verity, who was given a chance to shine out of the shadow of Larwood, bowled most overs and took 5 for 33.

Australia led by just 163. England knocked off the runs easily and won by eight wickets, giving them a 4:1 series victory.

Jardine's dictatorial and hard-nosed approach was the difference. His planning and tactics had paid off more than he would have dreamt. His main weapon was Larwood, and he had the figures: 33 wickets at 19.51. He removed

Bradman four times in eight innings, although a plus for the batsman was that he scored more runs—151—than anyone else from Larwood's bowling. Bradman's series average was 56.57, better than any other top batsman on either side. In addition, his strike rate of just under 75 was far faster than anyone else in the series.

In that regard he had fulfilled his aim of entertaining paying customers—albeit to the disgruntlement of his skipper, who would have preferred half the rate and twice the runs. Bradman's fans were disappointed too. They had wanted more big match-winning innings, which only came once in Melbourne.

Bradman's aggregate was 396 runs, or 99 runs per Test, which was the highest of both sides. He was the only player to reach 50 in at least one innings of each Test he played. By any measure he was the best batsman of the series.

The fact that he avoided being incapacitated by heavy hits allowed him to perform at the standard of the rest of the best Test batsmen in history. The other Australian key bats showed the real impact of Bodyline. Multiple bruises to flesh and bone slowed their effectiveness through the series to a point where they were uncompetitive.

McCabe got away to a flyer in Sydney with 187, but after being battered in that innings, his next nine visits to the crease yielded just 195 runs at an average of 24.37. Woodfull, hit more than any other Australian, averaged 33.80 at a strike rate of 37.00; Richardson averaged 27.90 at a strike rate of 46.73; Fingleton 25.00 at 32.96; and Ponsford 23.50 at 39.60.

In other words, the Bodyliners, aided by Allen and supported by Verity, had reduced Australia's best, apart from

Bradman, to averages mainly in the mid-20s, and at slow scoring rates. These returns were never going to win an Ashes or any other five-Test series.

Bradman's good average and speedy rate of scoring had not been enough to carry the team when three or four more batsmen were needed to average as he did. He proved that his method of avoiding debilitating hits had been the only way to remain competitive. Yet it had been a failure by his standards.

*

Jardine and England celebrated. They looked forward to a less demanding mini-series in New Zealand, followed by the long trip back to England for a heroic welcome.

However, the bad blood between the Ashes combatants meant that no Australian made the effort to see the tourists off as they set sail across the Tasman, a neglect that had not been experienced by any England team ever before.

43

1933: BODYLINE—'IT'S A NOTTINGHAM PRODUCT'

In April 1933 Arthur Carr stepped into the breach in an attempt to 'control' Larwood, the hottest property in English cricket. They met in Port Said, Egypt so that Carr could shepherd him home to Nottingham and make sure he didn't say anything to the press that would worry the county committee. Many journalists wanted to interview Larwood, and to a lesser extent Duleepsinhji, who had left the tour party to return early. Larwood's bruised bone in his foot seemed to have healed but he had not put any pressure on it after bursting himself to please Jardine in the Fifth Test in Sydney.

The main topic for journalists was Bodyline. Not having been in Australia, Carr was quick to support it as if it were the weapon that everyone would want.

Journalist L. V. Manning travelled with Carr and Larwood across the Mediterranean to France. They took the Blue Train from Toulon to London's Victoria Station.

Manning used a radio link to report his interview with Carr, who, within a few breaths, went on the defensive and then attack as if he were making a century for Nottinghamshire. 'Nothing short of a legislative move by the MCC would prevent Nottingham using leg theory,' he said.

It was a cute early ploy to scare the other counties. The message was clear: nothing was going to stop Nottinghamshire from enforcing the tactic. Counties had complained sporadically about Bodyline over the last four seasons but since the potency developed by Larwood and Voce in Australia there was now much more of a sustained threat.

'Are you afraid of retaliation?' Manning asked Carr.

'No,' Carr replied, scoffingly, 'and anyway, who is going to bowl it? There is no one in first-class cricket with Larwood's accuracy.'

Manning suggested Bowes.

'Bowes can bump,' Carr said, 'but that is not the Larwood ball.'

'Could leg theory tactics ruin English cricket as a spectacle?'

'Rubbish!' Carr said. Nottinghamshire was going to make the game more attractive using it. Long innings were becoming a bore. Carr went on to praise Larwood who in turn grumbled about his experiences in Australia, saying he'd been pestered and maligned.

The MCC secretary, William Findlay, met Larwood at St Pancras later in the month and reminded him like a schoolmaster that his contract with the MCC forbade him from speaking to the press about the Australian tour.

Newspaper speculation soon began about Nottinghamshire's plans to use the new 'weapon'. The *Nottingham Press*

News opined about leg theory, which no one was prepared to call Bodyline, saying it 'won the Ashes in Australia, and it is a Nottingham product . . .'.

The paper was well aware that Nottinghamshire and Carr had developed Bodyline, and gotten away with it with Carr's hit-and-run tactics against certain counties and batsmen since 1929. Now it was sanctioned at the highest level, the county and its supporters wanted to claim and defend it.

Media reaction reflected the hidden concerns.

*

Douglas Jardine was feted as a hero upon his return to England, soon after Larwood arrived with Carr. The England captain was greeted at Euston by the most powerful group in cricket, the MCC's Lord Hawke, Lord Lewisham, Sir Kynaston Studd and William Findlay. They all shook hands with him as if he were a winning battle commander from the Western Front. It was not dissimilar. The Test battles had been closer to war than any team sporting competition before it. The object of Bodyline had a 'win-at-all-costs' sense to it, no matter, within limits, who was hurt mentally or physically on the pitch.

And Jardine himself was damaged mentally after all the abuse, unprecedented in international sporting competition. Yet he would never show it, especially in front of such an illustrious group at a reception with hordes of press and cameramen in attendance. In true stiff-upper-lip manner, he would have seen tears as a sign of weakness.

There was no chance that Jardine would get a swollen head. He had been through too much during what he regarded as a sort of holy crusade. He even called his book on the Bodyline tour *In Quest of the Ashes*. As the main guest at Foyle's book-store for a literary lunch he was introduced as 'Douglas the Killer', at which—out of necessity—he winced a smile.

In his speech, he quoted several times from the Ancient Greeks in relation to what he had just achieved in Australia. First, Periander, the sixth century BC tyrant of Corinth: 'Pleasures are transient; honours are immortal.' This was in relation to the exhaustive efforts and sacrifices of his squad. They had won the Ashes against all odds. Now they would be honoured for a long time.

Second, he turned to sixth century BC Greek lawmaker and philosopher, Solon: 'Religion and laws; If they are exercised well, are beneficial; If exercised badly, they do not benefit at all.' Here, he was referencing the use of tactics that were within the laws of cricket, claiming that at no point had laws been contravened or the game's 'spirit' violated.

He was safe in his remarks. No one at the lunch was going to question him with other than reverence at worst and adulation at best.

On cricket he quoted fellow Oxonian, poet and writer Edmund Blunden: 'Cricket to us was more than play, it was worship in the summer sun.' Pertinently, the audience was given a small window into Jardine's thinking when he said, as he often did, 'Cricket is battle and service and sport and art.'

The battle over Bodyline was just beginning and Jardine's demeanour reflected it. He remained unmoved by flattery while taking every chance to defend his efforts in Australia.

Plum Warner's report to the MCC spelt out the respected manager's fears during a time of national hero worship for the entire English squad. Early in the 1933 season, they predictably did not take heed of the warning, or they put it aside.

Jardine was asked if he wished to captain England against the West Indies later in the 1933 summer. He had to say yes. Otherwise it would have seemed like he was running away—or felt guilty.

The Lord's spectators got to their feet when he led the MCC onto the field against the tourists. They rose again when he batted, even if he did not play attacking cricket. He could do no wrong.

It was such a pleasant contrast to Australia.

44

JARDINE FOR
THE DEFENCE

Much to Carr's and the Nottinghamshire supporters' disappointment, Larwood's injured foot diagnosis—or *mis*diagnosis—prevented him bowling in the 1933 season, although he did play sometimes for the county as a batsman. Voce was also out of sorts, with niggling little injuries that kept him from bowling at his top. As a consequence, the dangerous Bodyline combination was missing for the Tests versus the West Indies.

This meant that Nottinghamshire's use of the tactic was not on view much throughout the season. However, there were others who liked the idea of crunching batsmen and taking wickets with the new method, which was the old leg theory, revitalised and with menace. One such experimentalist was rangy Ken Farnes, who celebrated his 22nd birthday by taking seven wickets for Cambridge against Oxford.

Now the game's power brokers sat up and took notice.

They suddenly saw the past in the 1932–33 Ashes and a very ugly future together in one timeless moment. This was not the old leg theory that Hawke and the other MCC Committee men had seen or experienced. This was something different. The object was not to stop runs, but to stop batsmen by two obvious ways—belting them into submission or forcing them to give up their wickets, usually with a catch. Farnes managed to hit each of the first six Oxonian batsmen. Two of them had balls smash into their necks.

While England was drawing most national attention at Lord's thrashing the West Indies in the First Test, Larwood, as a batsman only, and Voce were playing for Nottinghamshire against Yorkshire at Trent Bridge. Voce, whose form had been poor, turned to Bodyline and gave all Yorkshire bats a torrid time. Bowes, playing for Yorkshire, retaliated with a series of searing bouncers, in the process knocking out Walter Keeton.

Carr, who had been batting with him, helped carry the stricken player, who was as limp as a rag doll, to the pavilion where a hostile crowd vented its collective spleen against Bowes. However, the incident barely rated a mention with nearly all press eyes on the one-sided Lord's Test.

Arthur Carr had turned 40 and was not nearly as agile as in previous seasons. He suddenly had visions of his own demise from a hit similar to that received by Keeton. His fear was to be expected. He had overcome it on the pitch and in war, but he was older now and he could see himself being badly injured.

In a game against Leicester, which had some useful quicks, Carr talked the opposing captain into not bowling head-high bouncers. He wrote in the *Daily Sketch* that he had made the agreement, which had been much maligned in the press, because he feared someone would be killed. Carr said, unconvincingly, 'Larwood is the only bowler capable of delivering "safe" leg theory because he is so accurate.'

This comment was seen by *The Times* as the oxymoron of the year and Carr was labelled a hypocrite. A week later Nottinghamshire played Surrey at The Oval and Voce let go a volley of Bodyline deliveries at Jack Hobbs. He was hit on the chest once, and narrowly missed other strikes, but Carr remained mute in his newspaper column about the subject. Hobbs, regarded as the finest English batsman alongside Hammond, had never been a Bodyline convert. Now he was more vocally against it, using his newspaper articles to express his attitude with more vigour.

Bodyline reared its head again, at least for national viewing, during the Second Test at Old Trafford in late July. The West Indies tried it with Learie Constantine and Manny Martindale hurling themselves at the England bats with a leg-side field. It was a slow wicket and they had to thump the ball in to get lift. They made several hits, especially on Hammond, who had to have stitches in a split chin, and a massage for a hit to the back.

'If this is what the game has come to,' Hammond said, 'it's time I bloody well got out!'

But Jardine had a point to prove. He too received bruises in a painful five-hour stay at the crease in scoring 127, his only Test century. He used his height to stand up straight and leave the bat perpendicular in front of his nose. The ball fell at his feet. It was a dramatic show of defiance in defence of his wicket and his own tactic to destroy opposition teams. The excessive use of the flying bumper elicited a typical reaction from Jardine. He more than once wandered down the wicket between deliveries and patted down the pitch in the bowler's half. But the pitch was slow. Had he been at Lord's or The Oval he would have had a greater challenge.

Feeling his tactic had passed censorship for the moment, Jardine returned the favour, letting Edward Winchester 'Nobby' Clark loose on the West Indies. Clark of Northamptonshire had observed Larwood and Voce beating up Victor Rothschild and others in the 1929 game. Batting at number eleven, he had watched in awe, and partly in admiration, as all Northamptonshire batsmen were attacked. He was himself given a fearful working over by Larwood before he was bowled for a duck.

A left-armer who favoured bowling around the wicket like Voce, Clark was by 1933 the second fastest bowler, after Larwood, in England. He was also an angry character. He enjoyed hitting the batsmen's bodies as much as taking wickets, and upset several of the West Indians without regard to their position in the batting order.

Now the unpretty show was on display for English audiences. Journalists pounced on it. References to the tactic were suddenly peppered with the word 'Bodyline'.

Plum Warner, smarting from the way Jardine had ignored his pleas, told the *Daily Telegraph* that Bodyline was causing 'anger, hatred and malice'. He had become utterly disillusioned with Jardine and his tactics.

The MCC was alerted now but not yet alarmed. They would back their man Jardine, but criticism from both *The Times* and *Wisden* gave cause for concern.

Jardine, himself battered from the Second Test, injured his knee in a county game and was happy to miss out on the

Third Test against the West Indies, who this time did not have the Constantine–Martindale attack combination.

Warner was pleased with Bob Wyatt, who took over as captain for the Third Test and did not allow Bodyline. Wyatt was against it.

It meant Bodyline was put away in lockers for the rest of the 1933 season.

But the tactic was not yet dead.

MCC President Lord Hailsham and Treasurer Lord Hawke, under the committee's directive, called Jardine in for a 'chat' at Lord's HQ about an offer to captain the MCC on a tour of India. On one hand, Jardine was perfect for the position. He had been born in India, as had his father. On the other hand, England could not afford another reaction to Jardine and the MCC tourists in the Jewel in the Crown, as had been experienced in Australia. There had been wild talk about breaking off diplomatic relations. Already Australians were not buying English goods as they once had. There was a lingering economic depression, and the Australian government was looking for better loan terms by attempting, unsuccessfully, to pressure the British in the wake of the Bodyline fiasco.

The lords put their offer to Jardine. He was thrilled at the chance and their support for him. Hawke added the proviso, 'You must give us your word that you will not do anything to provoke the Indian public or government.'

Jardine gave them his word.

'You know what we are talking about,' Hailsham said. 'Fast leg theory, or whatever you wish to call it.'

Hawke added they did not want another 1857-style 'uprising'. It had been put down by the Scottish thirteenth

Lord Elphinstone, governor of Bombay. But, he said, there were none of his type around anymore.

India would be a tricky assignment. Jardine would not have accepted any other MCC tour, but he was up to this challenge.

45

1933–34:
AS YOU WERE

Bradman spent the Australian winter of 1933 attempting to keep fit, despite intermittent abdominal pains and a 'dispiriting languor' which had dogged him since before the Bodyline series. Doctors were mystified. They prescribed 'relaxation'. But he was just turning 25 with a solid year of cricket, possibly, in front of him.

In August he taxed his mind rather than his body by sitting for and passing the umpire's exam. He was a student of the game and during the Bodyline furore had written to the MCC about the LBW law. He suggested that a batsman using his pads against balls pitched outside the line of the off stump should be given out if the ball was going on to hit the stumps.

Batsmen, especially in England, had made careers from padding or kicking away the ball with impunity. Bradman said his suggestion would lead to brighter cricket as bats would have to be used to defend the stumps. (It would be several decades before his advice was heeded.)

Bradman himself needed no such encouragement to use his bat and was renowned for hardly letting anything through to the keeper—or hit his pads. It was anathema to his obligation to entertain the fans.

He began his seventh Shield season with a dazzling 200 in 184 minutes against Queensland in Brisbane. There was something more adventurous in his batting as he launched into the bowling. No Bodyline tactics were in sight but one bowler tried the opposite: off theory. Bradman moved to the off and belted it with contempt through the vacant leg side.

In November he scored well enough in Test trials to decide the squad for the 1934 Ashes tour, if it were to go ahead. Cables were flashing across the world in an attempt to sort out the Bodyline controversy. The MCC held its ground. It would not make specific provisions to outlaw the controversial practice but it assured the Australian Cricket Board that a direct attack by a bowler on a batsman would be 'an offence against the spirit of the game'. This was not a concession. The MCC was being stubborn, although concerns were growing. The lull in Bodyline's use since the end of the 1933 season had allowed the committee members to bury their heads in the sand for the 1933–34 northern winter.

Finally, it was announced that the 1934 Ashes tour would go ahead. The Australians would leave on 9 March. Yet they would be sailing into the unknown. There had been no guarantees about stopping Bodyline. Jardine was leading the MCC on the Indian tour. Larwood was expected to be fully fit for the 1934 season, and Voce was vowing to do better after a poor and lethargic 1933, which he put down to the strain of the 1932–33 Ashes. The Australians were also reading about Bodyline having been used sporadically in 1933 in the county championship, and in the unpleasant and ugly Second Test at Old Trafford.

Bill Woodfull, captain again, would stand for no nonsense, which meant he could withdraw his team from the tour if someone used Bodyline against Australia. At the very least, such an eventuality would mean a disastrous financial loss for both parties, and a reignition of bad relations between the two countries.

46

ONE INDIAN SUMMER

Douglas Jardine was a different figure, at least on the surface, when he landed in Bombay with his second-rate, but still capable, fourteen-man MCC squad. Only Verity remained from the victorious Ashes team of 1932–33. Jardine was missing his Bodyline specialists, Larwood and Voce, although he had aggressive pacemen in Nobby Clark and Stan Nichols. But he was under orders not to allow Bodyline.

Jardine was determined to be his charming self among the Indians, whom he loved. There would rarely be heckling, booing or abuse as there had been down under. There was no sense of cynicism or sarcasm in the Indian mentality, and he would respond accordingly. If he'd had another chance in life, he would have lived and worked full-time in the vast Asian land with its huge population and diverse cultures and customs. Indians also loved cricket, which endeared Jardine more to them.

He knew how to behave in India. as opposed to Australia, where people could be judgemental and there were long-held grudges over backgrounds, the Irish conflict, and a sense of inferiority towards the seat of Empire. He'd fallen back on his stiff and repressed manner in that Anglo-Celtic environment.

But in India, the land where his parents and grandparents had lived for much of their lives, he felt freer, less inhibited and more open. The Indians were gentler and more appreciative of him and the game. Yet he was most aware too of sensitivities in India, which could lead to political violence that had never been an issue in Australia.

The Empire wanted to be seen as a benevolent ruler, yet certain elements, both political and religious, wanted independence. It had always simmered. Jardine had made himself an amateur expert on the country, and knew more than most about the machinations of the Indian Rebellion of 1857, to which the lords had alluded. He had read widely about how that had been adroitly handled by a Scot he ranked as highly as anyone else in history—the little known thirteenth Lord Elphinstone, a favourite of Queen Victoria.

In spite of his knowledge, Jardine was uneasy about the dual political and sporting roles expected of him, believing that sportspeople should not be used in this way. His masters at the MCC—most of them conservative political figures—disagreed and saw it as perfectly acceptable. Then again none of them had been put in such a demanding position. In Australia, Jardine's fervent drive had left a political mess in his wake that others were still cleaning up.

In India, he aimed to avoid any trouble.

When he arrived in Bombay, he made a radio broadcast speech in response to an effusive welcome in front of a big, loud crowd that interrupted him without being offensive. The tour squad looked on in astonishment as Jardine carried on with a relaxed almost permanent smile.

The team members realised then that only a person such as Jardine with his aristocratic bearing, grand cricketing status and comprehension of this special culture could run a successful tour. He had adjusted to the two different tour challenges with two contrasting faces and approaches. As Hedley Verity, the only common denominator in the two tour parties, told Bradman, 'He felt he had to be the hard bastard to defeat you, and the sweetest of fellows to pull off the Indian business.'

Jardine spoke with unabashed and enthusiastic sincerity of Bombay, 'the Queen of Cities', and how proud he was of the honour bestowed on him 'by the Marylebone Cricket Club to lead their team in the land of my birth'.

In Australia, his taciturn manner and disdain for plati-tudes had seen him dubbed an inadequate speaker. In India, his integrity came through and he was regarded as a more than adequate, even passionate speaker, not an adjective used loosely if at all before. As the tour progressed he felt at home in the last vestige of an Edwardian way of life which still had remnants of Victorian mores. The old Queen's nineteenth-century effigy in statues and portraits was seen everywhere and in far greater numbers than any other Briton. She had never set foot on Indian soil but had made herself Empress of the Nation.

Jardine's ease in this environment added another piece in the puzzle of his complex character.

Australia, with its more egalitarian ways, where the easy familiarity of crowds and individuals was rampant, offended him. He didn't want sycophants, just respect and at arm's length, a bit like a royal.

India's choice of captain, Colonel C. K. Nayudu, gave him that. An educated man from a wealthy Nagpur family, Nayudu was a hard-hitting bat who promised bright cricket against the 'English'. He set the pattern himself with 116 in his first game. He led a troupe of cricketers around the country, which each time made up half of the sides playing Jardine's team.

Cricket often took second place to socialising. Lavish parties and banquets laid on by maharajahs, nawabs and European dignitaries were more than distractions.

'There were dancing girls who quite often attended to the [tour] members' needs, so to speak,' Verity said.

Such nocturnal antics were often followed by an early morning hunt. The cricketers then turned up bleary-eyed, hungover but happy at cricket matches, for which they had to steel themselves. It was an adventure for most of the MCC squad that they would never forget. The cricket was a mere quaint façade.

Jardine was not always present at the after-function 'festivities'. Yet he was content to let them go on, as long as the press was not privy to anything, and if it were, the reporting was discreet enough, although later book publications included revealing passing comment about the 1933–34 tourists.

To ensure that diplomacy ruled, Jardine invited maharajahs to pad up and play against his team. Once he invited the Maharaja of Patiala to actually bat for the MCC team. The rotund, turbaned 42 year old, who apparently had more than 350 concubines, somehow found enough energy to make a half-century, much to the delight of cheering spectators. They included many of the veiled women from his court, not to mention the eunuchs who attended them.

Jardine's largesse in inviting Patiala to play for the MCC and be photographed in the sacred MCC blue jacket with the St George and dragon crest was a fine public relations call. But it was a liberty too far for the viceroy and governor-general, the Marquess of Willingdon. An Eton and Cambridge man, Willingdon was a reasonable cricketer for the university and the county of Sussex. He was born in 1866 and therefore steeped in the Victorian era. Letting a 'native', albeit a wealthy, well-placed one, wear an MCC blazer and actually *play* for Marylebone was altogether too much. He believed strongly that Indians should be kept in their place. His wife the Vicereine, the Honourable Marie Brassey, was incensed by Jardine allowing such a licence. No wonder this Scot was so unpopular in Australia, she said, according to the Marquess's private diaries.

Brassey went to see Jardine and tried to persuade him from his 'folly' in fraternising in such a way with the maharajah. Jardine politely refused to heed her. He took the approach as a slight. He was captain of the MCC. Who was the wife of a viceroy and governor-general to tell him what to do?

He clashed again with Willingdon three days later in the MCC v Viceroy's XI game. Willingdon's team was forced to follow on. Before it batted a second time, the Marquess wanted a very flat deck to bat on and had the groundsmen use a heavy roller for three times the allotted minutes under MCC rules.

Jardine, a stickler, was furious.

'I want an apology,' he told Willingdon, 'or my team will not come onto the field.'

Willingdon capitulated, much to the fury of his wife. Jardine instructed Clark and Nichols to deliver Bodyline but with an off-side field. In effect this meant fast bumpers sent down as much at the batsmen as the wicket. The result was Willingdon's team being rolled for a meagre 63.

Jardine refused the hospitality of the viceroy and vice-reine after the game.

'Hell hath no fury like a Jardine scorned,' said Verity, who witnessed the confrontation.

Willingdon wrote a letter of complaint to the MCC saying that his team had been a victim of Bodyline, which was not strictly true, and easy for Jardine to rebut from a distance. But it went down as a black mark against him in the consideration of who would lead the MCC against the Australians in 1934.

It didn't help also that he clashed with an umpire, Frank Tarrant. The Australian official had played for Victoria and Middlesex and was employed by two maharajas. He had been warned by the MCC to stop any Bodyline bowling.

Despite being told not to indulge in it, Jardine had Nobby Clark and Stan Nichols do just that. Tarrant confronted Jardine when two Indian batsmen in the Second Test were hit in the torso, and a third had his topee dislodged.

India retaliated, copying the field placings.

Tarrant complained to the MCC. Jardine hit back in a counterclaim by saying that too many LBW decisions had gone against his men.

Tarrant was relieved of referee duties for the Third Test.

*

Jardine's captaincy had varied from over-officiousness to a certain flexibility, while all agreed that he was an exceptional tactician. He used Bodyline and the fast bowlers were encouraged to be at their most aggressive. The Indians had two capable quicks, Mohammad Nissar and Ladha Ramji, leading into the Tests. They were hard, give-no-quarter affairs with both sides receiving their share of bouncers and hits. So much so that Jardine insisted that his batsmen all wore the topee, or the Indian helmet.

Jardine's own form was good in the three Tests (which the tourists won 2:1) scoring 60, 61, 65 and 35. He was ready to lead again in the 1934 Ashes, if the conditions were right for him, and if he were invited to do so by the MCC.

His form with the gun, however, was even better, much to the chagrin of the large animal population. He was a very good shot, as would be expected of someone so flinty-eyed, steady of hand and cool of manner. Several maharajas were more than happy to take him on hunts. Jardine had the best record by far of the tour group, killing a panther, a leopard and a tiger. Stags were a challenge and he bagged many, along with smaller prey, mainly rabbits.

He was disappointed not to go after an elephant. It was prohibited on many estates. Crocodiles took a special kind of courage. They had to be stalked on river banks. If you didn't hit them between the eyes from close range, they would escape or turn stalker themselves, which had ended the lives of many Indians. Lions and tigers had this inclination too. On two different occasions, 'beaters' employed to hit the undergrowth with sticks to force the wildlife into the open were mauled by wounded animals. One Indian never recovered.

Jardine, tongue-in-cheek, commented at the end of the tour that it was a little different from shooting grouse in Scotland.

Despite these 'sporting' relaxations, Jardine felt jaded after two years of continuous cricket. He loved the Indian experience but there were strains in competing as captain that drained even those with the hardiest of constitutions.

47

1934:
BODYLINE ON THE LINE

In early 1934, Bradman was in a good frame of mind, despite the occasional recurrence of the mystery illness that kept him underweight and easily fatigued. He had not taken up an enticing offer to play as a professional in the UK. He turned down a fresh contract with the Sydney *Sun* and more opportunities in radio. He had work in promotions at Palmer's department store, which was an upmarket version of his job at Mick Simmons' sports store.

He was a skilled journalist, although he eschewed the sensational and preferred the factual, which did not always rivet readers. Nevertheless, there would always be papers sold on the basis of his name. Radio too was not his forte. He had a quick wit and enjoyed a humorous observation in his analysis, but he would never progress to being a radio 'personality'.

His intellect required deeper challenges. They were provided by Harry Hodgetts, a member of the Australian

Cricket Board, with which Bradman had not always been on good terms. Hodgetts offered him a career in stock-broking. It was all about stocks and shares and numbers: figures involving buying and selling, and sometimes quick decisions. Broking suited his good numeracy skills. Bradman was keen to accept the offer. The only issue was moving from Sydney to Adelaide. On the one hand, he and Jessie would have to leave family and friends; on the other, it would mean escaping the glare of publicity in Australia's biggest city.

Jessie was not all that thrilled at first, but in the end, she gave the move her blessing. Bradman would join the local Adelaide Club, Kensington, and, in due course, South Australia. His salary would be 700 pounds a year, reduced to 500 pounds when he toured abroad. The contract was for six years. After a long time of disenchantment with his employment and his future, he now had stability. Soon he was learning about bulls, puts and options and reading up on stocks from blue chips to speculative shares.

*

Surrey wanted Jardine to captain the club in 1934 and sent three cables to him in India. He did not reply. Speculation began in the press about whether he would captain England in the Ashes. The Australians were on the way and the MCC needed to settle on a leader before the season began.

The MCC seemed undecided about him. Those who had not yet grasped the true intent and meaning of Bodyline didn't understand what all the fuss was about. Others could see trouble ahead.

Most of the committee still viewed Jardine as the best man to lead, and his conduct in India had generally drawn praise. Warner hoped he would retire after India, but by late February there was still MCC support for him captaining England in June for the First Ashes Test of the season.

Surrey was first to announce that Jardine's business commitments would keep him from playing much in the county games, so he had declined the offer to be its skipper. The MCC then got in touch, saying that if he wished to continue captaining England the same demands placed on him in India would be imposed on him when playing Australia.

There would be no Bodyline.

Jardine saw this as an ultimatum too far.

Warner noted in a private letter to the then Governor of South Australia, Alexander Hore-Ruthven, 'I am not sure I would trust him [as Ashes skipper again]. He is a queer fellow. When he sees a cricket ground with an Australian on it, he goes mad.'

Jardine mulled over his plans. He knew that without Bodyline he would have little chance of beating Bradman who was an even better batsman than he had been in 1930. Jardine needed something to stop or destroy him. If he had known of Bradman's illness, he may have been inclined to use conventional means to get on top early. But Bradman had kept his condition quiet. He didn't wish to give the enemy any advantage. All England saw coming out of Australia regarding Bradman's batting were more telephone numbers.

Jardine felt he was being left impotent. Better to end his career himself rather than have the MCC announce it. He was as proud as any national captain but he was upset by the indirect manner with which he had been pushed aside. He saw it as a betrayal. He had brought back the most prized item in sport, symbolically at least—the tiny Ashes urn—which the two teams had fought over for 53 years in the longest-running international contest between two countries. Not even yachting's America's Cup had been going on as long, and it initially had several teams competing. On 31 March he was reported in the *Evening Standard* as saying, 'I have neither the intention nor the desire to play cricket against Australia this summer.'

It was a bitter pronouncement made without informing the MCC directly. Jardine was the first major casualty of Bodyline, and the most important in terms of the Tests. He had implanted Bodyline with cold clinical precision and tactical brilliance. No one else except Arthur Carr could manage it as well and he had not done it in Tests. It was one thing to cunningly use Larwood and Voce in county games; quite another to do it in the ultimate contest in front of huge national and international audiences.

Jardine needed Bodyline in order to subdue Bradman. Now his main weapon had been taken away. It was as if he had been left standing alone without a big gun facing a lion or tiger. He felt abandoned by the MCC, and that its lack of support was tantamount to a condemnation of his leadership in Australia. He also viewed his effective sacking as a victory for 'the little bastard', who he knew was denouncing Bodyline behind the scenes. This rankled most.

*

Arthur Carr would be 41 during the 1934 season, and was overweight and past his best. He was most popular with the root-and-branch Nottinghamshire members, who had enjoyed their club being at or near the top of the county table for many seasons under his leadership. He had always been a great drawcard, a man who entertained with aggressive, match-winning cricket. There was a feeling of pride in Nottinghamshire, from the high tables of castles and manor houses to the coal mining villages' more modest homes, in knowing that the coming spring months meant another competitive season in the nation's national game.

But the Nottinghamshire Committee was having second thoughts about their biggest drawcard next to the legendary Harold Larwood. The complaints had begun to pile up. Other clubs were upset by his tactics. Lancashire, for one, stated it was considering not playing Nottinghamshire again (it didn't in 1935). This was about as serious as it got in English cricket. On top of that, the drinking culture sanctioned by Carr, along with his careless carousing, was setting an unfavourable tone, which was not advisable for younger players entering the club. It fitted his swashbuckling nature and image but some board members were willing to move past the Carr era. It had been whispered about for several seasons.

Now matters were coming to a head.

48

THE KILLING
OF BODYLINE

Don Bradman did not want to play in the opening tour against Worcester in 1934. He just didn't feel he had the strength, given his lingering mystery illness. But skipper Woodfull would have none of it. He wanted Bradman out in the middle making runs and sending another early message to the opposition. The media turned up in force to see if the champion had lost any of his capacities since they'd last seen him in England in 1930. The 109 journalists, 57 photographers and two film crews waited patiently in their overcoats for Bradman's appearance, which had become a national 'event'. He came to the wicket late in the afternoon after Worcester had been dismissed for 112, and Ponsford had been caught for 13.

He began shakily and then hit a magnificent 206 in 198 minutes before throwing his wicket away. The malady that shadowed him had sapped his strength. Four years earlier he was hungry to go on to 300, 400 and beyond if weather, time and captains would let him. But at 25 years of age, his condition made him think those days were behind him, except if a Test or series depended on it. Already in the calendar year, he had scored 851 runs at the staggering average of 283.66.

Some photographs of the thousands taken picked out a wan and gaunt expression despite his ship-board tan. Yet no one watching doubted that Bradman was still Bradman and would be near impossible to overcome in 1934 if his opening form was any guide.

*

Larwood had been demoralised by Jardine refusing to play against the tourists. Furthermore, he claimed he was not fully fit, which was false.

Mid-May, Larwood was among the few hundred spectators at a game at Sir Julien Cahn's palatial estate. At lunch, his now eight-year sponsor asked him for a private meeting in the pavilion. After some small talk, Cahn, a member of the Nottinghamshire Committee, got to the point. He wanted Larwood to sign a drafted letter to the MCC in which he apologised for his style of bowling in the 1932–33 Ashes.

Larwood was stunned, but had the presence of mind to say, 'I have nothing to apologise for, sir.'

Cahn pointed out that if he did not sign, he would not be selected to play for England. It was an awful blow to Larwood, who always saw Cahn as a moral as well as a financial backer. Now, at a crunch moment, he felt betrayed by a man for whom he had the utmost respect; someone who had hitherto vouched for him since the Bodyline crisis had begun.

The Nottinghamshire champion felt suddenly adrift and alone, a small boat without a rudder in a vast ocean.

Jardine had been cast aside by the MCC, now it was happening to him, and at the hands of the most important Nottinghamshire supporter, who in this case, had been the MCC's emissary.

But Larwood was stubborn. He was not about to grovel to the 'posh' MCC or anyone else for what he had done. He had been ordered by his England captain to bowl in the planned way to destroy Bradman. Larwood would claim he was just obeying orders. This was true. But felling batsmen with vicious deliveries was now becoming commonplace for him and half a dozen other speedsters in the 1934 season. Cricket fans from the village green to Lord's were witnessing what the fuss had been about in Australia. Bodyline was like a viral infection being transmitted to all levels of cricket, even at schoolboy level. It was rapidly losing support in the media and public.

Larwood's oft-repeated remark that 'he just worked under orders' was not having the traction it once had. He was not a robot. He was very much his own man. He and Voce had joked their way through several seasons about who would knock a batsman's head off and earn a beer as a reward. The argument that it was the batsman's fault for not being quick enough to get out of the way of their laser-like deliveries was not washing anymore. They were bowling, not all the time, but in bursts, at the batsman's body with both leg and off fields. It had become a habit. Impartial viewers, with the exception of the loyal Nottinghamshire supporters, were now aware.

On 20 May, the *Sunday Dispatch* announced that Larwood would not play in the First Test at Trent Bridge. He was invited by the MCC to play in a trial match, which meant he was being considered to play for England again. But on advice from Carr, he pulled out of the game, feigning continuing injury issues. Their strategy was risky, believing that after the First Trent Bridge Test there would be a public demand for Larwood to be selected.

He would agree to play if he was allowed to use Bodyline.

Larwood's compelling form gave the plan a modicum of credibility. In three county games in June he took 21 wickets at 11 runs apiece.

Australia's easy win in the First 1934 Ashes Test seemed to help, although his replacement Ken Farnes took ten wickets. Still, Larwood would walk into the national team if he agreed to terms. But the MCC made clear to him that the team captain would set the fields, not the bowler.

Larwood continued to refuse to declare and sign that he would adhere to the MCC's wishes. If he remained obdurate in his principled way, he was on the road to the most cele-brated martyrdom in cricket.

*

While the tourists practised at Lord's in the week prior to the Test there beginning 22 June, Nottinghamshire played Lancashire at Trent Bridge. It was a Test trial for Larwood and Voce, who were contenders for a Test spot, with selector and MCC Committee man T. A. Higson looking on. Carr told his bowlers to deliver 'at their best, unhin-dered'. They did not set Bodyline fields but the placements were on occasions close to them, and their intent was clear. They were aiming at the batsmen and they continually struck Lancashire players. Voce bowled more bumpers, but Larwood was at his best, although not at the pace of earlier seasons. Yet he could still manage to get deliveries to rear into ribcages off good length balls.

At one point he had taken six wickets for 29 runs, conceding just one run.

At the end of the innings the Lancashire management protested, claiming Nottinghamshire had contravened the agreement reached by county captains after the 1933 season that they would not allow 'direct attack' bowling. The newspapers had photos of bruises sustained by deliveries. It meant that any sympathy and support for Larwood would be countered by a growing distaste for Bodyline. The outcry from Lancashire and the press about the bowling method, which had been witnessed by Test selector Higson, forced the issue into the open.

Acting as journalists, Carr and now Jardine pushed for Larwood's selection without restrictions in the Second Test at Lord's, which of course would mean the use of Bodyline. Larwood himself used his writing to justify the technique against Lancashire. It was the last throw of the dice by all three, who had been the main instigators of Bodyline. But it was to no avail.

Then came the bombshell. Larwood declared in the *Sunday Dispatch* five days before the Lord's Test that he had 'definitely made up his mind not to play against Australia in this or any other Test'.

If he couldn't bowl Bodyline he wouldn't play. He admitted to those close to him, including Carr, that he was frightened of what Bradman would do to him. He'd been having nightmares about the 1930 season. His general fitness had slipped and although he was taking wickets with guile, experience and swing, his pace had dropped a yard. The pitches were much slower than in Australia, which meant Larwood would be further retarded. Under these circumstances, Bradman would dispatch him everywhere, an increasingly terrifying thought. He said that 'he didn't want to be embarrassed in front of his own people' as he had been before.

The MCC had taken away his firearm, which he had used to hit slow moving pheasants and the wild duck—Bradman.

Larwood's only way out was to abandon Test cricket.

Bodyline was in danger of being consigned to the dustbin of Test cricket history.

49

HEDLEY MAKES SPIN 'KING' AT LORD'S

Ironically, England won the Lord's Test with ease thanks to the grand spin of Hedley Verity, who took fifteen wickets for 104 runs. Bradman, whose form had slipped, was dismissed by the spinner on a pitch conducive to turn for 36 and 13.

Speed was not a weapon in England's victory.

The Third Test at Manchester and the Fourth at Leeds were both draws. The key factor was Bradman at Leeds who reversed a slump that had kept him from scoring a 50 in six successive Test innings. This time he belted 304 in 430 minutes proving that in spite of his illness, he was back with a vengeance. This augured well for the tourists in the Fifth Test at The Oval with the Ashes up for grabs.

In the meantime, Australia had to play Nottinghamshire at Trent Bridge starting 11 August.

Bradman was injured with a torn thigh muscle and his leg was in a plaster cast. Larwood was judged unfit to play and Carr, who had suffered a shock heart attack, could not take part, although he would watch some of it.

This took the sting out of the game as a gladiatorial event, but still 10,000 spectators turned up to watch. Voce, in better form and fitness than at any time in 1934, decided he had nothing to lose by delivering with a Bodyline field. He took 8 for 66.

Woodfull stood as firm as ever with a defiant 81 and the tourists were dismissed for 237. The Australian skipper said nothing, although he was livid at Voce's reckless display.

Nottinghamshire replied with 183 and Australia was in again late on the second day, and in poor light. Voce sent down two overs—twelve balls including eleven head-high bouncers—before bad light ended the day's play.

Woodfull was now most annoyed by Voce's dangerous and provocative display, which was a protest for not being selected in the Test side, so far. Yet it was an ill-timed, futile act similar to his and Larwood's efforts against Lancashire in mid-June.

The Australian management complained to the MCC. Voce withdrew from the match the next morning, citing 'shin soreness'. There was speculation that he had been ordered not to play, with Carr saying he would have told Voce to play. Woodfull countered by saying that if Voce were selected for the Fifth Test, and he bowled Bodyline, as he had done at Trent Bridge, he would lead his team off the field.

Bluff or not, Voce was not selected.

*

Woodfull won the toss and batted at The Oval, beginning 18 August. Bill Brown was bowled by Clark for 10. Bradman (244) joined Ponsford (266) for a record 351 partnership.

To the surprise of some, Nobby Clark, with the score on 1 for 365 and the batsmen in control, took the new ball and bowled with a full-blown Bodyline field. Jardine and Carr in the press box applauded, along with some in the crowd.

Bradman reacted by hooking Clark's first delivery, a head-high bouncer, for six over square leg. He then hammered a four through mid-wicket. Clark, chastened, was also dealt with by Ponsford, and taken off.

Australia were all out for 701, and 327 in the second innings (Bradman 77), in defeating England by 562 runs to take back the Ashes 2:1.

Bradman's tally was 758 runs at 94.75. Ponsford pipped him with a 95.83 average from 569 runs.

Jardine and Carr both reflected for decades on the 'what-might-have-beens' had Larwood and Voce been allowed to play in the series.

It was the second successive time Bradman had made double hundreds in series-deciding final Tests and winning the Ashes at The Oval, with Larwood playing in one game and not the other. In so doing, Bradman had maintained his position as the world's premier batsman, illness and Bodyline notwithstanding.

*

Nottinghamshire played its last game for the season at Lord's. Voce used Bodyline and hit lower-order Middlesex batsman Len Muncer with a ball that knocked him out cold. He was carried from the ground and took twenty minutes to regain consciousness. Muncer took no further part in the match. Unrepentant, Voce struck others in the chest and head, putting two more players in hospital for checks.

Almost the entire MCC Committee was at the game to witness the onslaught, just at the time they were considering how to handle Bodyline legally. Any reaction under the standing law was still in the hands of umpires, who had yet to deem anything they had seen as a direct attack on a batsman. Clearly, the on-field adjudicators were shying away from being the centre of any controversy.

The last casualty of Bodyline was Carr, its originator. At the end of 1934, he was forced to resign as captain of the county and was dropped from the Nottinghamshire team after fourteen years' service. He still had his interest in hunting, which he loved second only to cricket. His favourite horse for this pastime of chasing foxes with hounds in rural England was called Bodyline.

After a turbulent two years, the three main instigators of direct-attack bowling had been outed and ostracised. The MCC shunned Jardine and Larwood, and Nottinghamshire had ended Carr's long career abruptly.

After being feted and celebrated as heroes on returning from Australia in April 1933, Jardine and Larwood, just eighteen months later, faced bleak years of being ignored and vilified. Carr, too, as an ardent supporter and practitioner of Bodyline, went through a period where he was spoken and whispered about in unflattering terms. He had to wear the opprobrium of accusations about him ruining the game.

It seemed the spirit of cricket was exacting draconian penalties.

*

A month after the Ashes victory, Bradman fell ill with peritonitis, which doctors diagnosed as a slow bursting appendix.

It was the mystery illness that had debilitated him over two years since the end of his US tour in 1932. He had an emergency operation but the surgeons were not confident of his recovery. An infection of the abdominal lining looked likely to succeed where Bodyline had failed.

King George VI was informed that Bradman might not make it. Jessie decided to travel to him and was most relieved to learn while on board a boat that he had recovered. She arrived on 27 October 1934 to be with him in his convalescence, which doctors said had to be at least six months and preferably a year.

*

While Bradman was recovering in London, the MCC was attempting to bury Bodyline by altering, not the laws of the game, but its 'instructions to umpires'. They were directed to intervene in the case of 'systematic bowling of fast, short-pitched balls at the batsman standing clear of the wicket'.

The measure was mild, but it effectively outlawed Bodyline. The umpires were given more power but the issue of field placings, with seven on the leg side and five or six players clustered around the bat, had not been resolved.

*

The British establishment was now certain where it stood on the issue. In November 1934, King George, who noted in his diary how much he admired Woodfull, offered him a knighthood 'for services to cricket'. A prepared citation made an indirect reference to his actions during the Bodyline episode. But Woodfull surprised the Australian governor-general and the King by knocking it back.

Woodfull, who had retired, did not wish to 'inflame' the relations between the UK and Australia by accepting it. Later he explained that if he had been offered the award as an educationalist, he would have accepted it. 'But not for playing cricket,' he said, implying it was just a sport, and not to be treated so seriously.

Bodyline's main perpetrators, Jardine, Larwood and Carr, were finished as influential voices and Test-level performers. The recidivist Bill Voce's career was on life support unless he complied with the directives not to use Bodyline.

The moral and physical courage of Woodfull, Bradman and others had succeeded in saving cricket by not replying with a speed quartet such as Nash, Gilbert, Alexander and Wall.

Bradman would continue as the world's greatest batsman for the next fourteen years. As captain he would win and retain the Ashes in four more contests until he retired after the 1948 tour of England. If anything, he was a tougher cricketer post-Bodyline and more than ever determined to defeat England—within the laws of cricket and in keeping with the spirit of the game.

PART SIX
1936–2021

50

INTIMIDATION
FOREVER

The whiff of Bodyline's corpse lingered at the end of the 1936–37 Ashes in Australia. It was the first Ashes England tour since the controversy and there was still a lot of feeling about an MCC team visit. Local fans wanted revenge, and the choice of Gubby Allen as captain of the touring team was an intelligent move. He had been against Bodyline then and remained so.

Voce was in the squad and had given an undertaking not to use it.

The series was locked at 2:2 when the MCC played Victoria at the MCG beginning 19 February 1937. Laurie Nash, who had been referenced as the answer to England's use of Bodyline in 1932–33, was in the Victorian team. He delivered hostile bumping spells in both England's innings, taking 2 for 21 and 2 for 16. He had a conventional off-side field and bruised six batsmen, including Wally Hammond, with his extra speed and dangerous bounce. He and another speedster, Ernie McCormick, demonstrated what would have happened if Australia had used such bowlers in an answer to Larwood and Voce.

Bradman heard and read reports of the game and England's reaction. He suggested to fellow selectors that Nash should be included in the Australian squad of thirteen for the Fifth and deciding Test. There were objections from Board members on the grounds that a thirteenth person would add an extra unnecessary expense. Bradman pointed to the fact that Nash lived in Melbourne, meaning that there would be no further cost involved.

Gubby Allen was apprehensive about Nash's inclusion. He complained to the Board, saying that Nash should be dropped. But the selectors held firm and Nash remained.

Allen and Hammond then asked for a meeting with Bradman and the trio met for lunch in Melbourne on 25 February. Hammond expressed his annoyance at Nash's behaviour and bowling.

'It would be better all round if you didn't select him,' Allen said.

'No Englishman will decide who Australia selects,' Bradman said. It was not a snap-back, but relayed with his usual directness.

'You want to start a bumper war, do you?' Hammond remarked.

'I can assure you there will be no excessive use of bumpers,' Bradman said, adding, 'it is only a matter of adhering to the spirit of cricket.'

His comment was a reference to Bodyline being outside the game's 'spirit'.

Bradman reckoned 'excessive' was anything over two in an eight-ball over. The English accepted the assurances but remained worried about Nash's inclusion. He was easily the fastest man they'd ever encountered in Australia, and they had no real counter to his aggression, unless they let loose Voce and Farnes, and they were not as quick.

When the Board asked the selectors to drop one player, it was not Nash. Bradman had learnt much about intimidation over the years, particularly during the Bodyline series four years earlier. He said nothing, but let the tourists stew over the possibilities of Nash being picked in the XI.

On the morning of the match, in front of 50,000 fans, the two captains exchanged team sheets. Nash was in Australia's line-up.

'You're not going to have a go at us, are you?' Allen asked. 'We've got Voce and Farnes, you know.'

Bradman replied, 'I told you, there will be no bumper war.'

Bradman batted, and he top scored with 169, following his 270 in the Third Test and 212 in the Fourth to bring Australia back into the Ashes. Australia reached 604. Farnes took 6 for 96, including Bradman, in an excellent lone-hand of pace bowling.

When England's innings began, all eyes were on Nash, a very popular figure for his sheer brilliance as a high-marking, goal-kicking forward for South Melbourne. His deliveries, with the big crowd behind him, were the quickest seen in the series, but he was erratic and inaccurate. Nevertheless, he had all opposition bats jumping, although he didn't hurl down more than half-a-dozen bumpers. He took 4 for 70 and 1 for 34, with a useful bag of English bats: opener C. J. Barnett, Ames, Allen (caught behind for a third-ball duck), Verity and Joe Hardstaff Jr (bowled for 1).

O'Reilly, with 5 for 51 and 3 for 58, had the best figures and benefitted from the lightning speed at the other end.

Australia won by an innings and 200 runs. After a shaky start in the first two Tests, Bradman, in his first series as captain, found his mojo and ended the series with 810 runs at an average of 90.

His inclusion of the tearaway Nash went some way to winning the psychological stakes and the Ashes 3:2. He had learnt much from the approach of both Woodfull and Jardine.

*

After the Bodyline experience, Bradman was always on the lookout for good fast men to include in Australia's Test team. Post–World War II, he had a pair that would match any other opening bowling combination in history—Ray Lindwall and Keith Miller. Lindwall was one of the most lethal bowlers to ever pull on a boot for Australia. He said he had copied Larwood's run-up and action after seeing him bowl in the Bodyline series. Lord (Colin) Cowdrey played against him and another speed demon, Jeff Thomson. He ranked Lindwall as more dangerous.

'He had the capacity to deliver a lifting ball off a good length,' Cowdrey said, 'and his yorker was deadly. You never knew when one or the other was coming.'

Bradman called upon Miller to open the bowling when the all-rounder wanted to concentrate on his batting. Miller was reckless and unpredictable with the ball in hand. He never even took heed of where he dropped his marker, and could run in from a few paces and send down a very fast bumper.

Bradman loved this combination and they were an important factor in Australia winning two Ashes series in 1946–47 and 1948.

In the years after World War II, every cricket-playing nation did its best to nurture and develop pace bowlers who could intimidate and occasionally bruise or injure batsmen. It was a way of life in cricket long before Bodyline, although the 1932–33 series exposed what a highly disciplined tactical attack could 'achieve' in the interests of national pride, a sense of masculine superiority, and winning.

51
JARDINE: DR JEKYLL
OR MR HYDE?

Early in 1959, J. G. Miles, a teacher at leading Melbourne private school, Scotch College, set an essay for his English class: 'Compare and contrast, Douglas Jardine, England's Test Captain during the Bodyline Series, with the main (fictional) character in Robert Louis Stevenson's classic novel *The Strange Case of Dr. Jekyll and Mr. Hyde*'. The project came soon after Jardine's death in 1958.

'Johnny' Miles was a stylish, accomplished district cricketer and 'tragic' who would often talk cricket when he should have been teaching English, history or literature. This unusual exercise was a good excuse to combine two of his loves. He justified it by noting that the school was Scottish, and that both the author and cricketer in this case were also Scots.

Miles had to lecture his class on Jardine and set Stevenson's book as a reading exercise before letting the students tackle the challenging essay. Miles wished to draw out the concept of the duality in man, the good and the evil. This was a big obviously unfair stretch in considering Jardine's character, but there did seem to be two distinct elements to his personality, at least in terms of others' reaction to him, and his acts in regard to others.

R. C. Robertson-Glasgow said of Bradman, in reference to his batting, 'Poetry and murder lived in him together.'

With Jardine, considering his cricket *and* his character, it was charm and brutality together. Robertson-Glasgow thought he could be the best and most considerate of pals, but also a terrible opponent. The writer, himself loquacious, noted Jardine's 'Scottish economy with words and material', which was a way of saying he was laconic and thrifty.

Gubby Allen said he wanted to 'kill him [Jardine]' and found him often infuriating, but also claimed to be his best friend on the Bodyline tour.

Jardine's vice-captain during the 1932–33 tour, Bob Wyatt, was always loyal to him although he disdained his intimidatory tactics. 'He could be "insufferably offensive",' Wyatt noted. There were frequent spontaneous displays of invective in front of other team members that left the victim numb and humiliated. Jardine also showed a 'cold air of disdain' for anyone who crossed him or let him down, with the bat, bowling, behind the wicket or in slack fielding.

Jardine had a lack of empathy in regard to those under him. He showed scant regard for others' feelings. It was very much the way of the military, which underpinned the British Empire, but it did not have to apply so rigidly in sport. Jardine never considered buying a player a beer and telling him that he may have gone over the top in something said.

It was as though he didn't understand the impact of his emotional outbursts and didn't think they could offend in any meaningful way. However, he didn't hold grudges, even though he could be vindictive, such as when he had Frank Tarrant, the umpire in India, fired simply because Jardine felt he was making incorrect LBW decisions.

Bill Bowes stood up to Jardine over Bodyline, not because he was against it, but because he wanted to set his own fields for his bowling style. Long after the series, he said that on reflection he liked and respected his captain for his determination to win, and his meticulous planning.

Duleepsinhji had no time for Jardine and refused to field in the leg trap. He was discarded during the Bodyline series when he was in good form. Jardine's remark about him being a 'conscientious objector' for not fielding in the leg trap was a bullying put-down in front of others.

Those who toured with him to India were split on his character, and there were similar reactions to him from those on the Bodyline tour the year before.

Bryan Valentine, on the 1933–34 Indian trip, thought Jardine the best tactical captain he had played under. Jardine wanted everyone to do exactly as he wished without regard for different personalities, their needs and ways. Some players had to be driven, others encouraged and still others needed coddling. But Jardine ignored all this as 'sissy'. His approach was all in the interests of getting the best out of the team as a unit, regardless of individuality. Jardine often 'rode' the more gifted cricketers to stretch their capacities.

Another tourist, Hopper Levett, didn't think there were many laughs in him and his stern visage. He took it all too seriously. Levett recalled that one morning during the Third

Test, which England was losing, Jardine spoke to the team and quoted from Rudyard Kipling, 'Keep your head when all about you are losing theirs and blaming it on you.'

'I loved it,' Levett said. 'I used it often after that.'

Levett was enjoying the scenic (fun) route of the tour, and the partying, which did not always fit with Jardine's plans; certainly not during the Tests, where the captain stepped up his aggression towards the opposition.

It was not the same as targeting Bradman as 'the little bastard', and attempting to kill him off, tourist John Human said. He had come straight from playing for Cambridge to the tour matches. But still, he added, the leader wanted to win badly enough. Human found him quite *human* and held no grievances. Jardine had taken him under his wing; after all, he was an Oxbridge man.

A contradiction was that Jardine did care for his men, a long way from home and family, especially when they were ill. A few players contracted mild malaria, which was of concern for their families. Jardine went out of his way to write and reassure them. He had done this on the Bodyline tour as well, writing to relatives to ease their fears about what was happening in Australia.

But there was also an element of cruelty in handling his men. Harold Larwood had given his all by the Fifth Bodyline Test, and was hurting from an injured foot. He wanted to leave the field, but Jardine ordered him to remain on the SCG until Bradman was out.

The Ashes had been won easily in the previous Test. There was really no need to grind out a victory at the expense of an injured player, and certainly not the man who had done most to give Jardine the series victory he so obsessively desired.

He played the psychological game with Bradman to the finish, as if not doing so would indicate a slackening of his rectitude; an admission that continuing his cold-hearted drive to win was superfluous.

This was Robert Louis Stevenson's Mr Hyde on the loose.

Yet Larwood never said a bad word about his skipper, to whom he was forever loyal. They would never be close and there would be little fraternising beyond reunions or certain festive occasions—the class divide would not allow it—but that did not downplay mutual respect, a bond of friendship and a liking for each other. Larwood, a man of unsophisticated pleasures, was touched when Jardine gave him a silver ashtray after the Bodyline tour inscribed with the words 'from a grateful skipper'.

Another significant gesture on the positive side for Jardine was that Hedley Verity, who toured twice with Jardine as skipper, named his son after him.

Jardine's most egregious action, for which he has been long remembered, occurred in the Adelaide Test of 1932–33, when a Larwood delivery hit Woodfull over the heart and almost felled the gritty Australian skipper.

'Well bowled, Harold!' Jardine had cried.

Then in Larwood's next over, he clapped hands and six players moved from the off to the leg—'like a school of sharks'—for the Bodyline field. It may have been a provocative action to further rile the baying crowd objecting to Larwood's bowling, but it was a callous, unthinking move, by Mr Hyde again. Twenty years later, when prompted by Australian Prime Minister, Sir Robert Menzies, Jardine did say it may have been a move with which he would like to have had his time over. It took a cricket-loving, high-powered Imperialist to draw out this small concession.

Jardine did have a fanatical side, which was a further peep at Mr Hyde. His messianic desire to defeat Australia was fortunate not to have had more dire consequences, with injured players and rioting crowds.

*

The 'iron in his soul' recognised by his critics was tempered after he married Irene 'Isla' Margaret Peat in London on 14 September 1934, notably after he was done with cricket at the Test level. His new life led to him giving away his first-class career. He was 33 and ready for a change after such an arduous period during and post-Bodyline.

Yet an unfulfilled yearning remained. He could not walk away from the game he loved, which had given him Jekyll and Hyde adrenalin rushes. Jardine's father and father-in-law both wanted him to continue in the law, which added significant family pressures that he could do without.

He stayed with Barings Bank as a clerk so that he could write articles and books on cricket. But this was not particularly successful for him. Jardine carried the stigma of Bodyline. Even *Wisden*, which had been an effusive supporter, did not bother to write an article about him when he retired. It was the ultimate snub, and it hurt the proud Scot.

He was forced to earn money from playing bridge. He tried his hand as a salesman for Cable & Wireless and in marketing for a coal mining company. Then came World War II, and as with Arthur Carr, it was almost a relief for him. Jardine joined the Territorial Army. He served in Dunkirk and was wounded, and eventually posted to India for the remainder of the war. It was no burden. He loved the country and took time to learn Hindustani, saying that if it was good enough for Queen Victoria, it was good enough for him.

After the war, with Bradman employing Lindwall and Miller to upset England, Jardine's standing in the UK cricket community revived. Australia was not using Bodyline, but intimidatory and bruising tactics were on display. English writers began to hark back to 1932–33, the last time England won an Ashes series. There was a nostalgia for winners, and Jardine, regardless of all else, had been one of those on a grand scale.

He found himself being invited to dinner with members of Bradman's 1948 team—the Invincibles—such as Miller, Lindwall, O'Reilly and Lindsay Hassett, although Bradman avoided all contact. Images of Jardine with the old enemy, which was cutting a swathe through English cricket, beating the Test team and counties alike, acted as a rehabilitation of sorts for the outcast, Indian-born Jardine. He even travelled to Australia on business and was surprised to see he was well received with no sense of hard feelings.

In 1954 in England, he and Bradman were in the press box sitting next to each other as journalists covering the Ashes. There could be no love lost between them, but they did often discuss what was happening on the field.

'I would see it one way,' Bradman said, 'and he would see it differently.'

Jardine contracted tick fever in Rhodesia in late 1957. Treatment didn't help his condition. He went to Switzerland for more tests. Doctors discovered his main ailment was lung cancer, which had spread to his stomach and brain. He died on 18 June 1958, aged 57. Isla did what grieving spouses have often done; she threw out or destroyed all his cricket items, including his harlequin cap. It was her way of ridding herself of all the reminders of angst and pain for both of them. Some in the family believed that the stress of the post-Bodyline experience may have contributed to Jardine's cancer.

Bradman refused to comment on Jardine's death, rather than saying anything derogatory. He could never forgive Jardine for the damage he wreaked on the game, and for his efforts to destroy him. Larwood, poignantly, expressed his love for Jardine, which was quite an admission for a man of that era.

With time, and as the memories of adversaries faded, Jardine has come to be seen in a better light. Some commentators with obvious motives and others have revived and complemented his memory and image as a ruthless, yet outstanding tactician.

Only Dr Jekyll is seen now.

*

In 1963, after rejecting a knighthood nearly 30 years earlier, Bill Woodfull was invested with an Officer of the Order of the British Empire (OBE) for services to education. He was headmaster for six years at Melbourne High School, one of Australia's top educational institutions. Two years later, aged 67, he collapsed and died playing golf in Tweed Heads, New South Wales.

Just as the Jardine family believed that the mental pressure had foreshortened Jardine's life, the Woodfull family were adamant that the Bodyline attack had permanently damaged Bill's health and curtailed his life. Both are likely.

Furthermore, Woodfull took more hits on the body—and particularly the area above the heart—than any other Australian, including Ponsford, who also took a hammering. Several batsmen have been struck over the heart and killed on the pitch over the decades.

Bill Woodfull, showing the courage he demonstrated on the pitch, managed to live on with a disability for another 34 years after Bodyline. His moral fortitude meant he should take most credit for ending the tactic that would have ruined cricket as a spectacle, not to mention the injury and misery it would have caused.

52

REDEMPTION

Harold Larwood was not done with first-class cricket after Bodyline finished his Test career. He battled on with Nottinghamshire, playing well, but enjoying it less. Carr's absence meant that the game was not the same at county level. Yet he kept on taking wickets, up, down and across England. In his benefit year, 1936, he took 119 wickets at 12.97, which indicated that he was still as effective as ever at first-class level. It brought the inevitable speculation that he might make a comeback for England. It was always open to the MCC to invite him, but he would not play unfettered. However, his closest mate, Bill Voce, capitulated to MCC terms not to bowl Bodyline, and was selected to play Australia in the 1936–37 Ashes campaign after the captain, Gubby Allen, had talked him into it. It caused a serious rift between the Nottinghamshire close pals. Not even a 'beer or two' at the local could solve their differences.

Voce's defence was that he was 27 with possibly a decade left at the top. He was struggling with income, even playing semi-professional football in the winter to bring in some much-needed money. He now felt it was folly to be stubborn about a principle which affected his family's well-being. It was a heart-breaking moment for both.

Larwood walked away feeling more betrayed and isolated than ever.

His support base had eroded. Jardine was gone from the game; Carr was on the fringe without influence and the MCC had abandoned him. Now his best mate, the man whom he admired as much as anyone in life, was leaving him stranded. After a few months' estrangement, his wife, Lois, said he had to patch up the disagreement. Voce was too good a friend to lose. The two got very drunk together, argued more and yelled at each other. Then they buried their differences which were never spoken about again.

It showed Larwood as a good character, who could not hold a grudge for long. He wished Voce well on the 1936–37 tour.

But it led Larwood to drinking more, and enjoying that less also in the lowest ebb in his life. He turned up drunk for the first day's play for Nottinghamshire a couple of times, which did not endear him to the club or the new captain, the straitlaced George Heane.

Carr would have slapped him on the back and laughed it off, but those days were long gone. A player complained about Larwood and Voce getting drunk and demonstrative in a pub after a game in 1938. Their behaviour was not a secret, and had been going on for a decade.

The committee summonsed them. Its members wouldn't say who had pimped on them.

Both the Bodyliners were angry. At net practice that night, Larwood bowled faster and more dangerously than anyone had seen him at three players suspected of being the complainant. George Heane received the roughest treatment with two hits on the shoulder and chest. Another split his box open.

All the victims were said to be non-drinkers.

Larwood was using his exceptional skill again in an effort to hurt someone, making a mockery of his claims that he never deliberately sought to do so. His argument that the batsmen were not good and fast enough to get out of the way had long ago run dry. He had been hitting others ever since he knew he had something special in the power of his right arm.

Larwood was not alone. A legion of speed bowlers had done the same for a century and would within the laws for another. It was not a new attitude. But Larwood's gifts for being able to aim the ball at any target, stationary or otherwise, with more speed than almost anyone made him that much more dangerous. It was a big part of the sport's attraction to most except the recipients of the deliveries.

England and Nottinghamshire had had their moments of glory because of it.

The club asked Larwood to play for it in a last hurrah against Bradman's touring Australians in 1938. He refused. He was ill again at the thought of delivering at less than his former full pace with Bradman knocking him around the field. It was the old nightmare, which he'd lived so much of, returning to haunt him. It made him anxious. Larwood also was depressed at the idea of meeting any of the Australians he had played against, even some he liked, such as Bert Oldfield.

The committee had their eyes on the gate receipts if there was another Bradman–Larwood confrontation on the pitch. They tried goading him, writing, 'It would redound to your credit if you did play.'

There would be no redounding. He was traumatised at the thought of it.

*

The reported drinking incident was the final straw for him and the Nottinghamshire Committee. They parted ways at the end of 1938.

He joined Blackpool in the Ribblesdale League for the 1939 season, and moved with his family to the working-class seaside holiday town. The ground he played on was not the MCG or Trent Bridge and a long way from his highs and lows in Sydney. But humble Larwood did not care if the Blackpool Tower overlooked the ground and not the gasholder at The Oval. He was at home with the working-class inhabitants and passing parade of holidaymakers, who might gawk at Larwood the legend in the thin afternoon light and then play in the beach-front amusement arcades.

No one who stopped for an hour or so to watch him bowl would forget his perfect action, silent run to the wicket and rhythmic delivery. He was too much for his opponents even bowling at half-pace. Every now and again, the crowd would urge him to let one rip at a batsman, and Larwood, for the fun of it, would oblige with a throat-high short one. He had lost none of his accuracy. He clean-bowled 41 batsmen of 68 wickets at 10.57 apiece, and bruised plenty more.

War ended his cricketing career. He worked as a market gardener and when the conflict was over bought a Blackpool sweet shop, which was a struggle to run, especially with post-war rationing.

In 1948, as Bradman and the Invincibles were winning their way around the UK, Bert Oldfield bumped into Larwood at a Blackpool bat maker's outlet. This led to Jack Fingleton and Oldfield visiting Larwood at his sweet shop, followed by beers and reminiscences about cricket. The two Australians realised that Larwood was lonely and disillusioned, fed up with his treatment by his own countrymen at the top of cricket and in the media. It hurt that they ignored him. He was reclusive and dispirited.

Fingleton waxed lyrical about Australia, and surprisingly saw a spark of interest in his old foe. Larwood recalled the wonderful reception he received after his 98 in the 1933 Fifth Ashes Test in Sydney, and regarded the population as fair-minded. He realised then that despite the booing and howling at Bodyline, the cricket fans were discerning. They were angry at Jardine for his hard-nosed destruction of Australian batsmen, yet thrilled at a player who would 'have a go' to entertain them with the bat.

It was a simple, yet contradictory reaction based on emotion, but reassuring for Larwood, who would never forget it.

Fingleton tried to arrange for Larwood to come to the 1948 Old Trafford Test. Lindwall, in particular, wanted to meet his inspiration to bowl fast. O'Reilly also wished to make his re-acquaintance without a ball coming at him at 160 kph.

In the end, he didn't show up. Larwood had for years been struck by anxiety and concern about how people judged him. He was tempted but did not want the attention.

Then Larwood received a shock invitation to attend a grand luncheon at the Savoy Hotel in London, which would include many dignitaries, the high and mighty of the UK, and players of note. It had been arranged by *the people* to farewell Bradman after his last Ashes tour. He had been shown the list of possible invitees and had approved Larwood coming.

Again, Larwood worked himself into a lather of nerves over attending despite the enthusiasm of Fingleton, Lindwall, Miller, Oldfield and others.

He said no. But then Lois stepped in again and told him to turn up.

It was September 1948, and one of the most magnificent all-time bowlers left Blackpool and the isolation he'd felt since before World War II. He enjoyed the event and felt appreciated. He was even photographed having a smiling chat with Bradman. They shook hands. They could be cordial at best, but never close. The Australian was at the peak of his career and polled as the most popular man in Britain in 1948, even ahead of King George VI.

Larwood felt the gulf between them, but Bradman's welcoming of him, along with the attitude of a score of Australians in attendance, gave him an idea. He had a wife and five daughters and he began thinking about their future in sunny Australia, as opposed to their grim outlook for England post-war.

Fingleton portrayed the land down under as an alluring, classless Utopia.

Larwood and his family eventually decided to make the move.

53

A RAPPROCHEMENT
OF SORTS

In 1949, the MCC included Harold Larwood in a list of
26 players to be made honorary Club members—the most
exclusive in the cricketing world—and one redolent of the
British establishment. It had taken fifteen years for his
rehabilitation and his public handshake with Bradman had
much to do with it.

A year later, the Larwoods emigrated to Australia and
received a warm welcome. They stayed at first in a Sydney
hotel. In secret, former Australian prime minister, Ben
Chifley, a cricket fan, picked up half the bill. Soon afterwards, accommodation was found for them at Kingsford
in Sydney's east, and Larwood was quickly employed by
a soft-drink company. The general reaction from Australians astonished the new immigrant. He realised that his
bitterness and fears were unfounded.

Late in 1950, Larwood was in George Street in the city with
his daughter Mary when they bumped into (now Sir Donald)

Bradman, who was up from Adelaide for a business meeting. He had become a successful Adelaide stockbroker as well as being a member of the Australian Cricket Board. They shook hands and exchanged pleasantries. Larwood would like to have spoken longer but didn't know what to say. Both men preferred to forget what had put them in the ring together.

Reaching for something, Larwood remarked, 'It's not like the old days.'

Bradman asked what he meant.

'Well, 20 years ago,' Larwood explained, 'there'd be a hundred people around us by now.'

It wasn't quite the same for Bradman. He had retired from all cricket a year earlier but was still the most recognisable face in Australia. But he agreed with Larwood. Both had abhorred the overreaction of fans and the media, and were happy to go through life without that sort of attention. Both hated intrusion into their private lives.

They chatted for several minutes. Bradman was pleased that Larwood had settled in well in his adopted country and that his daughter was happy with the move too.

Then they parted with no plans to meet again.

*

Larwood always praised Bradman, the batsman, but in private, the differences between them had festered in the Englishman's mind. He had never liked Bradman since Jardine had drilled a negative attitude into the Bodyline team about him. Now Larwood was living in Australia, he envied Bradman's wealth and detested the public adulation for him. Bradman's success in the game and his professional life had allowed him to move on. Larwood dwelt often on the cards he'd been dealt. His mindset was rooted in the traumatic events from 1932 to 1934.

But as the decades rolled on, and after a few more polite chats with his former archrival, Larwood mellowed in his attitude. They had a more affable, long chat at the Centenary Test in Melbourne in 1977, which Larwood had to be cajoled in to attending. Once more, it took Lois's directive to show courage and attend.

Bradman was no longer a Cricket Board member. He had left stockbroking and journalism. He still had several company directorships. There was also unpaid work on occasion for the South Australian Cricket Association, and he was endlessly being asked to help charities, but otherwise he had 'retired' while keeping his mind very active. His time was consumed by golf, playing bridge, watching sport on TV, reading, and replying to some of the 2000-odd letters he received each week.

He too had mellowed, and gave the impression to close friends that he did not dislike Larwood. Regardless of their feelings for each other, they were locked together forever in the pantheon of great sporting combatants.

In 1993, big cricket fan and British prime minister, John Major, engineered an MBE for Larwood, then aged 88. Fingleton and others had tried for decades for some official recognition, but they were ignored. Larwood himself thought it was long overdue and was convinced Bradman had been behind it. When asked by several interviewers why the honour had come so late in life, Larwood replied, 'I think The Don had something to do with it.'

'I heard that,' Bradman said, when asked at the time about the MBE, 'but no, I didn't know Major.'

'You didn't say anything to anyone [of influence in the UK] about him [Larwood]?'

'I've been asked about my opinion of him countless times, but not specifically about honours, no.'

It was probably wishful thinking on Larwood's part, and demonstrated a sad obsession with not being able to embrace Bradman late in life. If Larwood felt any recriminations for his actions in the Bodyline series, they were forever outweighed by his duty to Jardine and England. For Bradman's part, supporting a high recognition of Bodyline's finest purveyor would have been tantamount to condoning Jardine's methods.

Bradman could forgive, but he could not forget.

Harold Larwood died on 22 July 1995, aged 90. (His loyal wife, Lois, who he said was the true strength and love of his life, died in 2001.) His life had not been foreshortened because of physical injury. But his prolonged apprehension over the way people reacted to him caused sixteen years of insecurity and intermittent misery until he settled in Australia.

Bradman did not wait for the media to ring him to comment on Larwood's passing. He pre-empted a rush of calls by phoning two major newspapers to read out a one-line statement, 'Harold Larwood will live in history as one of the greatest bowlers of all time.'

It was an honest assessment, and supreme praise from the greatest ever batsman and cricketer, who rarely spoke in superlatives, mainly because he had attained the highest standards in the game.

54

THE VICTOR IN LIFE

The ultimate target of Bodyline, Don Bradman, came through the ordeal and went on with his life undaunted for nearly the next seven decades. He was Australia's tallest poppy, and many wanted to cut him down. Some are still attempting it, posthumously. The Bodyline experience prepared him for most negative or tough issues he would face in his 92 years of life as a cricketer, an administrator, a businessman and a family man.

After Bodyline, he had doubts about continuing on with cricket for his country. He considered becoming a professional in England, or a journalist, and decided instead to become a stockbroker in Adelaide. This was about as conservative and invisible as one could get in Australia, alongside banking or undertaking. It showed where his mind was. He hated the limelight. Broking gave him the security he wanted, although upheavals in that world in 1945 also challenged him when his boss, Harry Hodgetts, acted fraudulently and nearly dragged Bradman's career down too.

The steady broking job allowed him to continue with his career post-Bodyline from 1934 to his retirement from the sport in 1949. He combined his cricket administration duties with the job until 1954, when mentally exhausted from doubling up, he gave away broking. He took up some of the many offers for business directorships, which, along with covering Ashes series as a journalist, gave him enough income to continue with his prime unpaid jobs in national, state and club cricket.

In so doing, he gave back to the game more than any other cricketer in Australian history. He eschewed the celebrity status of many former stars, which would keep them in the public eye, and stayed in the background as the éminence grise of Australian cricket. Even after retirement from the Cricket Board, he was the 'go-to man' with whom Australian media mogul Kerry Packer negotiated after his disruptive World Series Cricket circus foray. As Richie Benaud told Packer, nothing at the top level got done without Bradman's approval.

Bradman held his privacy dear. He submitted to just one proper biography, in which he was interrogated over six years. Yet he was accessible to journalists. Many cricket writers and top paper editors had his number, but they dared not use it unless they had something 'important' or specific to ask. Some reporters tried to turn conversations into interviews that would end up as full-blown articles based on one or two Bradman responses, which he detested. He put a stop to that abruptly.

Prominent cricket journalist Robert Craddock once rang him to ask him something. 'Just one question,' Craddock said, and then got side-tracked on another topic, to which Bradman responded. Without trying to con Bradman into responses that might lead to a newspaper article, Craddock then returned to his original query, but was cut off.

'You've had your one question,' Bradman said.

He responded to interviews in books and radio and TV programs about Bodyline for more than 60 years, and said much the same as he had in his autobiography, *Farewell to Cricket*. In essence, it was disastrous for cricket and had to be nipped in the bud.

Bradman was patient with all questioners, as tedious as he must have found the repetitive queries. He realised that everyone, from the less informed and those who had little or no interest in cricket, to historians and 'experts', wanted to hear from him on the hottest ever topic in the game, if not all sport.

Second to none on the field, he also excelled as an administrator, working on a range of difficult topics, from Bodyline to the law on throwing, which he ironed out with George 'Gubby' Allen when he became a key committee man at the MCC and president in 1963.

Bradman also consulted Allen on the Apartheid issue when South Africa refused to play against England with a so-called 'Cape Coloured' player, Basil D'Oliveira, in its team in 1968. Bradman further quizzed the two British prime ministers handling the topic (Harold Wilson and Ted Heath), and also the fascist South African prime minister, John Vorster. Armed with adequate information, Bradman then decided that Australia would not play South Africa until they chose 'a team on a non-racial basis'. That ruling stood from 1971 to 1993 when Apartheid was well finished.

It was his most important, and least publicised achievement of many in the interests of the game.

Don Bradman died on 25 February 2001, aged 92.

55

FEAR AND DANGER

Intimidation will never be taken out of cricket. It is part of the game, and crude as it may be, it's still an art form of the game. It was most notably reintroduced in the 1940s by Australia's Ray Lindwall and Keith Miller. England countered with Frank 'Typhoon' Tyson in the 1950s, one of the more eloquent pacemen. He spoke of a sense of 'omnipotence' at the impact of his furious pace and bouncers over batsmen.

Tyson was followed in the 1960s by the lethal West Indian combination of Wes Hall and Charlie Griffith, described by English writer Ian Wooldridge as 'hired assassins'. They ran a swathe through England, Australia and other opposition. Hall knocked out Australian Test player, Bob Cowper, one of the finest ever players of bouncers, in a game against Victoria. Hall also menaced one of England's greatest batsmen, Colin Cowdrey, and broke his arm in the Lord's Test of 1963.

South Africa had its angry pacemen too. Peter Heine was so annoyed by the blocking skills of England's Trevor Bailey that he let go a stream of invective, ending with an unthinking, 'I want to hit you over the heart!'

England was never far away from coming up with a speed merchant. John Snow fitted the bill at the beginning of the 1970s when he was the most effective player in the 1970–71 Ashes in Australia. Less articulate than Tyson, but more coldly vocal, Snow told the media he was unashamed of leaving a trail of broken fingers and hands.

'That's what I'm there for,' he said.

He qualified this by saying he was not there to inflict deliberate injury, but did not explain *how* he would manage that while smashing limbs. His words had a shade more integrity than the 'I just take orders' commentary from Larwood, but were nearly as disingenuous. No one could ensure, when bowling in order to smash hands or ribs, that the balls would not collide with skulls or chests.

That sort of open, public pronouncement led to the era of Australia's Dennis Lillee and Jeff Thomson. They spoke of *loving* to hit batsmen. Lillee revelled, he said, in striking batsmen in the ribcage with bouncers. Thomson went one further, with the appalling statement, 'Hitting a batman's skull was music to my ears.'

Larwood and Voce couldn't have expressed it better, had they been bowling in that era.

The peak of the Lillee–Thomson terror occurred in the 1974–75 Ashes series. No part of the body was sacrosanct or missed, with heads, boxes, limbs, chests and hands all targeted.

Colin Cowdrey, aged 42, and with a figure more pyramidic than in his earlier days when Wes Hall broke his arm, was England's most experienced player in facing cricket's cannonballs. He was flown out from London on a jumbo jet to replace the battlefield wounded.

It was a Trafalgar/Dunkirk moment for the brave veteran.

Despite considerable and necessary padding, Cowdrey took a fearful battering from Thomson.

Both speed demons were revved up by the Australian crowds, who at one point chanted, 'Kill, kill, kill!' Some fans, intoxicated or otherwise, had in mind John Snow's torment of Australian bats four years earlier. Those with longer memories recalled the Bodyliners of four *decades* earlier.

It was only by chance that Thomson did not get his wish to see English blood on the pitch, and certainly not by umpires doing their duty in stopping intimidatory bowling.

Yet death on the pitch was just a breath or two away.

After the 1974–75 Ashes series, England moved on to New Zealand, which was always more relaxing after the intensity of Australian tours. But it was anything but that when New Zealand number seven, Ewen Chatfield, was felled by a bouncer from England's Peter Lever. It deflected from the bat into Chatfield's temple. He collapsed. His heart stopped beating. Prompt mouth-to-mouth resuscitated him. Chatfield lived.

This terrible incident caused much comment in the world's media, but did not stop the dangerous tactics. In the next Australian summer, Australia's body hunters went on with their methods against the West Indies. In turn the West Indies ditched their spinners in favour of vicious pace against India in 1976 in the Caribbean.

Michael Holding led the way, smashing skulls, faces and hands. Later that year, the West Indies began with their run of the great and fearsome quartet of pacemen: Andy Roberts, Holding, Wayne Daniel and Vanburn Holder.

In the late 1970s, Kerry Packer salivated over all this and saw the potential in TV broadcasting and creating a breakaway 'Test' competition. His 'World Series Cricket' institutionalised the gladiatorial elements of the game, but the sense that they were fabricated contests, no matter how combative, soon saw a drop in TV viewers and spectators. Yet still, helmets became part of most batsmen's protection.

By 1980, the national Test sides were back in action as before with the West Indies resuming their presentation of 'awesome foursomes' of clinically intimidating bowlers through the 1980s and into the 1990s. Their tactics were successful but damaging to cricket as a viewing spectacle. The bowlers were taking six or seven minutes to deliver an over of their short stuff, which took away many batting strokes, particularly off the front foot.

Only the advent of Shane Warne and his great leg spin in 1991 turned the game on its head. Pace was still a pre-requisite to win Tests, but Warne and other spinners added the dimension of the turning ball, which had been largely neglected for two decades. It also brought back front-foot batting strokes, and made the contest more entertaining—and quicker. Warne was known to deliver six balls in less than two minutes, which was far better viewing at the match or on the TV screen.

Added to this, at last, were laws in the game. The liberal use of the short ball was eventually thwarted in late 1991 when bowlers were restricted to one bouncer per batsman an over. In 1994 this was increased to two, which remains today.

While Bodyline no longer exists, its intention to intimidate, and if necessary, bruise a batsman into submission or a mis-stroke in self-defence, remains.

Even with the law and body protection that the Bradman era did not have, batsmen facing the fast men of the modern era will have to show as much courage and skill as their predecessors.

56

NOT BODYLINE, BUT INTENTION THE SAME

At least sixteen known fatalities have occurred in major cricket matches since 1624 and many more in lower grades. About a third of them were because of short-pitched deliveries that struck batsmen in the head or over the heart. The most tragic in recent years occurred on 25 November 2014 when South Australian Test cricketer, Phillip Hughes, was hit on the base of the skull below the ear by a fast, lifting ball from Sean Abbott of New South Wales. Hughes had tried to hook, which countless batsmen at every level of the game try or do every day somewhere cricket is played.

Aged just 25, he died two days later.

Abbott, who was not a venomous fast-medium bowler, also felled Victorian batsman Will Pucovski during another Shield match on 4 March 2018. Lower grades of the game have also had their fatalities. Forty-three years earlier, Martin Bedkober, aged 22, playing for Toombul in Brisbane, was hit by a medium-fast delivery on the chest just above the heart.

He died in hospital soon afterwards. These and other incidents have all been branded as 'freak', or 'one-in-a-million', or pure bad luck. The frequency of the deadly strikes has been limited, and this underplays the very real dangers of the game.

*

A further incident occurred in the 2019 Ashes involving the prolific Australian batsman Steve Smith who was emerging as at least Bradmanesque. After much leather chasing during his innings over two Ashes series in 2015 and 2017–18, England was thrilled to add the Barbados-born Sussex speedster Jofra Archer to its bowling squad in 2019, especially after the First Test at Edgbaston when Smith scored big centuries in both innings.

Archer, aged 24, was chosen for his international debut in the Second Test at Lord's only nine years after moving to England at age fifteen. He was billed as a 'master-blaster'; a modern-day Harold Larwood. Many newspapers revelled in saying that if England couldn't bowl Smith out, they would blast him out. The pre-match media coverage was similar to the build-up to the Larwood–Bradman contests nearly 90 years earlier.

Smith reached 80 at Lord's. Archer managed to deliver him a painful blow on the forearm at the beginning of the over, which was recorded as the fastest ever. The English crowd bayed for more. In seconds, the atmosphere at gentle, polite Lord's turned into something like a Roman colloseum. In the language of the boxing ring, the arm smash had softened Smith up for another hit. It came in the form of a ripping throat-high bouncer that pole-axed the batsman.

The crowd in some sections of the ground clapped and cheered as Smith went down hard. Then even the part-intoxicated in the Compton Stand—the cheap seats at 300 dollars each—went quiet. Australians in the audience wondered if this was another Phillip Hughes moment. Had Smith been killed? Movement and being helped to his feet buried that fear, for the moment. Smith retired hurt, returned at the fall of a wicket, and batted like a concussed individual riding his luck, which he was, on both counts. He was removed LBW for 92.

The British media rejoiced. This was a 'gotcha' moment, so grotesquely expressed by a tabloid during the war with Argentina in 1983 when the battleship *Belgrano* was sunk. During the Lord's Test, there was glee as salivating writers spoke of their new Ashes-winning 'weapon'.

Jofra Archer is terrific and terrifying. He bowls his short ball with the same ferocity and level of bounce as Lindwall and Malcolm Marshall before him. The big difference is that those two top-class pacemen dropped their shoulders a fraction and whipped the ball at Adam's apples with a sling-shot action approaching round-arm. It was a split-second indicator for the receiver to take evasive action. Archer, however, bowls his carotid delivery without a discernible difference in his high arm delivery movement, making it even more problematic for the intended victim, and very similar to Larwood's explosive style.

England was lifted. Smith was knocked out of the rest of the Lord's Test and all of the Third Test at Headingley, which was won by England, thanks to a miraculous innings from Ben Stokes.

A recovered Smith was selected for the Fourth Test at Old Trafford. British cricket commentary went into overdrive about what Archer would do to him and the other Australian bats.

When pushed in a media conference about this, Smith delivered his boyish grin and said, despite all the hype, Archer was yet to actually get him out. He reminded the media, sagely, that if England was bowling at his head, they were not aiming at his stumps, or for a catch. The implication was that this approach would bring the English bowlers under his control. He would wear them down, which he did to the tune of 211, and a quickfire 82 in a second innings when chasing runs for a declaration.

For the record, Smith punished Archer in this Test and ended the series with 774 runs at an average of 110.57, exactly 200 short of Bradman's 1930 aggregate from the same number of innings.

Archer said he was cold and tired at the Old Trafford Fourth Test, in a game which was a leveller for him following the overblown media reaction after Lord's. (He never did take Smith's wicket in the series, yet ended with the top-class return of 22 wickets at 20.27 runs per wicket.)

Smith's courage in the way he prepared for the return and his performance were exceptional and admirable. In this way, he was similar to Bradman in 1934 in the Fourth Test at Leeds with his score of 304. For different reasons they showed courage beyond the call and were fortunate to survive.

Since that start to his international career, Archer has been over-bowled and an elbow injury to his delivery arm kept him from playing at all in the first half of 2020. But he was back in the second half, causing trouble with explosive deliveries to Australian batsmen in the three One Day Internationals in England in September.

England was doing its best to manage him through 2021, hoping he would be primed for the Ashes, the biggest contest in international cricket. But by August 2021 he was declared unfit for the Ashes series (which was in doubt because of Covid restrictions).

*

In the first Test in Perth of the 2019 series, Australia v New Zealand, Australia captain Tim Paine commented to the media about the Kiwis' short-pitching plan that had worked so well in the home team's collapse of 7 for 58. The burst included an extraordinary passage of play where batsman Matthew Wade stood his ground and let paceman Neil Wagner hit him several times on the arm. Wade had also shown enormous grit facing Archer in the 2019 Ashes.

'It was great theatre, wasn't it?' Paine said. 'We were just having a laugh before when we were bowling at their tail; we think it's going to be a bit of Bodyline for a lot of the series.'

Paine was trying to drum up interest in a lopsided contest which Australia won easily 3:0. Technically it was dissimilar to Bodyline, which in theory had been banned in 1934, but not actually outlawed. That did not occur until 23 years later in 1957, when the laws were changed so that only two fielders were allowed behind square (close in or not) on the leg side.

It killed off Bodyline forever as it was delivered by Larwood, Voce and others. But its reinventions within the laws are as dangerous as ever.

BIBLIOGRAPHY

Arlott, John, *Gone to the Test Match*, Longmans, Green and Co. London, 1949.

Barnes, Sid, *It Isn't Cricket*, Collins, Sydney, 1953.

Bedser, Alec and Eric, *Following On*, Evans Brothers Ltd, London, 1954.

Bradman, Don, *Farewell to Cricket*, Hodder and Stoughton, London, 1950.

—*The Bradman Albums*, Rigby, Sydney, 1987.

—*The Art of Cricket*, Hodder & Stoughton, London, 1990.

Bromby, Robin, Ed., *A Century of Ashes*, Resolution Press, Sydney, 1982.

Carr, Arthur, *Cricket with the Lid Off*, Hutchinson and Co., London, 1934.

Douglas, Christopher, *Douglas Jardine: Spartan Cricketer*, Methuen, Slingsby, 2003.

Fingleton, Jack, *Brightly Fades the Don*, Collins, London, 1949.

Frindall, W. H., *The Wisden Book of Cricket 1887–1984*, MacDonald Publishing, Guild Publishing, London, 1985.

Frith, David, *Bodyline Autopsy*, ABC Books, Sydney, 2002.

Geddes, Margaret, *Remembering Bradman*, Viking, Sydney, 2002.

Hamilton, Duncan, *Harold Larwood*, Quercus, London, 2009.

Harvey, Neil, *My World of Cricket*, Hodder and Stoughton, London, 1963.

Heald, Tim, *Denis Compton*, Pavilion, London, 1994.

Hobbs, Jack, *My Life Story*, 'The Star' Publications, London, 1935.

Howat, Gerald, *Len Hutton*, Heinemann Kingswood, London, 1988.

Jardine, Douglas, *In Quest of the Ashes*, Rigby, London, 1984.

Larwood, Harold, *Bodyline?*, Elkin Mathews & Marrot Ltd, London, 1933.

Lillee, Dennis, *Over & Out!*, Methuen, Sydney, 1984.

Lindwall, Ray, *Flying Stumps*, Stanley Paul and Co., London, 1954.

McHarg, Jack, *Arthur Morris, An Elegant Genius*, ABC Books, Sydney, 1995.

Mailey, Arthur, *And Then There Came Larwood*, The Sportsman's Book Club, London, 1933.

Martin-Jenkins, Christopher, *World Cricketers: A Biographical Dictionary*, Oxford University Press, Oxford, 1996.

O'Reilly, W. J., *Cricket Conquest*, Werner Laurie, London, 1949.

Perry, Roland, *The Fifth Man*, Sidgwick & Jackson, London, 1994.

—*The Don*, Macmillan, Sydney, 1994.

—*Captain Australia*, Random House Australia, Sydney, 2000.

—*Bradman's Best*, Random House, Sydney, 2001.

—*Bradman's Best Ashes Teams*, Random House, Sydney, 2002.

—*Miller's Luck*, Random House Australia, Sydney, 2005.

—*Bradman's Invincibles*, Hachette Australia, Sydney, 2008.

—*Tea and Scotch With Bradman*, ABC Books, Sydney, 2019.

Pollard, Jack, *The Complete Illustrated History of Australian Cricket*, Viking, Melbourne, 1995.

Preston, Hubert, Ed., *Wisden Cricketers' Almanack, 1949*, Wisden, London, 1949.

Rae, Simon, *It's Not Cricket*, Faber and Faber, London, 2002.

Rippon, Anton, *Classic Moments of the Ashes*, J. M. Dent, Melbourne, 1982.

Wakley, B. J., *Bradman the Great*, Mainstream Publishing, London, 1999.

Wallace, Christine, *The Private Don*, A Sue Hines Book, Allen & Unwin, Sydney, 2004.

Webster, Ray, *First–Class Cricket in Australia*, Volumes 1 & 2, Victoria, 1997.

William, Charles, *Bradman: An Australian Hero*, Abacus, London, 1996.

Wynne-Thomas, Peter, *Arthur Carr*, Chequered Flag Publishing, London, 2017.

Yardley, N. W. D. and Kilburn, J. M., *Homes of Sport*, Peter Garnett, London, 1952.

ACKNOWLEDGEMENTS

I wish to thank Allen & Unwin's Tom Gilliatt for the opportunity to publish this book, my thirty-seventh.

Thanks also to my agent Jo Butler. Those who contributed specifically on the topic with interviews, correspondence, files, information, photographs and inspiration over 50 years include Sir Donald Bradman, Lady Bradman, John Bradman, Geoff Collins, Dean Golja, Professor Mary Finsterer, Dr Felix Nobis, Thos Hodgson, Bruce Woodley, Neil Harvey, Keith Stackpole, Sam Loxton, Arthur Morris, Lindsay Hassett, Richie Benaud, Martin Ashenden, Alec Bedser, Eric Bedser, Denis Compton, Lord (Colin) Cowdrey, Godfrey Evans, Gus Glendinning, Jack Grossman, Ian Johnson, Ross Johnston, Bill Johnston, Ray Lindwall, Grant McAlpine, Tony Maylam, Ken Jungwirth, Keith Miller, (also Miller's family, notably Denis Miller, Bob Miller and Miller's niece Jan Beames), John Miles, Mary Newham, Lady Pippa O'Brien, John MacWhirter,

Rod Mater, David Temple, John Hay, Alan Young, Ian Craig, Alan Davidson, Basil Grapsis, Peter Philpott, Doug Ring, Ron Hamence, Paul Ritchie, Vicki Ritchie, Sachin Tendulkar, Barry Richards, Boss Tapia, Bamboo Tapia, and Tony Walker.

INDEX

Roland Perry OAM is one of Australia's most prolific and versatile authors—from biography to politics, espionage, military history, royalty and sport, and including six novels. His sports books include biographies of Sir Donald Bradman, Steve Waugh, Keith Miller, Shane Warne and sailor Rolly Tasker.

His awards include the Fellowship of Australian Writers National Literary Award for Non-fiction in 2004 for *Monash: The Outsider Who Won a War*, and the UK Cricket Society 2006 Cricket Biography the Year for *Miller's Luck*, which was also named the UK *Daily Mail*'s Sports Book of the Year. In 2011, Roland Perry was awarded the Medal of the Order of Australia for services to literature and was made a Fellow of Monash University. In 2012, he became Monash University's first Writer-in-Residence, lecturing PhD students on writing and Australian history.

Allen & Unwin has published his three bestsellers on animals at war, *Bill the Bastard*, *Horrie the War Dog* and *Red Lead*; two fiction works in the Assassin series, *The Honourable Assassin* and *The Shaman*; *The Queen, Her Lover and the Most Notorious Spy in History*; and *Monash & Chauvel*.

Bradman vs Bodyline is his thirty-seventh book.